T0378021

Washington's Lieutenants

Also by Douglas M. Branson

WASHINGTON'S LIEUTENANTS

Major versus Brigadier Generals in the Revolutionary War

DOUGLAS M. BRANSON

STACKPOLE BOOKS

Essex, Connecticut

STACKPOLE BOOKS
The Globe Pequot Publishing Group, Inc.
64 South Main Street
Essex, CT 06426
www.globepequot.com

British Library Cataloguing in Publication Information available

Library of Congress Cataloging-in-Publication Data
ISBN 9780811777131 (cloth)
ISBN 9780811777148 (electronic)

∞™ The paper used in this publication meets the minimum requirements of American National Standard for Information Sciences—Permanence of Paper for Printed Library Materials, ANSI/NISO Z39.48-1992.

Contents

CHAPTER ONE

Overview

MANY REVOLUTIONARY WAR GENERALS STOOD OUT AS "TALL TREES," WHO FOR six to seven years led men on marches and countermarches, across rivers, on roads that were no more than Indian or game trails, and through forests and unknown territory. They ate bad food; slept rough in rudimentary camps; communicated up and down the chain of command as best they could; and led their men in skirmishes and battles, suffering wounds, capture, and death (thirteen brigadiers died in combat or from combat-related causes). Over the course of the war, fifty-eight men served as brigadier generals, who for the most part remained loyal to their commander in chief and to the cause of independence and liberty.

By contrast, among the higher-ranking major generals (of whom there were twenty-three Americans), there were few, if any, "tall trees." Instead, almost to a man, the major generals were "bent trees" in the Revolutionary War forest, pursuing selfish agendas, often profiting from conflicting transactions one after another, disloyal to and even contemptuous of the commander in chief. This book contrasts seven of the major generals, "bent trees," with four brigadiers, three of them "tall trees," whose efforts, leadership, and loyalty played an outsize part in winning independence for the fledgling nation.

Of Brigadier General Hugh Mercer, Dr. Benjamin Rush wrote, "His character was marked with all the traits of one of the heroes of antiquity." General Nathanael Greene added, "He was a fine companion, a sincere friend, a true patriot, and a brave general. May heaven bless his spirit."[1] British cavalry had bayoneted an incapacitated Mercer, knocked from his horse while leading troops at the Battle of Princeton. He died several days later.[2]

By contrast with Mercer and many of the brigadier generals,[3] commander in chief General George Washington's senior leaders, the major generals, were a disappointment. They pled old age, illness, or urgencies at home as grounds for their resignation from service in the midst of war. Several major generals were more notable failures than that. Several, such as Thomas Mifflin, Thomas Conway, Adam Stephen, Arthur St. Clair, Charles Lee, and Horatio Gates, were badly bent, crooked trees in the forest. Metaphorically, Washington's contretemps with Lee and Conway resembled modern-day cage fights, while his longer-range relationship with Thomas Mifflin came close. This book singles out those seven notable failures: seven sins and the sinners, so to speak, the bent trees in the forest.

Washington commanded fifty-eight brigadier generals.[4] As aforesaid, thirteen died in combat or had combat-related deaths.[5] By contrast, the Continental Congress commissioned twenty-eight major generals, twenty-three American and five foreign. Only two American major generals, Richard Montgomery and John Thomas, died, both in the disastrous 1775 winter expedition to Canada. Quebec defenders shot and killed Montgomery at the very commencement of the patriot attempt to capture Quebec City.[6] While leading a retreat from Canada, Thomas died from smallpox. Thereafter, from 1776 to 1783, no American major general perished, either from wounds or as a captive.[7]

Thus, on a proportionate basis, 23 percent of the brigadiers died; only 4 percent of the major generals did. The late historical novelist Hilary Mantel reminded us, "History is [often] about what people are trying to hide from you.... You search for it in the same way you sift through a landfill: for evidence of what people want to bury."[8] Because finding corroborating evidence that reflects negatively on the major generals has been difficult, little has been written about the group's decided failings.

The record shows that at least ten major generals resigned their commissions, returning home before the war ended.[9] One famous (or infamous) major general, Benedict Arnold, committed treason and deserted, ultimately escaping to live out his days in England. Based on "problematic performances," Major Generals Israel Putnam and William Heath were "shunted to less important commands" but not neutered completely.[10]

We would think that the senior commanders, the major generals, would have led American forces to the war's conclusion. That proves not to have been the case. Amazingly, only two major generals were active for the duration: Nathanael Greene (Rhode Island) and Benjamin Lincoln (Massachusetts). Despite his record, Henry Knox of Massachusetts was not made a major general until 1782.[11]

Calculations account for sixteen of the war's major generals. This book is about seven others, all of whom came to be under dark clouds, suffering less than laudable outcomes. Their behavior and ensuing punishments ranged from suspension from command to courts of inquiry and courts-martial. For some, dereliction of duty resulted in separation from the service when they were cashiered following a court-martial:

- Arthur St. Clair, suspended from all combat duty after surrendering the American stronghold Fort Ticonderoga without ordering the firing of a shot, regardless of commanding a three-thousand-man garrison.
- Adam Stephen, court-martialed and cashiered for drunkenness at Germantown, there for prematurely ordering a retreat.
- Richard Howe, suspended for womanizing, relieved as commander of the Southern Department, and further downgraded for leading an ill-considered and outmanned defense of Savannah, Georgia.
- Charles Lee, cashiered for refusing to follow orders from Commander in Chief Washington at the 1778 Battle of Monmouth Courthouse.
- Horatio Gates, suspended for extreme cowardice and abandonment of his troops at Camden, South Carolina.
- Thomas Mifflin, under a cloud for participation in a plot to overthrow Washington (the Conway cabal); poor performance as quartermaster of the army, contributing greatly to misery and deaths at Valley Forge; and self-dealing, selling goods procured with government money for his own account.
- Thomas Conway, an Irishman who had served in the French army and was the prime mover of the plot seeking Washington's dismissal as commander in chief.

FIVE FOREIGN MAJOR GENERALS

In May 1777, France's Philippe Charles Tronson du Coudray pried a general's commission from the Congress. Unwilling to foist the arrogant du Coudray on troops, General Washington assigned him to inspect Forts Mifflin and Mercer, guarding the Delaware River below Philadelphia. Meanwhile, du Coudray sought the major general's commission that Congress had promised him. Among others, brigadiers Henry Knox, Nathanael Greene, and John Sullivan vowed to resign if Congress promoted the Frenchman over their heads. On September 11, 1777, while returning to the American camp, du Coudray's horse bolted on a wooden pontoon bridge spanning the Schuylkill River. Thrown into the river, the general drowned.[12]

Another Philippe—Philippe Hubert, chevalier Preudhomme de Borre—commissioned only as a brigadier, commanded troops but considered himself a de facto major general and thus a better tactician than his superiors. At Brandywine he argued with Generals Sullivan and Washington. He publicly complained that he had been given "bad troops." Disgraced, de Borre resigned his commission, returning to France after a few months of service.[13]

Great in number were the flameouts of those to whom, based purely on paper records and relentless self-promotion, Congress handed out commissions and ranks. One of the more spectacular was General Matthias Alexis Roche de Fermoy. In charge of a major contingent of troops before the Second Battle of Trenton, Fermoy mounted his horse and simply rode away before combat commenced. Called a "worthless drunkard" by his American contemporaries, Fermoy resigned his American commission, returning to France in 1777.[14]

Appointments of foreigners to high rank in the American army, premised on genuine experience, could nonetheless constitute a blow to morale. On December 13, 1777, for example, Congress appointed the Irishman and former French officer Thomas Conway a major general. Conway was more than a pretender. He led troops in combat, seeing action in several major engagements.[15] Initially, however, giving no thought to potential effects on existing brigadiers and major generals, Congress appointed "Thomas Conway to Major General over twenty-three [American] brigadier[s]. . . . Several major generals and nine brigadier generals . . . protested to Congress and threatened to resign."[16] George Washington protested.[17] Their protests availed them not.

In asserting its desire to control military matters, the Continental Congress listened to scores of foreign would-be adventurers. Often, the latter would present Congress with fabricated or exaggerated credentials:

> *A Swiss officer wished to become a lieutenant colonel under George Washington, despite never having risen higher than lieutenant for the Dutch. A veteran of ten years in the French army . . . thought he should be a regimental quartermaster. A student from Lyon declared that the time had come for him to do something grand: he would start by killing redcoats.*[18]

Especially in the war's earlier years, Congress would award senior officer ranks to foreign supplicants.

No less an authority than the Pulitzer Prize–winning Ron Chernow, in his *George Washington: A Life*, came to a negative view of the war's major generals and a positive one of the brigadiers: "In the end, the generals who succeeded in the Continental Army weren't grizzled veterans, such as Charles Lee or Horatio Gates [or most of the other major generals], but young, homegrown officers who were quite daring and stayed loyal to George Washington."[19] This book chronicles the exploits of three brigadiers—Hugh Mercer, Peter Muhlenberg, and William Davidson—whose exploits and deaths in combat stand in contradistinction to senior commanders' less-than-praiseworthy records. Greatly assisted by the men they led, the brigadiers, not the higher-ranked major generals, won the war and could be considered "other" founding fathers of the new nation. That is the thesis that the ensuing chapters seek to support.

Part I
Arthur St. Clair

CHAPTER TWO

Banned from Combat Duty

ARTHUR ST. CLAIR'S PRINCIPAL BIOGRAPHER, R. W. PHILLIPS, WENT TO GREAT lengths to laud him with superlatives. St. Clair was "a great American hero," an officer "whose courage knew no bounds," "an honorable and courageous officer," "one of the most brilliant military strategists of his era," and a general "rightfully considered by many to be an American Founding Father."[1] He was "one of Washington's most trusted major generals" and one who walked with the giants of the American Revolution—Washington, Franklin, Adams, Jefferson, Greene, and Lafayette.[2]

These characterizations are not accurate. Arthur St. Clair's accomplishments—at least the military ones—have gone down as including two of the most shameful blots on Revolutionary War ledgers. In July 1777, St. Clair was in command of the three-thousand-man garrison at Fort Ticonderoga, the first line of defense against British General Johnny Burgoyne. With his eight-thousand-man force, Burgoyne was descending from Canada into upstate New York, intending to split the fledgling nation in half. Under cover of darkness, with Burgoyne a threat, St. Clair abandoned the fort without his men having fired a shot or having impeded Burgoyne's advance in any other way. Both military and political establishments were so shocked that Congress decreed that St. Clair "never be given any future military commands."[3] The episode stamped Arthur St. Clair with the indelible mark, a grievous sin, a stain from which he never fully recovered. After the Ticonderoga surrender, its commandant, Arthur St. Clair, was a bent tree in the Revolutionary War forest.

Postrevolution, in the fall of 1791, George Washington directed St. Clair, as first governor of the Northwest Territory, to deal with the recurring Indian raids in the Ohio Country.[4] On November 4, 1791, in the Battle of the Wabash, St. Clair commanded a fourteen-hundred-man force on an expedition against Chief Little Turtle and one thousand warriors. Utterly vanquished, St. Clair's brigade lost 914 men killed and 276 wounded. This encounter remains the American military's greatest loss to a Native American force, garnering the moniker "The Battle of a Thousand

Slain."[5] Last of all, the 1775 Battle of Trenton aside, little or no evidence exists that Arthur St. Clair ever participated in combat during the Revolutionary War.

Yet there must have been some trait that the Continental Congress and George Washington saw in St. Clair. Congress passed over more senior, distinguished officers (Connecticut's Benedict Arnold and New Hampshire's John Stark) to promote Arthur St. Clair to major general.[6] General Washington appointed St. Clair to the important post of Ticonderoga commandant. Later, St. Clair was appointed governor of the Northwest Territory, a position he held for fourteen years. Still later, Washington and Secretary of War Henry Knox assigned St. Clair the task of dealing with the Native American confederation in the Ohio Country, taming the warriors' bellicosity.

Handsome, Tall, and Affable

Arthur St. Clair was tall, "raised as a gentleman . . . said to have carried himself with aristocratic bearing."[7] Born at Thurso (the exact date being uncertain, probably in 1734), in the far north of Scotland, the northernmost town on the Isle of Britain, St. Clair was a descendant of the Earls of Caithness. "Being of a noble family, he inherited the fine personal appearance and manly traits of the St. Clairs."[8] Being tall has always given one an advantage, a commanding presence in one's community. In the eighteenth century, the average male stood five feet, five inches.[9] St. Clair grew to six feet, two inches—the same height as George Washington. Also, as with Washington, "[t]hroughout his life [St. Clair] exhibited a faultless precision in dress, regarding a person's apparel as an outward sign of inner order."[10] A contemporary 1776 portrait of St. Clair, age forty-three, captured a well-proportioned countenance, alert eyes, and thin lips, with a tricorn tipped short of rakishly but less than modestly to one side.[11] According to Professor Stephen R. Taaffe's research, "St. Clair was a handsome, well-mannered, and honorable man without the cloying ambition of some of his colleagues. His steadiness, prudence, and experience contributed to Congress' decision to promote him to brigadier [on August 9, 1776] and then to major general."[12]

Several American senior officers in the Revolutionary War (Hugh Mercer, Edward Hand, Adam Stephen, Arthur St. Clair, James Craik) were Scots physicians who had lived under English thumbs, immigrating to America to escape English oppression and later joining the American fight for independence. St. Clair was a surgeon, educated at the University of Edinburgh with further training in London. In 1756, St. Clair's mother died, leaving her son an inheritance. Leaving medicine behind, seeking adventure, he used funds to purchase an ensign's commission in the Royal American Regiment of Foot.[13] In 1758, the regiment came to North America to engage in the French and Indian War. St. Clair and the regiment, under the command of Major General Jeffery Amherst, were present at the successful siege of the French fortress at Louisbourg on Nova Scotia's Atlantic coast.

St. Clair spent much of his late 1750s service as a British subaltern stationed in Boston. He was well educated and articulate, pleasing in both personality and appearance. "He had the social skills required to" and did "function in the high societies of Boston." St. Clair "became an acceptable visitor to the best families."[14] He courted and married Phoebe Bayard, niece of the future Massachusetts governor, James Bowdoin II.

BECOMING AMERICAN

In 1762, St. Clair resigned his British army commission. He and Phoebe moved to the site of the future Ligonier in the Allegheny foothills of western Pennsylvania. He began to acquire land, eventually accumulating 10,881 acres (of which 8,270 were in the Ligonier Valley). Based on his prior military experience, St. Clair assisted Pennsylvania proprietor Richard Penn's son John Penn, also governor, in defense against Indian raids. In 1769, St. Clair resigned his Pennsylvania military commission but continued to receive service appointments, such as the surveyor of Cumberland County, from John Penn. Because Indian raids persisted, however, St. Clair moved his family east to Bedford, Pennsylvania, and then later to Pottstown outside Philadelphia (then known as Pottsgrove).

COMMISSIONED IN THE CONTINENTAL ARMY

Historians hazard the opinion that George Washington's higher-ranking officers lacked military experience.[15] St. Clair's biographer appears to have joined the chorus, stating that "St. Clair was one of the few experienced generals."[16] That assertion was wrong; many (if not most) were battle-tested veterans. For instance, seven of eight Virginia brigadiers (George Weedon, Charles Scott, Andrew Lewis, Hugh Mercer, William Woodford, George Rogers Clark, Edward Stevens) had served with George Washington in the Virginia regiment supporting the British during the French and Indian (or Seven Years') War. Major Generals Charles Lee and Horatio Gates, both of Virginia, also served in the French and Indian War, as British army officers. So had Arthur St. Clair.[17] A supermajority of the brigadier generals from the Carolinas (William Moultrie, Andrew Pickens, Griffin Rutherford, Richard Caswell, Francis Nash, William Davidson) gained extensive military experience in the Cherokee Wars (1758–1761), fought in the dense woods of the hill and mountain country of western Carolina.[18] So, too, in New England, where Revolutionary War officers (Generals John Stark, Moses Hazen, and Israel Putnam, for example) had gained military experience in the French and Indian War, fighting with Roger's Rangers.[19] Contrary to many historians' versions, for higher officer positions, Washington chose (or recommended to the Congress) men with prior military leadership background. That included Arthur St. Clair.[20]

Besides military experience, St. Clair possessed another attribute that Washington valued: St. Clair was a Mason, a member of the Scottish Rite, as was Washington. Masonic Lodge Number 4, known as Washington's "Mother Lodge," had as members future generals Hugh Mercer, Gustavus Wallace, George Weedon, and William Woodford (as well as the Marquis de Lafayette, an honorary member), all of whom knew Washington.[21] The Fredericksburg lodge counted ninety-four members who fought in the American Revolution.[22]

Last of all, St. Clair was Scottish. In *Born Fighting*, former US Senator James Webb wrote, "The Scots-Irish heritage has been defined as . . . [an] extreme mistrust of government authority and a propensity to bear arms." Webb elaborated: "Between 250,000 and 400,000 Scots-Irish migrated to America in the eighteenth century . . . bringing with them not only long experience as rebels and outcasts, but also unparalleled skill as frontiersmen and guerilla fighters. Their cultural identity reflected acute individualism as well as a dislike for aristocracy and a strong military tradition."[23] More accomplished in the drawing room than on the battlefield, St. Clair was nonetheless experienced in warfare and in leading troops.

FIRST ASSIGNMENT

Naively, members of the Continental Congress, pundits, military leaders, and George Washington thought that if a military excursion achieved some success, Canadians would transfer allegiance from Britain to the neighboring newly independent nation. The widely held belief was that Canada would become the "fourteenth state."[24] Accordingly, in 1775 Washington sent a sizable force under Major General Richard Montgomery (another former British military officer) up the Hudson River, across Lakes George and Champlain, up the Richelieu River flowing north out of Lake Champlain, and to the St. Lawrence River, then as now Canada's principal aquatic highway.[25] Somewhat later, in early winter, Benedict Arnold would lead one thousand men from Boston up the Maine coast, into the center of Maine on the Kennebec River, across several portages, and down several swift-flowing northbound rivers to the vicinity of Quebec, Canada's capital. Miraculously, in an extraordinary exercise of bravery and leadership, Arnold bought his men north with minimal losses.

Richard Montgomery and his men captured Montreal, downriver from Quebec. Canadian Governor Guy Carleton fled upriver, east by northeast, to the walled Quebec City, where he assumed command of the city's defense. Montgomery followed, intending to rendezvous with Arnold's command. While enduring a protracted delay, though, Arnold's force lost the element of surprise, retreating a short way down the St. Lawrence. With enlistments set to expire, the Americans attacked on December 30, 1775.

The attack was an unmitigated disaster. Montgomery was killed before even breeching the city walls. On the other, northeast side of Quebec, Arnold was severely wounded. Virginia's Daniel Morgan assumed leadership of the attackers. Canadian and British forces captured Daniel Morgan and others, imprisoning them for a year (under humane conditions and in more than tolerable quarters—a precursor of the Canadian way of doing things).

Retreating, the battered American force suffered from cold, inadequate clothing, greatly worn shoes (or no footwear at all), and desertions. Most of all, the retreating army became infected with the age's scourge—smallpox. In retreat, the Americans' leaders quarantined over one-third of the force on a small island at the juncture of the Richelieu River. Most of them (plus others) died. Accompanying the doomed was the force's leader, Major General John Thomas, who, covered with oozing pustules and blind from the pox, died a pitiful death.

Commanding General George Washington and Major General Philip Schuyler, commander of the army's Northern Department, sent Arthur St. Clair north to lead the force's remnants home, which he did. No high praise or fluttering flags ensued, nor should they have. The Canadian episode was a sow's ear that remained a sow's ear.

St. Clair's biographer, though, elevates the retreat into a silk purse. He extols St. Clair's exploits in retreat from Canada. When St. Clair arrived, "he found [the] army in full retreat from a British force. . . . St. Clair's fast action turned what would have been a certain massacre into a controlled retreat that saved the lives of more than one thousand American[s]."[26] The treatment of St. Clair's first action contains no citations to authority.[27] Left unsaid was the lack of any significant combat.

FUTURE ASSIGNMENTS

Leading the retreat from Canada, St. Clair accomplished the mission, always deserving of an accolade—indeed, praise. But high praise? No. The Quebec saga had a certain tawdry aura that detracts from any exploits associated with it. The opportunity for St. Clair to garner high praise was in the future: his 1777 assignment to command the imposing stone fortress at Fort Ticonderoga on Lake Champlain, with a three-thousand-man garrison.

CHAPTER THREE

Credit Was Not Due

ARTHUR ST. CLAIR RECEIVED BLISTERING CRITICISM FOR HAVING COMMITTED the first of his major "sins"—namely, in 1777, ordering Fort Ticonderoga's abandonment. The fort controlled the chain of rivers, lakes, and portages that made up the 195-mile strategic route between New York and Canada. "When news of Fort Ticonderoga's fall reached London, Britain's King George III . . . exclaimed, 'I have beaten them. I have beat all the Americans.'"[1] On the American side, "[b]lame for the debacle"—loss of a supposedly impregnable fortress—"fell on Ticonderoga's commander, Arthur St. Clair. People accused him of cowardice, even treason. . . . Washington was, like everyone else, shocked that St. Clair abandoned the fort."[2] Throughout the Continental Army's officer corps, ranging from a soft hiss to vocalized belittlement, officers condemned Arthur St. Clair.

Earlier, in 1755–1757, the French had built a formidable star-shaped fort of stone, Fort Carillon, at Lake Champlain's southern terminus. The lake there had narrowed for some distance, approaching a 3.5-mile portage to another long, narrow lake to the south, Lake George. After fighting two battles there against the French, in 1759 the British captured Fort Carillon, renaming it with the Iroquois word for junction of two waterways, corrupted into "Ticonderoga." The British garrisoned the fort with declining numbers as the years ticked by.

In 1775, without firing a shot, the American Green Mountain Boys from the Catamount Tavern in Bennington, Vermont, whose leader was the tall, bearded Ethan Allen, captured the fort. Ticonderoga further became a symbol because of a second legendary exploit when Henry Knox, the Boston bookstore proprietor, recovered the fort's twenty-nine cannons. In 1775–1776, Knox, who was to be Washington's artillery chief for the war's duration, used oxen and sleds to transport the heavy cannons, in midwinter, over the snow-covered Berkshire range to Boston, a journey in those times thought impossible. There, placed on Dorchester Heights and commanding a perch above Boston, the cannons rendered the British occupation untenable. The British abandoned the city, departing on Royal Navy transports for Nova Scotia.[3] Based on these two events, Ticonderoga took on iconic status for American revolutionaries.

A Commanding Perch at Ticonderoga

St. Clair's "sin" was that before he ordered Ticonderoga abandoned, he had failed to take measures to hold the advancing British at bay—or at least to slow their descent toward New York. Previously, while in command of the Americans' northern army, "General Philip Schuyler decided that Fort Ticonderoga could be defended," even though a tall hill across the waterway, Mount Defiance, paradoxically also called—benignly—Sugar Loaf Hill, could constitute a commanding perch if the British were to site artillery atop it.[4] In midspring 1777, Major General Arthur St. Clair assumed command of Ticonderoga. Contrary to Schuyler, then colonels Benedict Arnold, Anthony Wayne, and John Trumbull thought that an undefended Sugar Loaf Hill constituted a major threat. The colonels reported that "there was vulnerability to cannon from above": "Trumbull, Wayne, and Arnold, borrowing the commandant's barge, crossed [Lake Champlain] and landed where Mount Defiance was rocky and perpendicular. [T]hey began to climb. The ascent was difficult but in a little time they reached the top. . . . [T]hat it would be a simple matter to build a carriage road and haul cannon up the side of Mount Defiance was obvious to all."[5] Later, Colonel Wayne, the retiring Ticonderoga commandant, reported the foregoing to St. Clair, who made the command decision to leave the hill undefended. He failed to do what would not have been difficult to accomplish.

Arrival of the British

Clanking down the route from Canada came British General Gentleman Johnny Burgoyne, accompanied by three or four wagons of champagne (Burgoyne being much enamored of champagne) and an army of eight thousand "British regulars, Hessian mercenaries, American Loyalists, and Native Americans," plus ladies with whom Burgoyne mingled and played cards, as well as assorted camp followers.[6] British General William Phillips of the Royal Artillery headed Burgoyne's artillery detachment. As the British approached Ticonderoga, they reconnoitered the fort's surroundings. On July 5, under the cover of darkness, General Phillips and his men "managed to put guns atop Sugar Loaf Hill."[7]

General St. Clair made a second decision. When St. Clair and his staff "spotted the British troops and campfires on the summit of Sugar Loaf Hill, General St. Clair ordered the immediate evacuation of the fort . . . to be carried out at night."[8] Ticonderoga fell, for the second time without a shot having been fired.

John Burgoyne
ART.COM

As has been seen, the abandonment of Ticonderoga set off extreme criticism of Arthur St. Clair, both by officers and men of the Continental Army and by the politicians. In the Continental Congress, John Adams and Samuel Adams publicly called St. Clair "a coward."[9] Congress passed resolutions that the army was to court-martial Arthur St. Clair. The legislators further decreed that St. Clair be barred from "any future commands."[10] Major General Arthur St. Clair entered a limbo that lasted the remaining four Revolutionary War years, relegated to recruiting duties in Pennsylvania.[11] When fifteen hundred Pennsylvania troops mutinied early in 1781, killing three officers, the mutineers "kicked St. Clair out of camp."[12] In the same year, as Stephen Taaffe recorded it, St. Clair "wrote to Washington to ask for a more active job. . . . Washington responded that there were not enough . . . units in the main army to accommodate another major general."[13] He closed by "urg[ing] St. Clair to remain in Pennsylvania for now to focus on his recruiting duties."

APOLOGISTS FOR THE EVACUATION

Enter again St. Clair's principal biographer, who calls St. Clair "one courageous general who defied the expectations of a misinformed Congress and risked his career to save his troops from annihilation." Mr. Phillips's perspective was that "Congress

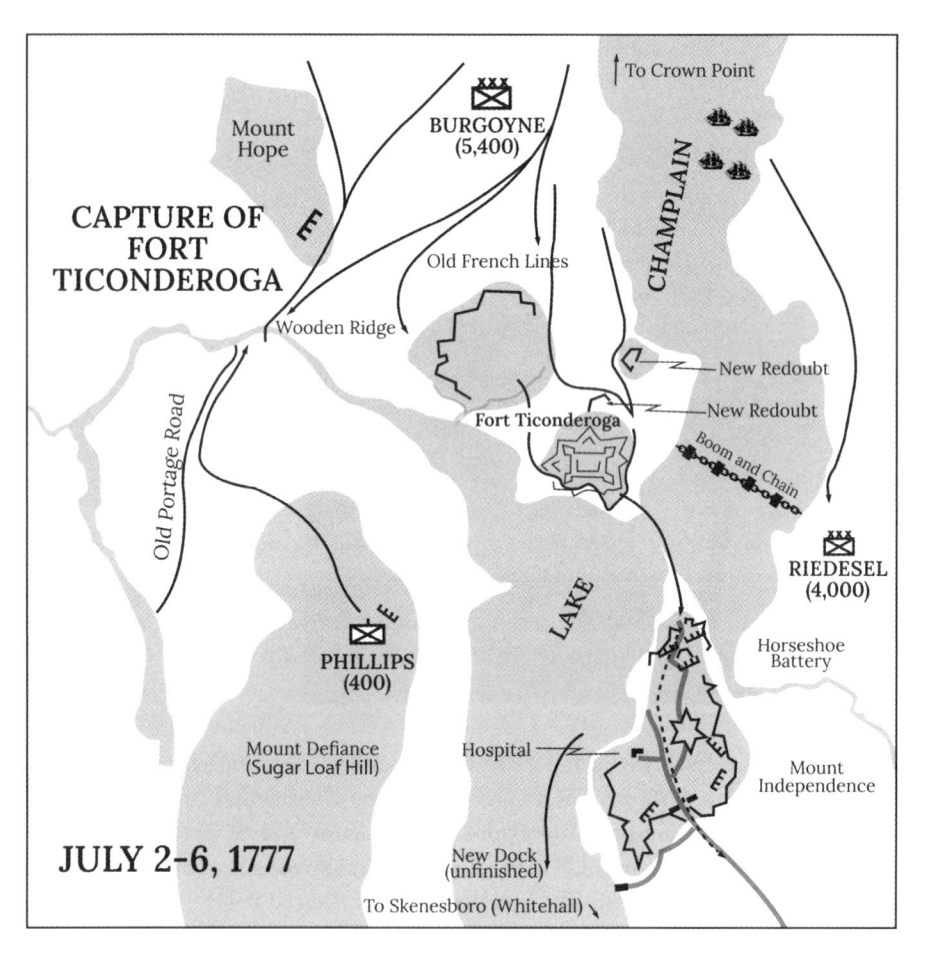

CAPTURE OF FORT TICONDEROGA

JULY 2-6, 1777

could be lightening [*sic*] fast in finding a scapegoat when their decisions didn't work out . . . as with St. Clair's unauthorized strategic retreat from Fort Ticonderoga to save his army."[14] Alleged ancillary explanations buttress support for St. Clair's command decision to abandon Ticonderoga:

- The fort's "dismal condition": The fort was large, built of stone, and sturdy. Earlier, in spring 1777, on being relieved, Anthony Wayne had told St. Clair that "all was well [with the fort] and that the fort would never be carried without much loss of blood" by the attacking force.[15]

- The fort's age: Completed in 1757, the fort was but twenty-two years old.

- St. Clair's conscious decision to ignore the obvious: Congress and General Washington sent St. Clair to Fort Ticonderoga in April 1777.[16] For two and a half months or more, St. Clair left Mount Defiance undefended. Trenching, abatis, a redoubt perhaps, and a contingent of American troops could have prevented (or at least greatly hindered) British attempts to summit the hill, especially when dragging heavy cannons up steep slopes.

- The poor health of the three-thousand-man defending force of Americans, with "a third unfit for duty": Poor food, contaminated water, poor sanitation, and the like rendered the American men unable to fight. Yet the same would have been true of the British/Hessian force. A level of unfitness for duty plagued every regiment and brigade throughout the war, on both sides, British as well as American. To the north, in the Richelieu River vicinity, Burgoyne's men had had to pass through an area infected with smallpox (Isle aux Noix). Moreover, the Native Americans accompanying Burgoyne and his men were beginning to defect. American loyalists—Tories, as they were known—accompanied the British force but were becoming fainthearted, deserting from the expeditionary foray. Of a force estimated at eight thousand fighters, something like fifty-three hundred would have been available to Generals Burgoyne and Phillips.

- The daunting size of the attacking force: Military analysts posit a five-to-one numerical advantage as necessary to overcome an entrenched opponent such as Ticonderoga.[17] Burgoyne had a numerical superiority equivalent to 2.6 to 1, hardly representing a daunting force opposing the entrenched Americans.

ONE BRUSH WITH COMBAT

The factoid left undisturbed all these years is the reality that Arthur St. Clair had only one combat experience in the war. Early on, in November 1776, Washington had led his small, decimated, and demoralized army in retreat diagonally across New Jersey, from Fort Washington in the northeast—across the Hudson to the west of New York City—to Newtown, Pennsylvania, in the southwest, across the Delaware River. Toward the march's end, St. Clair and five hundred troops joined Washington, beginning reinvigoration of the American forces.[18] Besides erroneously crediting St. Clair with bringing two thousand fresh troops into camp, St. Clair's biographer credits him with engineering the entire reversal of fortune that Washington's army experienced in late 1776 and early 1777: "Arthur St. Clair's fresh troops, military strategy, and brigade leadership pumped life into Washington's deflated army, helped defeat the Hessians at Trenton, the British Army at Princeton, and drive the British completely out of New Jersey, in nine days . . . turn[ing] the tide of the war."[19] These exploits constitute, the author tells us, "The Untold Story of the New Jersey Victories."[20]

Did St. Clair devise the strategy of crossing the Delaware on Christmas night, surprising the Hessian Trenton garrison the following morning? Probably not. Writing about the crossing in *The British Are Coming*, Rick Atkinson concludes that "[f]or over ten days" prior to the Delaware crossing, "Washington had contemplated a bold lunge into the enemy's flank."[21] St. Clair would not even have been physically present at those times. The second reason to doubt that the crossing and attack were St. Clair's ideas emanates from Washington's practices. He frequently convened senior officers in "councils of war," analyzing and choosing between strategies, later to vote on alternatives.[22] Washington recognized that he alone was not a great strategist. Further, the early engagements of the war had made Washington aware that his impetuous side caused him to overcommit, taking unnecessary risks.[23] Thus, almost never was the strategy crafted by a single officer or even two or three. Washington operated by consensus.

THE SECOND BATTLE OF TRENTON

After the Americans' complete defeat of the Hessians at Trenton, Lord Cornwallis was infuriated that a ragtag army of rebels had defeated professional British soldiers. Six days after the Hessian embarrassment, Cornwallis, at the head of eight thousand British regulars, set out from Princeton, thirteen miles to the north, focused on teaching the Americans a lesson. Lord Cornwallis and his officers thought the British would obliterate the American army and its camp, now below the town of Trenton and behind the Trenton River (Assunpink Creek).[24] In his haste, though, Cornwallis did not observe the practice of armies on the move—setting out picket and skirmish lines along with scouting parties southwest and southeast of the main body's line of march—thus facilitating what happened later that night.

"St. Clair was the only officer with the courage to suggest the bold strategy which outflanked Cornwallis's army at Trenton," wrote Dick Phillips, conflating St. Clair into the principal hero of the Second Battle of Trenton.[25] But the true hero of the Second Battle of Trenton was Colonel (later Brigadier) Charles Scott, the rough-hewn and profane Virginian. Several miles above Trenton, Scott and his troops began a strategic retreat, slowing Cornwallis and ultimately facilitating the strategic move that followed.[26]

The American advance force slowly retreated. Colonel Charles Scott's force waded across Shabbakonk Creek, passing through the village of Trenton. Southeast of Trenton, the mission for Scott and his men became defending the single bridge over Assunpink Creek—that is, beyond Trenton where the Assunpink curved west to flow into the Delaware River. The British halted opposite the American encampment, on the creek's opposite shore. In his memoirs, Virginian Robert Beale remembered:

Our brigade, consisting of the Fourth, Fifth, and Sixth Virginia Regiments, was ordered to form a column at the bridge. General Washington came, and in the presence of us all, told Colonel Scott to defend the bridge to the last extremity. Colonel Scott answered with an oath, "Yes, General, as long as there is a man left alive."[27]

Scott's subordinate, Major George Johnston, publicly stated that by his actions, "Colonel Scott acquired immortal honors from his performance" at the Battle of Assunpink Creek, as the engagement also became known.[28] Although greatly outnumbered, Scott and his men repulsed three British attempts to take the bridge. With darkness approaching, "General Cornwallis suspended his attack."[29]

The American delaying tactic had succeeded.

DIVERSION AT ASSUNPINK

That night the Americans left campfires burning, tended by five hundred soldiers who stayed behind. The remainder of the American army marched quietly out to the east, bending north, toward Princeton. Thus, enabled by Scott's men and their earlier valiant defense against a superior British force, under cover of darkness Washington's army conducted an end run around Cornwallis's army. Again, the Americans were further aided by Cornwallis's failure to have outriders (scouts and skirmishers) east of his force, who would have impeded the American end run around the British eastern flank. The following day, the Americans went on to defeat, convincingly, several regiments of British troops camped on the grounds of the College of New Jersey (Princeton University).

Again, it was St. Clair, not Colonel Scott, who is accorded credit by Dick Phillips for the strategy and the victory at Princeton. The nighttime march was "St. Clair's brilliant strategic idea. . . . In St. Clair, Washington discovered a valuable military strategist . . . capable of assessing situations and making sound decisions. . . . We can only imagine the courage it must have taken to suggest this strategy."[30] Gerald Carbone, in his biography of General Nathanael Greene, hit closer to the mark when he put St. Clair's contribution into a modest perspective: "[T]he local knowledge of Arthur St. Clair revealed a new road from Trenton to Princeton. This road ran east, around the town, to the left of Cornwallis' troops. Washington, with the concurrence of his generals [council of war], decided to march along this road."[31]

ST. CLAIR'S SOLE COMBAT EXPERIENCE OF THE WAR

Flashing back to the earlier Battle of Trenton, once Washington had gotten his twenty-four hundred frozen men across the ice-strewn Delaware River, he divided them into two detachments. The first, under General Nathanael Greene, would march toward and attack Trenton from an inland road. The second, under General

John Sullivan, would approach Trenton along the river road, astride the Delaware River. Arthur St. Clair commanded a unit within Sullivan's force. The major thrust against the Hessians appears to have come from the upland force that attacked on Trenton's Queen's and King's Streets.[32]

Historical accounts do place St. Clair in the lower portion of the town, "bellowing" at the Hessians, "If you do not surrender immediately, I will blow you to pieces."[33] Evidently it did not become necessary to blow Hessians to pieces, as one thousand of the fourteen-hundred-man Hessian garrison surrendered.[34]

A PRELIMINARY ASSESSMENT

Arthur St. Clair obviously was a capable administrator. By contrast, claims about his courage and military prowess fall flat. Contrary to certain assertions, his abandonment of Fort Ticonderoga set off alarm bells, producing catcalls of "coward" and effectively sidelining him for the Revolutionary War's last four years.

CHAPTER FOUR

St. Clair's Generalship: Battle of a Thousand Slain

IN 1787, ARTHUR ST. CLAIR WAS APPOINTED GOVERNOR OF THE NORTHWEST TER-ritory, a post St. Clair occupied through four and a half three-year terms (fourteen years). Under the Treaty of Paris (1783) ending the Revolutionary War, the British ceded to the newly independent confederation the territory north of the Ohio River continuing west from Pennsylvania to the Mississippi River. The vast forested tract, the Northwest Territory, was more than two-thirds the size of the original thirteen colonies, 260,000 square miles compared to 360,000. In 1787, Congress enacted the Northwest Ordinance, setting forth the guidelines for America's development north of the Ohio River. Eventually the Northwest Territory became five states (Ohio, 1803; Indiana, 1816; Illinois, 1821; Michigan, 1837; and Wisconsin, 1848) in addition to containing a portion of a sixth state (Minnesota).[1]

The Northwest Territory's first seat of government was Marietta, on the Ohio River at its confluence with the Muskingum River, the first town in the new territory. Four Revolutionary War generals who settled there laid out the town's plan (Generals Rufus Putnam, James Varnum, Benjamin Tupper, and Samuel Holden Parsons).[2] They named the streets after military officers: Richard Butler, Nathanael Greene, Henry Knox, Richard Montgomery, Israel Putnam, Arthur St. Clair, Alexander Scammell, Joseph Warren, George Washington, Anthony Wayne, and Daniel Wooster.[3] In addition, following the general founders of the town, the first families' men "were all veterans of the Revolution."[4]

THE FIRST GOVERNOR
When appointed to the Northwest Territory's highest position, St. Clair was fifty-four years old. He moved his family to Marietta, where he began to administer the vast

area. "[St. Clair] soon discovered," though, "that his new job was replete with major problems. The British in Detroit and nearby Canada . . . seemed oblivious to the 1783 [Treaty of Paris]. [T]hey had been encouraging and supporting the hostility of the northwest Indians against the Ohio and Indiana settlers."[5]

In the Treaty of Paris, from the Northwest Territory the British carved out Detroit, where they maintained a small military force, a group of traders who dealt with the Indians, and an administrative staff who supported small British centers throughout the territory. "The British were clever . . . cultivating and trading with the northwest Indians, encouraging them not to sign treaties [and] encouraging development of a confederated army of Indian tribes, while supplying them with the latest weapons and munitions."[6] The British objective was to prolong the supply of pelts to the Canadian fur trade. So, for fifteen or more years after the 1783 treaty ended the Revolutionary War, the British continued treating the Northwest Territory as British territory. With British assistance, Little Turtle, chief of the Miami, helped create an army of several thousand Native American warriors.[7]

In 1789, St. Clair moved the administrative capital west to Cincinnati on the Ohio River, more centrally located in the Northwest Territory, where he would be better able to assess the Native Americans' growing restlessness. As often is its wont, Congress intervened. The legislators decreed that President Washington and Henry Knox organize a force to deal with the Indian threat. In 1790, Secretary of War Knox designated a commanding officer, General Josiah Harmar, a Revolutionary War veteran, to lead fourteen hundred men to deal with the Indian threat. In *The Pioneers*, the late David McCullough summarized how Harmar led forces against the Shawnee and Miami: "Harmar was known to be a drinker, prone to 'indulge . . . in a convivial glass,' as his friend Secretary . . . Knox expressed it."[8]

Harmer sent out a reconnaissance-in-force detachment of several hundred men, who unexpectedly engaged a party of one thousand Indian warriors. The American troops sent word back to Harmar, requesting reinforcements. However, Harmar had drunk himself into oblivion and was "in no condition to respond."[9] Two hundred men perished. The Harmar-led force never mounted an offensive as the authorities had tasked them with doing. In the aftermath, said Knox, "I expected little from the moment I heard he was a drunkard."[10]

THE BATTLE OF THE WABASH

The following year, 1791, Congress and Secretary Knox initiated a second attempt to quell the Native American threat. On this occasion they chose Governor Arthur St. Clair to lead the expedition. He organized a force of fourteen hundred, including eight hundred six-month volunteers, four hundred regulars, and some Kentucky militia, as well as a small party of cavalry.[11] The force departed Fort Washington

(Cincinnati) with winter on the horizon. In addition to the mission to confront the confederated Indian force, Congress detailed St. Clair's army to build forts spaced a day's horseback ride apart along what today is the Ohio-Indiana boundary.

In early November, the Americans finally reached the south bank of the Wabash River, below Fort Wayne, Indiana, 140 miles north of Cincinnati. St. Clair rode in a wagon, as at age fifty-seven he was stricken with gout in both feet, unable to walk. St. Clair's first error was to split his force, as he sent his best soldiers, the American Regiment, off in search of the Indian supply lines. Second, the night before the battle, he and his executive officer, General Richard Butler, sent a thirty-two-man scouting party across the river. The party reported back that the Indians were mustering, preparing to attack the next day. This report never reached St. Clair. Third, although equipped with three-pounder cannons, St. Clair's men either mistakenly or carelessly sighted the guns, a deployment an experienced officer such as St. Clair should have detected. The gun emplacements were such that even at the cannons' lowest elevations, shot would sail over the heads of an attacking force.

The following day, November 4, "St. Clair's Defeat" took place. Over four hours, the Indians attacked, fell back, and then attacked again, and again, and again, until combat degenerated into hand-to-hand fighting. Indian rifle fire was particularly effective, as the British had supplied the Native American warriors with the latest Enfield rifles, while many of the Americans had obsolete smooth-bored barrel muskets with a range of fifty to sixty yards. The outcome was the greatest defeat Native Americans ever visited on government troops, greater even than General Custer and the Seventh Cavalry's 1876 defeat at Little Bighorn. The Native Americans decimated the American force, leaving 918 killed in action and 276 wounded.[12] Among the deceased was General Richard Butler.[13]

Excuses, Excuses
The loss at the Wabash River was "the most egregious scandal of the time." Most commanders would have stood erect, accepting blame in accordance with the military tradition of "total responsivity." Not so Major General St. Clair, who offered only excuses for the defeat:

- He was too old (fifty-seven) at the time he accepted the commission.[14] St. Clair, or his biographer, asserted that "his overwhelming sense of duty" caused him to do so.

- He was ill, suffering from gout.[15] Bouts of gout come and go; the condition does not persist.[16] St. Clair was in charge. He could have waited until his condition ameliorated, commencing the excursion in the spring.

- Congress conveyed to him a sense of haste.[17] Again, St. Clair was the commanding officer, whose discretion would have permitted ordering a more auspiciously timed start in the spring.

- Misprision by Secretary of War Henry Knox, who had an investment in the principal outfitter for the little army. Everything the outfitter supplied was inferior in quality (food, tents, blankets, tools, weapons, horses, wagons), according to biographer Dick Phillips.[18] The assignment of blame to Knox was vocal and consistent: "Knox was mostly to blame for the defeat."[19]

- The Native Americans had superior weapons and ammunition.[20] The outfitter had supplied defective powder and shot, so the Americans' firepower had an even shorter range.

- St. Clair's force came from the dregs of frontier society. Accordingly, the volunteer force was undisciplined, plagued by desertions.[21]

- Slowed by the necessity of building the forts Congress had required, St. Clair's army arrived late at the battlefield, further beset by deteriorating weather.[22] Supposedly an experienced commander, St. Clair should have prioritized the main objective—quelling the Indian militancy and the Native confederation—and built the forts later.

- "St. Clair had another job"—namely, as governor of the Northwest Territory.[23] Apparently, all he had to do was to plead his age and office to pave the way for command by another.

- He faced increasing hostility by the settlers, predominantly Jeffersonian Republicans, who resented having a Federalist governor.[24]

- St. Clair's executive officer, General Richard Butler, failed to post pickets, who in turn would have detected Indian stirrings across the Wabash.[25]

The military code of total responsibility negates the foregoing excuses.

Total Responsibility

A commanding officer's complete responsibility has always been a central feature of military life. When he was president of the United States, Harry S. Truman prominently displayed the sign "The Buck Stops Here." While that may (or may not) have been descriptive of most politicians' beliefs, the sentiment expressed applies universally to the captain of a ship or aircraft, the leader of a detachment, or the commandant of a base or post.[26] It is a central, dominant feature of military command.

Arthur St. Clair and his biographers seemed unaware of this principle as they piled excuse upon excuse for why General St. Clair should not be assigned blame for the defeat at the Battle of a Thousand Slain or for Fort Ticonderoga's abandonment. In both incidents, Arthur St. Clair was commanding. On November 4, 1791, the "Battle of a Thousand Slain" ended St. Clair's military career.

Little Harm Done

Following the Battle of the Wabash, Arthur St. Clair returned to Cincinnati, serving ten additional years as the Northwest Territory's governor, a position for which he was well suited. In the election of 1801, however, Thomas Jefferson, who favored a decentralized republic of farmers and merchants with stronger states' rights (Jeffersonian Republicanism), succeeded John Adams, a Federalist who had served a single term. After his inauguration, Jefferson implemented his ideas. In 1802, he removed Arthur St. Clair, an avowed Federalist, from his gubernatorial position.

The St. Clair family returned to Westmoreland County in Western Pennsylvania. To pay his debts, Arthur had lost most of the land he had once owned. There, near the Pennsylvania frontier, St. Clair lived out a humble but long life, dying in 1818 at age eighty-six. He is buried in St. Clair Park, Greensburg, Pennsylvania.

PART II
ADAM STEPHEN

Chapter Five

A Second Scottish Physician

A contrast to Major General Arthur St. Clair was Major General Adam Stephen, whose biography reminds us that "those who wore uniforms were not always uniform."[1] "Adam Stephen was always getting into trouble by doing things his own way, whether from antagonizing prominent men or skirting the edge of insubordination as a field and general officer. He had a self-inflated estimation of his own abilities . . . [and] occasionally [frequently?] he bridged propriety with conflict of interest,"[2] summarized Revolutionary War historian Harry Ward. In the vernacular, Stephen did what St. Clair seems never to have done—that is, "worked both sides of the street," on both sides of transactions, as a seller while simultaneously affiliated with the buyer. There were far more than a few conflict-of-interest transactions:

- Stephen's supply of provisions (grain, flour, cattle, hogs) from his plantation to the army
- Appropriation—nay, theft—of government property and services in using military personnel to herd his livestock and tend his crops
- Profiting from his grist mill converting grain to flour for sale to the Continental Army
- Ownership and supply of alcohol from the Stephen-owned distillery
- Selling to the Continental Army muskets and rifles from the Stephen-owned armory
- Providing lumber from the Stephen-owned sawmill to the Continental brigades and state militia

For his part, "Stephen's rapid rise in the army," from a colonel in 1776 to major general early in 1778, "seems to have bought out a greater vanity, even a flippant air, in him, and stirred his old sensibilities as a politician. [He] began to supply information to the newspapers, with the implication of his own importance."[3] Mystery writer Lauren Wilkinson's recent characterization of a male acquaintance fits the Adam Stephen of 250 years ago: "[H]e thought he was smarter than everyone else, and, by extension, that the rules shouldn't have applied to him."[4] George Washington described Stephen as "designing" and "unprincipled."[5]

Regardless, Adam Stephen spent more than fourteen years in nearly continuous military service, defending Virginia's territorial integrity and then the new nation's independence.[6]

SCOTTISH ROOTS

Shorter of stature, with a peppery disposition, Stephen professed himself "a little habituated to danger," which he attributed to abandonment of a stint as a surgeon with the Royal Navy.[7] No portraits of Stephen exist, so one can only guess whether he was a red-haired Scot.

Like Hugh Mercer (chapters 8 and 9), another Virginia general, Adam Stephen was from north of Edinburgh—namely, Aberdeenshire, born there in 1721.[8] Like Mercer and Arthur St. Clair, Stephen trained as a physician, in his case in Edinburgh. Mercer, St. Clair, and Stephen all fought in the French and Indian War. Mercer and Stephen became Virginians, settling in Fredericksburg, Stephen at Falmouth across the river from Fredericksburg proper. Stephen later relocated to Berkeley County in far northwestern Virginia (today West Virginia).

There were differences as well as similarities between the men. As a young doctor, Hugh Mercer stood with the forces of the Stuart pretender who claimed the Scottish throne.[9] After Bonnie Prince Charlie's defeat at Culloden in 1746, all who had stood with him became enemies of the British Crown. Mercer went into hiding, a few years later emigrating from Scotland to America (chapter 8).

Adam Stephen was on the opposite side. He became a servant of the Crown, serving as a surgeon on HMS *Neptune*, a hospital ship. He immigrated to America in 1748. After moving from Falmouth in 1753, he continued to practice medicine as well as raise cattle and crops on his plantation, the Bower, along Opequon Creek in Berkeley County.[10]

BRITISH AMERICAN COLONIAL SERVICE

In 1753, word came that the French were building forts on the western frontier, including at the Forks of the Ohio, and staffing them with fifteen hundred men. Virginia's House of Burgesses authorized a three-hundred-man Virginia regiment to be captained by Joshua Fry, assisted by George Washington as second-in-command.

Virginia's colonial governor, Robert Dinwiddie, named Adam Stephen third-in-command. Washington set out from Alexandria for Winchester, where he met Stephen, accompanied by the thirty-nine soldiers Stephen had recruited. Fry did not accompany the force; little was ever heard of him.

The Virginia group set off to the northwest. On May 28, 1754, George Washington, Adam Stephen, and their force encountered a thirty-five-person French and Indian scouting party at their encampment east and south of where Pittsburgh stands today (the Battle of Jumonville, or of Jumonville Glen). Early in the morning of May 28, 1754, the British-Colonial-American force ambushed the French party. Someone (possibly an Indian accompanying the British) murdered the young French officer in charge, Joseph Coulon de Villiers de Jumonville, kicking off the French and Indian War.[11] The American troops retreated to an alpine meadow thirty miles to the southeast, where they constructed a stockade, christened Fort Necessity.

Threatened with attack by a French and Indian party, and finding his soldiers drunk, on July 3 George Washington surrendered. Generously, the French commander (Louis Coulon de Villiers) permitted Washington, Adam Stephen, and their battalion to march out unscathed, beginning their march back to Virginia. These events marked the beginning of Adam Stephen's American military career.[12]

Brief Command

On the force's return to Virginia, Governor Dinwiddie promoted George Washington to colonel, placing him in command of the Virginia volunteers, with Adam Stephen as second-in-command. Soon afterward, though, "Washington, offended that [British] officers of less rank would have precedence over him, as a result resign[ed] his commission in November 1754."[13] Adam Stephen stepped into the commander's shoes.

Combat followed. In February 1755, Major General Edward Braddock arrived from England with the 44th and 48th British Regiments. Sixty years old when he arrived, Braddock's past posts had been sedentary, most recently as governor of Gibraltar.[14] Nonetheless, Braddock was, in author Walter Isaacson's estimation, "brimming with arrogance."[15] An interested party warned Braddock to be "wary of Indian ambushes." General Braddock replied, "These savages may be a formidable enemy to your raw American militia, but upon the king's regular and disciplined troops, sir, it is impossible they would make any impressions."[16]

Assembling 1,736 men, including the Virginians, Braddock and his force began the 144-mile march from Winchester, Virginia, to the French fort, Fort Duquesne, at the Forks of the Ohio, using the same northwesterly route the Virginians had used in 1754. The Braddock column moved at the snail's pace of two miles per day.

Wending through and strung out the length of a narrow defile, at the Battle of Monongahela Braddock's troops suffered a humiliating loss to the French and their Indian allies, who, as forecast, ambushed the strung-out British. Of 1,459 actives, Braddock lost 914 enlisted and 63 officers killed or wounded. Stephen himself suffered minor wounds.[17] Braddock suffered severe wounds, dying several days later as his force's retreat turned into a rout.[18] Braddock's troops buried him in the middle of the road, the National Highway today, southeast of Uniontown, Pennsylvania. They passed wagons over and back over Braddock's grave to disguise it, hoping to protect the grave from desecration.[19]

George Washington had joined the force as a consultant to Braddock, later reclaiming his role as commander of the American contingent. For his part, after the defeat and a further retreat to Virginia, Stephen stayed in service, at Fort Cumberland and at Winchester, fifty and twenty-five miles, respectively, from his Bower plantation.

First Spots on Stephen's Record

Colonial Governor Dinwiddie appointed Stephen to lead a Virginia expeditionary force to South Carolina. "Stephen displeased [Royal] Governor Dinwiddie in being dilatory in bringing the Virginia detachment down the James [River]."[20] The governor was further displeased when, on their return, Stephen's troop count was less than on departure, the inference being that Stephen had allowed women to accompany the expedition, misrepresenting them as soldiers. Earlier, Stephen had not seen to payment by the troops for fish ordered and left at Fort Cumberland. "Washington fumed at Stephen's giving so many of the regimental stores to the Catawba Indians, including 122 blankets." Stephen's earlier dereliction of duty at Fort Cumberland made Washington distrustful. "[In Washington's mind], Stephen depended too much on his own spot judgment."[21] Over and over, it seemed, Stephen interpreted orders as mere guidelines or thought that he knew better than his superiors.

Forbes Road and the Forbes Expedition

In 1757–1758, the British decided to attempt another assault on Fort Duquesne, but by a different route, cutting a new wagon road 220 miles from Carlisle, Pennsylvania, in a straight line, east to west, farther north than the angled northwesterly route Braddock had taken. Adam Stephen played a principal part in the road building, which involved one thousand mostly Americans, the manual labor assignment reflecting the British disdain for the colonials. Along those lines, British General Sir John St. Clair wrote to Prime Minister William Pitt that the Virginia and Pennsylvania officers "are an extreme bad collection of broken innkeepers, horse jockeys, &

Indian traders, and the men under them are direct copies of their officers, nor can it be otherwise, as they are a gathering from the scum of the worst people."[22]

Over that road, John Forbes's six thousand troops reached Fort Duquesne, finding it abandoned, and renamed it Fort Pitt. General Forbes himself, suffering from stomach cancer, returned to Philadelphia, where he died. By that point, Adam Stephen had been in service for five full years, an active participant in the struggle against the French and their Indian allies.

CHAPTER SIX

Business over Generalship

RETURNING TO BERKELEY COUNTY, IN 1760 STEPHEN ACQUIRED EIGHT HUNDRED additional acres along Opequon Creek, adding to the two thousand he had previously acquired (the Bower). In 1762, he bought 137 acres on the Cacapon River; in 1763, he bought 1,000 more acres on Opequon Creek. He continued to sell flour, cattle, and hogs to the British army, using American colonial soldiers to herd his cattle and bring in crops. He also returned to military service. In August 1761, Harry Byrd resigned as commander of a one-thousand-man expedition against the Cherokees in North Carolina. Adam Stephen succeeded him, soon thereafter negotiating a peace treaty and avoiding combat. In the main, though, Stephen continued with his main avocations: selling provisions to the British army and acquiring land.[1]

For the former, Stephen endured British officers' criticism. Captain Lewis Ourry wrote that to him, "Stephen's patriotism was affected by a profit motive."[2] Stephen made agreements (1763) with Plumsted & Frank, sutlers to British forces, to supply sixty head of cattle and sixty thousand pounds of flour to Bedford, Pennsylvania, where the British maintained a fort. Later, ninety cattle and a quantity of hogs were to be delivered. Shipments of flour were late and "fell short of the amount promised," which led to a falling out with Colonel Henry Bouquet, the Swiss officer after General Forbes's death in command; Bouquet ordered that no more army business was to be done with Stephen.[3]

FIRST LEGAL REVIEW OF STEPHEN'S ACTIVITIES

In 1763, the Virginia House of Burgesses opened a court of inquiry, which "gave the complaints against Stephen a . . . thorough and volatile airing." Three sets of charges were laid before the court. First was that he, "by Persuasions, Orders, Threats, and Influence prevented many Persons from joining as Volunteers in the Expedition commanded by Col. Bouquet against the Indian towns in Ohio, etc." Second was that he had used Virginia militia in his private engagements. Third was that he sent grain to his own mill to grind into flour, selling that to the army. Even though the court did not fully acquit him of the charges, Stephen escaped reprimand.[4]

Despite the legal contretemps, Stephen did not stop. All along he continued with land acquisitions: 212 acres on Mossey Creek (1764), 570 acres on the North River (1764), 255 acres on Tuscarora Creek (site of today's Martinsburg, West Virginia), 386 acres on Opequon Creek (1765), and 542 acres on Patterson Creek in Hampshire County (1770). For having served in the French and Indian War, in 1763 he also received from the Crown an award of bounty lands in Ohio territory and Kentucky.[5] By 1770, in addition to land he owned elsewhere, Stephen was the largest landowner in Berkeley County, with 5,381 acres.[6]

During an interruption from military service, Stephen engaged in more sharp dealing or outright theft, or so it appeared. Stephen had returned to medicine. For his practice, he ordered quantities of drugs from Hugh Mercer in Fredericksburg. Stephen welched on paying for the supplies, forcing Mercer to sue. Governor Francis Farquier signed an arrest warrant for Stephen, ordering him confined to Williamsburg until he paid the bill, which eventually he did.

MAINTAINING POLITICAL CONTACTS AND ADVANCEMENT TOWARD REVOLUTION

All along Adam Stephen maintained useful associations. George Washington had a cottage at Berkeley Springs (then called Warm Springs or Frederick Springs), not far distant from the Bower.[7] Stephen dined with Washington several times; they renewed their on again, off again "touchy relationship" that dated from French and Indian War service.[8] The relationship was exacerbated by Washington and Stephen's "rivalry" in Ohio land acquisitions and their dispute over House of Burgesses elections from Frederick County, a situs that Washington also called his residence for voting purposes.[9] The House of Burgesses did not hive off Berkeley County from Frederick County until 1772.[10]

By summer 1775, all fifty-one Virginia counties had formed Committees of Safety. At least anticipating skirmishing, "everywhere they were engaged in the vital role of raising volunteer militia companies."[11] Colonial Governor John Murray (Earl of Dunmore) dissolved the House of Burgesses for voicing its sympathies with and calling for a day of prayer for revolutionaries and their supporters. The First Virginia Convention (March 20, 1775) took its place. "[A]dam Stephen was warmly attached to the revolutionary cause," but perhaps not for patriotic reasons. "[T]here would be opportunity not only to achieve further military distinction but also to pursue economic gain," the latter of which Stephen did throughout the war.[12]

In midsummer 1775, the Third Virginia Convention appointed Stephen, James Wood, Andrew Lewis, Thomas Walker, and John Walker as peace commissioners to treat with the Indians in western Pennsylvania and Ohio. First aligned with the French and later with the British, Native Americans constituted a threat to the would-be new nation, raiding from the western frontier far into the colonies. During the war, after the war, and for several decades, raiding war parties terrorized western New York, Pennsyvania, Virginia, the Carolinas, and Georgia. The commissioners—Stephen, Wood, Lewis, and the Walkers—traveled to Fort Pitt, where "[p]robably at no other time in early America did so many great chiefs assemble in one place." They included Cornstalk and Blue Jacket of the Shawnees, Delaware Captains Pipe and Custaloga, Half-King representing the Wyandots, and Ottawa Chief Shaganaba. "What bothered Stephen most was evidence that the Indians were leaning toward an alliance with the British. . . . What Stephen observed was the beginning of a contest between the Americans and the British for the loyalty, or at least the neutrality of the western Indians; it was a struggle which would not end until forty years later," with the Treaty of Greenville (1795) and the Battle of Tippecanoe (1811).[13] The Pitt conference ended with an agreement that turned out to be no more than pieces of paper.

"Although [in Virginia] his public responsibilities" and preparations for war "made demands on his time, Stephen gave attention to his new industries—a distillery and an arms manufactory. As in the past, Stephen was viewed as creating opportunities for [personal] profit."[14] In April 1775, citizens accused Stephen of rigging the election for Berkeley County delegates to the Virginia Convention that took place in July 1775. No notice of election had been given in three other churches of the county, only in Stephen's home parish (Norborne Parish). Charges were bought before the Berkeley County Committee of Safety. The committee found Stephen "to have done nothing improper." Of course, Adam Stephen chaired the committee.

The Battle of Bunker Hill occurred on June 17, 1775, with the news reaching Virginia several days later.

THE WAR BEGINS

In December 1775, the Fourth Virginia Convention, to augment the two regiments already existing, created six additional regiments.[15] On January 12, 1776, the convention selected Adam Stephen as the 4th Virginia's commander, with orders "to take his post immediately at Suffolk. . . . [B]ut Stephen dallied, not getting into the field [far southeastern Virginia] until mid-May."[16]

Stephen's 4th Regiment replaced Muhlenberg's 8th, which Major General Charles Lee had ordered south to Charleston. Stephen's regiment assumed a backup role at Suffolk, Virginia. On May 22, 1776, Earl Lord Dunmore, former colonial governor, and his small fleet of ships had moved from Tucker's Point to Gwynn's Island, below the Rappahannock's mouth, at the foot of Virginia's Middle Peninsula. Away from the action, Stephen supervised his men in constructing fortifications at Portsmouth, to the southwest of (but adjacent to) Norfolk. "He acted independently of his superior, General Andrew Lewis, who . . . did not take offense that he was not consulted."[17]

It was William Woodford and his regiment who defeated Dunmore's army at Great Bridge, directly south of Norfolk. Brigadier Andrew Lewis later ordered the bombardment of Dunmore's little fleet, slightly wounding Dunmore, who ordered his ships to weigh anchor, sailing up the Chesapeake. So ended the Battle of Gwynn's Island, with Adam Stephen's involvement being in a backup role. Dunmore's fleet sailed down Chesapeake Bay, out into the Atlantic, and to New York.[18] Governor Dunmore left in his wake Norfolk, burned to the ground. "Norfolk became a vivid emblem of British cruelty."[19]

The Revolution in Earnest

Congress ordered the 1st (Woodford) and 3rd (Weedon) Virginia Regiments north to reinforce George Washington at Long Island, but they arrived too late to participate in the Battle of Brooklyn. The regiments did participate in battles at Kip's Bay and Harlem Heights (September 16, 1776) as the Continental Army retreated up Manhattan Island. Earlier, on September 3, 1776, Congress had ordered three more Virginia regiments, including Stephen's 4th Virginia, to go north. On September 4, 1776, Congress elevated Stephen to the rank of brigadier general, after which he assumed command of a brigade (four regiments).

In contrast to Woodford's and Weedon's brigades, Stephen's brigade never reached New York, instead wandering from place to place: Head of Elk at the top of Chesapeake Bay; east to Annapolis, Maryland; up to Trenton, New Jersey; and south to Wilmington, Delaware, finally arriving near Perth Amboy, New Jersey, on November 16, 1776. Despite receiving no "mention in the dispatches"—that is, no publicized combat exploits—Stephen had powerful allies. Benjamin Rush of Philadelphia, a signatory to the Declaration of Independence and leader in the Continental Congress, wrote to fellow legislators, "[I]n our next promotions we shall disregard seniority, [Adam Stephen] must be made a major general; he has genius as well as knowledge."[20]

After defeat upon defeat and a dispirited march half the length of New Jersey, George Washington got his troops across the Delaware River into Pennsylvania in early December 1776. Reinforcement by Generals John Sullivan and Horatio Gates, as well as by Stephen, lifted their spirits to a degree. But what one hand had given, the other took away. "Stephen's [force] had dwindled to 520 men." Overall General Washington had 10,804 men on paper, 8,000 on hand, but only 6,000 fit for duty.[21]

Stephen and his men made the historic crossing of the Delaware on Christmas night of 1776. As has been seen, nine miles above Trenton, Continental forces divided to approach the Hessian force quartered there, proceeding over two roughly parallel roads: Washington, Greene, Fermoy, Stephen, and Mercer took the upper road. General John Sullivan led his brigade, including Arthur St. Clair, on the lower, river road. Upland, Stephen and his soldiers nearly compromised the element of surprise, earning George Washington's rebuke. Fifty soldiers of the 4th Regiment, out on the left wing, were seeking revenge for colleagues who had been killed and had a firefight with Hessian guards, killing four and wounding eleven. "Washington was astonished and enraged. . . . He allegedly sent for Stephen and exclaimed: 'You, sir, may have ruined all my plans.' Washington was afraid that the whole Hessian camp had been alerted."[22]

Stephen now claimed participation in two American victories in eight months, Gwynn's Island and Trenton, although it is doubtful whether he saw real combat in the former, and the commander in chief had reprimanded him in the latter.

Other Engagements and Battles

Stephen's brigade saw little action in the Battle of Princeton (January 3, 1777), in which fellow Scot and physician General Hugh Mercer received fatal wounds (chapter 9).[23] On February 10, 1777, Congress promoted five generals to major general rank, including Stephen. The others were Lord Stirling, Arthur St. Clair, Thomas Mifflin, and Benjamin Lincoln. "Stephen's quick promotion, only six months after being commissioned a brigadier, ruffled the sensibilities of other brigadier generals, [many] of whom outranked him." Andrew Lewis, once in command of all the Virginia forces, "was one, and he resigned in April [1777] because he was not on the promotion list. . . . Washington . . . was disappointed that Lewis had not been promoted (implying a preference of Lewis over Stephen)."[24] The existing revolutionary force generals had other complaints as well: "The new [1777] promotions [Stephen, Lincoln, Mifflin, etc.] including the [congressional] arrangement of seniority within a grade, along with Congress's grant of commissions to foreigners over the heads of American officers, affected the pride and sense of honor of those who were slighted."[25]

For his part, "Stephen's rapid rise in the army seems to have bought out a greater vanity, even a flippant air, in him, and stirred his old sensibilities as a politician. [He began to supply] information to the newspapers, with the implication of his own importance."[26] He corresponded with Virginia Governor Patrick Henry and Congressman Richard Henry Lee. For a senior officer—a major general, no less, especially one who had seen little combat—openly to tread on the political stage usurped the prerogative of the commander in chief and gave offense to other major generals as well.

Chapter Seven

Egregious Sins

Political forays aside, Adam Stephen did gain exposure to combat in the time between the major battles of Princeton in January 1777 and Brandywine in September 1777. In the interval, two-thirds of the year, the American army camped at Middlebrook, seven or eight miles northwest of Brunswick, in the Watchung Mountains of New Jersey. During that time, British General William Howe attempted to lure the Americans out from their bivouac for an engagement.[1] Rather than risking a cataclysmic confrontation, though, "increasingly the American army turned to . . . light infantry and hit-and-run tactics, as the [American army was] reluctant to engage in pitched battle." The American tactics produced results, concluded Leonard Lundin in *Cockpit of the Revolution*: "The resulting constant harassment led to the drastic reduction of provisions and forage for the British."[2] The downside to this development was that "light infantry commanders [who had leeway to] conduct operations much as they pleased" abused the discretion entrusted in them.

Thus, relying on General Washington's discretionary orders, Stephen and his light infantry took outsize latitude. Washington upbraided Stephen, saying, "I am very sorry that my orders have been too frequently unattended to." In May 1777, Stephen earned further rebuke from General Washington by reporting inflated casualty numbers from an incursion on a detachment of the British army near Piscataway, New Jersey.[3] Stephen reported 70 British killed, 120 wounded. The Hessians and British later claimed only one sergeant was wounded after Stephen and his eight-hundred-man force had mounted a "disorderly attack."

Partial Paralysis in 1777

In late spring and early summer, Stephen, despite his faux pas, kept prodding Washington to mount all-out attacks on the British. On one occasion, Stephen "caught Washington off guard with a proposal to attack a British regiment quartered at Bergen New Jersey." General Washington, however, had to keep a larger picture in mind: Would he have to reinforce the northern army under Generals Philip Schuyler and Horatio Gates north of Albany? He had to be prepared to send reinforcements in case British commander William Howe went north to meet up with General Burgoyne progressing south from Canada, southward on the Champlain–Lake George–Hudson pathway. Or would Howe move against Philadelphia by a route across New Jersey? Or would Howe's forces embark on oceangoing transports, sailing southward and then up the Delaware Estuary, or Chesapeake Bay, to attack Philadelphia from the south or southwest? Washington knew that the army had to be nimble to be able to respond to widely varying scenarios, a factor Stephen did not consider.

Stephen was again at odds with Washington's decisions, disapproving of collection of all the troops at Middlebrook. In a letter to General John Sullivan, "Stephen rather clearly disputed Washington's military judgment. 'I know as little the reason for our present disposition as General Sullivan does.'"[4] More sniping by Stephen renewed communications with politicians. Regarding the loss of Fort Ticonderoga, abandoned by General Arthur St. Clair (chapter 3), Stephen wrote to Congressman Francis Lightfoot Lee, blaming the abandonment on New Englanders' refusal to raise troops: "For Want of the Quota, the Place [Ticonderoga] is lost and they [the New Englanders] stand answerable for the consequences." The criticism "[s]tirred Yankee blood," including that of Samuel and John Adams.[5] The latter, a Massachusetts Continental Congress delegate, regarded himself as something of an authority—an armchair general, if you will.[6] With this slap at New Englanders, Stephen seemed to stick his nose where it was not wanted, and where it did not belong, second-guessing General Washington and poking New England in the eye.

THE BRITISH ATTACK PHILADELPHIA FROM HEAD OF ELK

General Washington's guessing game ended in late August 1777. British General Howe made a choice from among his alternatives, sending eleven thousand men sailing down the Atlantic from New York and up Chesapeake Bay, to disembark from royal transports forty miles southwest of Philadelphia. Joined by Hessian mercenaries, Howe's force numbered over 15,000. Mustering a roughly equal number of 15,500 Americans, Washington chose to block the British advance at Wyatt's ford over Brandywine Creek. There the Philadelphia Road crossed the north-to-south flowing stream. Again, though, as at Long Island, in arraying his 15,500-man force, Washington left his flank unprotected, this time the right rather than the left flank. On the afternoon of September 11, as the battle developed, soldiers in Stephen's division had to wheel to the right from the main westerly facing defensive line, advancing to face Lord Cornwallis's British troops attempting to turn the American flank. With 9,000 or so men, Cornwallis had marched north several miles above where the creek branched, to the unprotected Trimble's (west branch) and Jefferies (east branch) fords, where they crossed the creek. From a position east of the creek, the British could turn southward, rolling up the American line.

Stephen's men fought well, though accounts of the eleven-hour battle record no exploits by General Stephen; subsequent accounts praise Stephen, albeit faintly. "At ... Brandywine," according to Gene Procknow, "Stephen acquitted himself as well as any officer. . . . However, before and after the battle, Stephen vociferously expressed his opinions in councils of war, many times in conflict with Washington's views."[7]

STEPHEN'S MILITARY CAREER ENDS

After Brandywine, General Washington's troops retreated northwest of Philadelphia while Howe's force continued east, occupying Philadelphia two weeks later. Smarting from the Brandywine defeat, Washington was determined to deliver a licking to the British. He saw the opportunity in the British bivouac of ten thousand troops in Germantown, five to six miles northwest of Philadelphia (today part of the city).

Beginning in the early morning on October 4, 1777, Generals Wayne, Sullivan, Conway, and Nash, with their troops, from several miles to the northwest, were to proceed in a direct route along the main road to Germantown. Off on the American left wing, Greene's division, subsuming Stephen's division and Scott's regiment, was to proceed down the Lime Kiln Road, northeast of the principal American force, eventually curving toward the British right flank. As Professor Harry Ward notes, "For the broad pincer movement it was of utmost importance that the advance be synchronized to the greatest precision."[8] It was not so synchronized, being thrown into disorder by Stephen's commands directing his division to the right and to the center, rather than staying on and proceeding forward on the left.

The explanations vary. Professor Ward records that "a guide led the American left wing down the wrong road." A second, overlapping explanation was that Stephen and his troops were "fatigued from the long march, and a fog limited visibility to no more than fifty yards," as Brigadier George Weedon explained.[9] A third and most frequently encountered explanation was that Adam Stephen was drunk, confusing his right for his left, thus spoiling the plan for a surprise attack. Confusion and troop movements worsened, with Stephen's men attacking comrades (General Anthony Wayne's men in the center, and Stephen's coming up from the rear).[10] Adding to the plausibility of the latter theory was a prior incident in which, at Brandywine, General William Maxwell had reportedly led troops while drunk.[11]

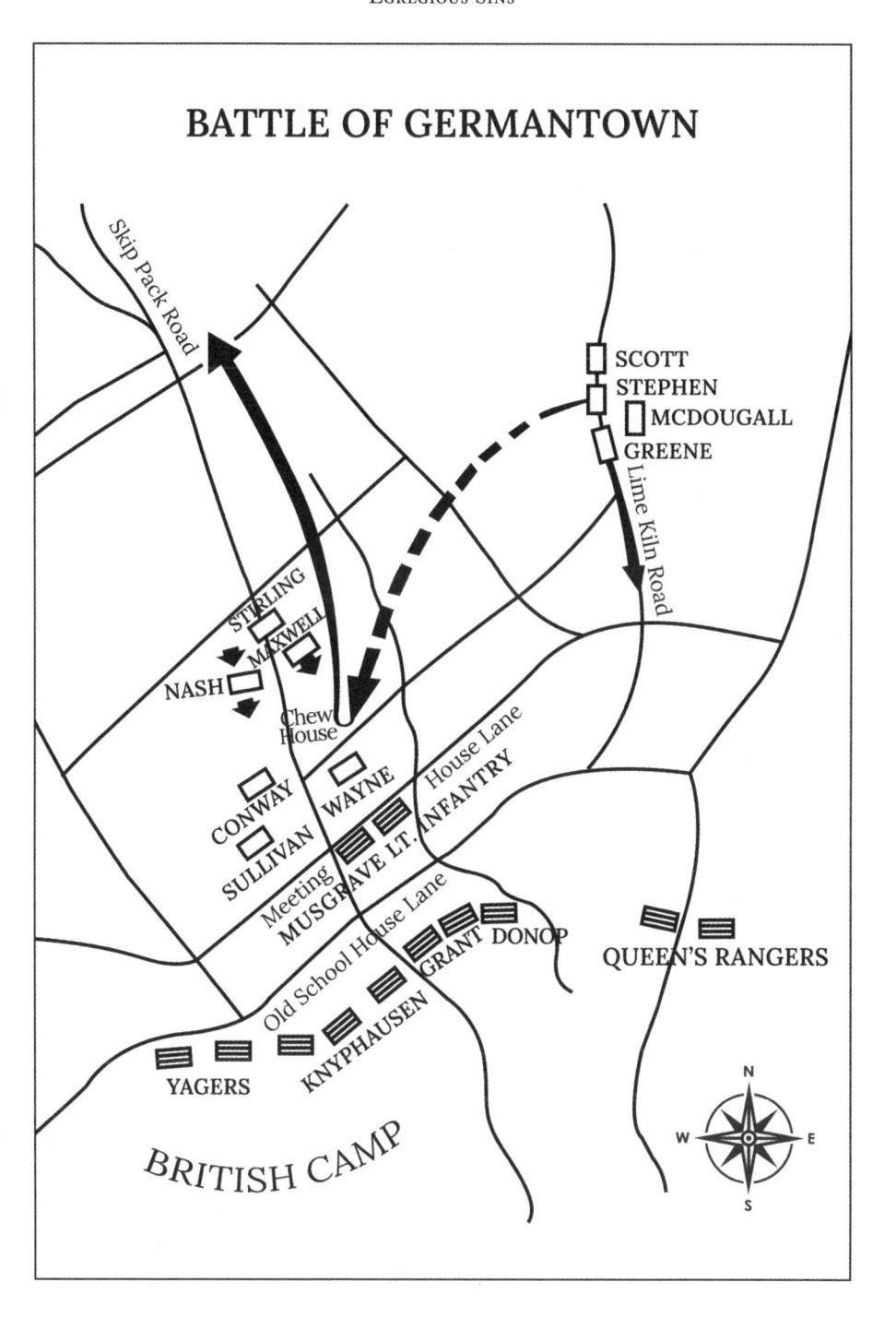

BATTLE OF GERMANTOWN

Again, on the Lime Kiln Road, Stephen's troops broke away from those of Nathanael Greene and headed toward the center, obliquely across Anthony Wayne's rear. Wayne heard firing behind him as Stephen's troops shot at a British redoubt (the Chew House). Wayne mistook Stephen's men for British, possibly from Chew House, the stone building over which Wayne's men had earlier leapfrogged. Wayne ordered his men to about-face and fire at what he assumed was the Chew House British contingent but was actually an American force. Stephen's troops replied in kind, continuing a heavy fusillade. So-called friendly fire killed many.

Other misfortunes flowed from Stephen's dereliction. His diversion left Greene's division hanging in the air, so to speak, unsupported by any advance in the center. A salient formed on the American left. The British surrounded the most advanced regiment of Greene's division, Colonel David Matthews's regiment, compelling it to surrender.[12]

ADDITIONAL MISFORTUNES

Further compounding his one-man effort to snatch defeat from the jaws of victory, Stephen prematurely signaled retreat to his troops, "paying no attention to the advice of his officers . . . to have his troops reform and post artillery to [cover other units' retreat] and to check the enemy's pursuit."[13]

After Germantown, a probable victory that ended as a devastating defeat, gossip and remembrances turned ugly. Several men reported that after the retreat Stephen was found lying on the ground next to a fence, sleeping off his alcoholic excess. Stephen did his cause no good by writing a long letter to General Washington, dated October 9, 1778, demanding that his name be cleared. Stephen denied being intoxicated as well as charges that he had abandoned his troops' retreat. "It was certainly a mistake for Stephen to write the kind of letter he did, especially in venting his petulance toward [General Charles] Scott," against whom Stephen harbored a grudge. "[S]tephen only further alienated Washington and the Virginia officers."[14] Charles Scott, who came from Virginia and had been the hero of the Second Battle of Trenton, bore witness to Stephen's derelictions.[15] In the past, too, Stephen had often contradicted or argued with the commander in chief, being blunt and impolitic in doing so.

FALLOUT FROM THE BATTLE

As the days passed, word spread throughout the army that Stephen had been drunk at Germantown. Acting on Stephen's request, Washington announced a court of inquiry. The court found the allegations against Stephen as proven more likely than not: "Drunkenness, or drinking too much, as to act frequently in a manner unworthy of the character of an officer" and "[e]vidence [serving to prove] that the General was not with his division during the Action." On receiving the court of inquiry report, Washington ordered Stephen to be tried by court-martial, commencing November 3, 1778.

DISMISSAL FROM THE CONTINENTAL SERVICE

Dating from French and Indian War days, authorities perceived Stephen as derelict in his duties while he was away tending his plantation, his real estate, and his commercial activities. The dereliction later "made Washington distrustful of Stephen. [In addition,] Stephen depended too much in his own on-the-spot judgment." Stephen had second-guessed his commander in chief on numerous occasions. Worse yet, Stephen leaked his criticisms to politicians and newspaper reporters. For example, learning that Colonel Joseph Reed and Major Thomas Mifflin had been appointed as Washington's aides, Stephen wrote, "I am glad to hear it for General Washington will require such men about him. He [General Washington] is *a weak man*. I know him well. I served with him during the late French war."[16]

In Stephen's defense, certain politicians and high-ranking military figures threw a few punches. James Madison, for example, "possessed a penchant for assuming the worst of others. [H]e castigated Washington as of a class of tidewater gentry that demonstrated 'a pusillanimity little comporting with . . . the name Virginian.'"[17]

Pusillanimous or not, General Washington ordered a general court-martial. Five generals (John Sullivan, George Weedon, Peter Muhlenberg, James Conway, and Henry Laurens) and five colonels (two full and three lieutenant colonels) constituted the court. "Stephen thought it was beneath the dignity of a court trying a major general to have three lieutenant colonels on the bench"; he stated his opinion to anyone within earshot, tipping a court member or two toward an unfavorable view before the trial even began.

Before the court, damaging testimony came from Stephen's own brigade commanders, William Woodford and Charles Scott. The court found Stephen guilty of "un-officer-like behavior, in the retreat from Germantown, owing to inattention, or want of judgement, and that he has frequently been intoxicated since in the service, to the prejudice of good order and military discipline."

During that period, there actually were four courts-martial—namely, of Stephen, Generals Maxwell and Woodford, and Charles Scott. All were acquitted save Stephen, who not only was found guilty but also received a drastic sentence: dismissal from the service. General Washington wrote to Congress, "I flatter myself that these examples will involve many favourable and beneficial consequences."[18]

Of patience, it is said, unlike hatred, humans have only a limited supply. That was certainly true of George Washington, a commander of nearly infinite patience with his squabbling subordinates. Nonetheless, Washington ran out of patience with his fellow Virginian, Indian fighter, and general.[19] The commander in chief affirmed the court's sentence: Stephen was to be cashiered from the army.

Stephen appealed the verdict to Congress in a letter including a "denunciation of George Washington" that "did not help his cause," stated Professor Harry Ward. "The rancor that Stephen bore Washington and his other alleged persecutors [was] quite evident" in the letter. "It has been my misfortune," wrote Stephen, "to become the Object of hatred of a person of high rank [Washington] for no other reason that I know but for delivering my Sentiments on the Measures pursu'd this Campaign, with that Candour & Boldness which becomes an old officer of Experience, who had the Interest of America at heart."[20]

Postscript

Adam Stephen returned to Berkeley County, where he relieved his overseer of active management of his enterprises (farming, cattle raising, horse breeding, grist milling, whiskey distilling, and operating an arms factory). Stephen also plotted 120 lots on land he owned, which became Martinsburg, Virginia (named after Lord Fairfax's favorite nephew, Colonel Thomas Bryan Martin). Stephen built an eight-room stone house, standing today and on the *National Register of Historic Places*, as is his plantation house, the Bower, near Shepherdstown, West Virginia. The in-town house and a monument to Major General Adam Stephen are among Martinsburg's principal attractions. General Stephen died on July 17, 1791, and is buried beneath the Martinsburg monument.

Doctor Benjamin Rush described Stephen as "a sordid, boasting, cowardly sot."[21] More generously, what made General Adam Stephen tick? Historian Paul David Nelson sums up Stephen as "attracted to trouble like iron to a magnet."[22] A less metaphoric surmise would be that Adam Stephen possessed a burning desire to join Virginia's elite, in terms of acceptance, prestige, and wealth, a task that others attempted and found "a complex social art."[23] As Professor Harry Ward concluded, "Stephen was an outsider to [Virginia's] elite," destined to remain so, "not only because of the area of his residence [Berkeley County in the far northwest] but also essentially because he was a parvenu and not of the kinship network of old families. . . . [H]e was a Scottish émigré, and thanks to the sharp practices of Scottish factors in Virginia, Scotsmen were viewed with suspicion. Stephen's own quick [financial] success could be seen as behavior of the typical Scotsman."[24]

Stephen's quest for accumulation of wealth seemed all out, unseemly to the landed classes. He achieved wealth but not acceptance from Tidewater Virginia and the clusters of gentry existent in those times.

PART III
HUGH MERCER

Chapter Eight

Yet Another Scottish Physician

Hugh Mercer is one of the more venerated Revolutionary War gener-als. No less than twelve United States counties and towns (mostly counties) bear the name "Mercer."[1] Even far-off Washington State has a Mercer Island. A principal Seattle thoroughfare is named "Mercer."[2] In the eastern United States, no less than five monuments are dedicated to General Hugh Mercer and his exploits.[3] During the Revolutionary War, on January 12, 1777, Brigadier Mercer passed away, suffering from bayonet wounds received in the runup to the assault on Princeton, New Jersey.

THE JACOBITE RISING

Mercer's early background involved famous historical events. In the 1740s, a "pre-tender" to the English throne was Prince Charles Edward Stuart, known as "Bonnie Prince Charlie." In 1745, the pretender returned from exile in France to lead a six-thousand-man Scottish Highlander army intent on restoring the Stuart dynasty to the throne. Historians refer to the uprising as the Jacobite Rebellion or Jacobite Rising.[4] Hugh Mercer was a veteran of the vanquished Jacobite rebel force.

Mercer came from a line of Presbyterian ministers, and his father was pastor of a church east of Inverness.[5] Mercer was born in 1726, "in the manse of Pilsligo Kirk."[6] He pursued medicine rather than ministry, studying at Aberdeen to become a physician.

Led by John Augustus, the English Duke of Cumberland, on April 16, 1746, the Crown's forces met the Jacobite rebels on Culloden Moor, east of Inverness. With a twelve-thousand-man force, the English thoroughly vanquished the six thousand Highlanders. Not only were the English victorious, but Cumberland also declared the rebels outlaws. With the English hunting rebels down, the Jacobites retreated into the Highlands.[7]

Hugh Mercer
COURTESY OF
YALE ART MUSEUM

The outlaw edict likewise applied to young Mercer, probably a surgeon or surgeon's assistant at Culloden.[8] So after the defeat Mercer fled south, staying on his cousins' farm west of Aberdeen, hiding for a year. He then found his way to Leith, the port city on the Firth of Forth, adjacent to Edinburgh. In May 1747, Hugh Mercer boarded a ship bound for Philadelphia and America.

Straight to the Frontier

Given his "outlaw" status, on arriving in colonial America, Mercer did not tarry in Philadelphia, departing immediately for the frontier.[9] He settled in what today is Franklin County, in south central Pennsylvania, west of Gettysburg, a score of miles short of the Alleghenies.[10] He began practice as a frontier physician.[11]

Those were perilous times on the frontier, perhaps more perilous than they had been in Scotland. Pennsylvania was a Quaker colony founded and dominated by pacifists. The colony's assembly refused to authorize a standing armed force, let alone public funds to buy weapons for a volunteer one.[12] Further, proprietors William Penn, Thomas Penn, and John Penn would not permit any tax on the vast Penn landholdings.[13]

After Mercer had been on the frontier eight years, General Edward Braddock, of the Coldstream Guards (former royal governor of Gibraltar), arrived from England.

Braddock, according to Benjamin Franklin, "[w]as a brave man, and might probably made a good figure in some European war. But he had too much self-confidence; too high an opinion of the validity of regular [British] troops; too mean of one of both Americans and Indians."[14] A Virginia regiment, made up of nine companies of fifty men each, led by a young George Washington, was to accompany Braddock to confront the French and their Indian allies. The goal was to recapture Fort Duquesne at the Forks of the Ohio, considered the gateway to the Ohio country and the west. The combined British-American force left Fort Cumberland, Maryland, on June 10, 1755, with 150 wagons and two thousand horses.

Ten miles short of Fort Duquesne, on July 9, 1755, the French and Indians ambushed Braddock's 1,400-man force, with devastating effect (see chapter 6). By one count, the British-American force lost 457 killed and 450 wounded. Braddock was mortally wounded, dying two days later as his army's remnants retreated southeast.

RANGER CAPTAIN MERCER OF THE PENNSYLVANIA MILITIA

Braddock's failure heavily influenced frontier moods. News of the defeat encouraged bolder Indian raids, which swept past the frontier into the colony's more settled regions. In his Hugh Mercer biography, Joseph Waterman recounted that "[a] wave of terror swept across Pennsylvania."[15]

Forty-five miles northeast of present-day Pittsburgh, on the eastern shore of the Allegheny River, sat the Indian village Kittanning.[16] "To Kittanning the [Indian] war parties returned with plunder and prisoners and here took place the orgies of triumph. . . . [H]ere lived the Delaware chief, Captain Jacobs, and here resided [Lenape Chief] King Shingas," also known as "Shingas the Terrible." Ranger Colonel John Armstrong, a surveyor familiar with the terrain and Mercer's friend, organized a seven-hundred-volunteer force to cross the Alleghenies, to subjugate the Kittanning. Armstrong organized the militia into six companies, with Hugh Mercer as a company captain.

The colonists' raid, "which was only nominally successful, given the number of casualties suffered by Armstrong," quelled hostile Indian activity for a time. The rangers killed forty Indians and burned down Indian structures while suffering the loss of seventeen. The Kittanning raid, though, "was a big success psychologically, boosting the morale of settlers throughout Pennsylvania," laid low as it had been by Braddock's defeat.[17]

HUGH MERCER'S RETURN TO CIVILIZATION:
THE STUFF OF LEGENDS

In the Kittanning raid, Indian warriors shot Mercer, shattering his wrist. Mercer's men commandeered a horse, placing their wounded captain in the saddle, and retreated southeast. Soon, though, an Indian group ambushed the militia party. The Indians shot three or four men. Two other men hopped on the horse, disappearing up the game trail they had been following. Alone, Captain Mercer hid behind a fallen tree.

After a close brush with yet another warrior, Mercer stood alone. He was more than one hundred miles from civilization, separated from familiar surroundings by a mountain range, with neither food nor weapons, badly wounded and bleeding. "This [was] the forest primeval. The murmuring pines and hemlocks, bearded with moss . . . indistinct in the twilight."[18] Thus began "an incredible ordeal."[19] Mercer survived for several weeks, following routes indicated by moss on tree trunks' faces and the sun's rising and setting, crossing mountain after mountain. He picked blackberries and killed and ate raw a rattlesnake. He arrived, nearly unrecognizable, at Pennsylvania's Fort Littleton.

"The story of Mercer's escape spread throughout the Pennsylvania Colony, repeated throughout all of the colonies."[20] The New York *Mercury* reported, "We hear that Captain Mercer was fourteen days in getting to Fort Littleton. He had a miraculous escape, living . . . on two dried clams and a rattlesnake."[21] He became widely known as a symbol of pluck and heroism.[22]

THE FORBES EXPEDITION

Another adventure followed. In 1758, the British colonial secretary sent General John Forbes, with twelve hundred Scottish Highlanders, to America, attempting to accomplish what Braddock had failed to do. Forbes, a Scot and (like Mercer, Stephen, and St. Clair) a physician, was known to be more attuned to the Indian way of warfare.

As chapter 5 recounts, the Forbes expedition's first order of business was to cut a new road, more east-west in orientation, from Carlisle over the mountains to Fort Duquesne, at the Forks of the Ohio. Forbes eschewed using Virginia as a launch point, as Braddock had done. In May 1758, Hugh Mercer became a colonel, commanding the Third Battalion, Pennsylvania Militia, serving the Forbes expedition. His men's first business was, along with Adam Stephen, six months spent constructing the rough-hewn route, "the Forbes Road."[23]

Second-in-command of the Scottish Highlanders was the arrogant Colonel James Grant. Forbes's men built a stockade, Fort Loyalhanna (later renamed Ligonier), on Loyalhanna Creek, forty-five miles east of Fort Duquesne. From Ligonier, Colonel Grant persuaded General Forbes to allow Grant to take an eight-hundred-man force to probe the French fort. In an aside, Colonel Mercer confided in George Washington, whom he had known for some time, about the irony of it all: The British had sent the Highlanders from Scotland to pursue British aims in America, foreclosing the possibility that the Highlanders could serve Scots' interests in another Scottish rebellion. Now the British were sending forth Scots as "the tip of their sword."

Grant's reconnaissance was a disaster. Of 813 men, 273 were killed or severely wounded. Grant himself, in a fit of narcissism, had bagpipes played and troops pass in review in front of the fort, dissipating any element of surprise. Alerted, the French and their Indian allies poured out of the fort, annihilating Grant's party.

VISIONS OF FREDERICKSBURG AND VIRGINIA

During the earlier journey on the Forbes Road, Mercer became close to George Washington. Mercer also met up with a fellow Scots physician, James Craik. Together the two men urged Mercer to open a medical practice in Fredericksburg, Virginia. "They pointed out to him that his old neighborhood [Franklin County, Pennsylvania] had almost been abandoned by the settlers," most of whom had migrated south, to Virginia's Shenandoah Valley, or farther south, to colonies that offered protection against Indian raids, as Pennsylvania did not.[24] Seeds had been planted in Mercer's mind.

In November, after the Grant debacle, General Forbes led a much larger, twenty-five-hundred-man force toward Fort Duquesne, learning on arrival that the French had abandoned the fort, setting fire to the log structures. The French had calculated the position was untenable, given the distances to Montreal and Quebec and the paucity of men and supplies.

Because the supply lines were so long and difficult to traverse, General Forbes left only two hundred Pennsylvania Militiamen at the fort, to be commanded by Colonel Hugh Mercer. British Brigadier General John Stanwix, who succeeded Forbes in command, sent Mercer additional men to help in construction of a larger fort.[25] Shortly thereafter, in 1761, Mercer saw his five years in the military ending. His thoughts turned to what he should do next and where he should do it.

BECOMES A VIRGINIAN

Mercer settled in Fredericksburg, a sizable Tidewater town on the Rappahannock River in Virginia. On arrival, Mercer went to John Gordon's tavern, where he booked room and board. The tavernkeeper introduced Mercer to Gordon's son-in-law, a fellow French and Indian War veteran. George Weedon was welcoming; he and Mercer became fast friends. Mercer opened an apothecary shop and a surgical practice on Caroline Street. He married Isabella Gordon, whose sister, Catherine, had married George Weedon.

Once in Fredericksburg, Mercer regularly saw George Washington, whose mother lived across the river, close by Fredericksburg. In 1767, Mercer joined Fredericksburg Masonic Lodge No. 4, to which Washington and other (now historical) figures belonged, including future president James Monroe and eight persons who became generals in the Revolutionary War.[26] Mercer became a colonel in the Spotsylvania County Militia. He frequented Weedon's tavern, rubbing elbows with George Mason, Fielding Lewis, Thomas Jefferson, John Dandridge, Alexander Spotswood, James Madison, and others, as well as with Washington and Weedon. He and Isabella had four children: William (born deaf and mute), John, George, and Anna. A fifth child, Hugh Tenant Weedon Mercer, was born during the Revolution.[27] Mercer enjoyed a thriving medical practice on top of a "quiet easy-going existence in Fredericksburg . . . where even the horses dozed in the streets."[28]

THE IRON IN THE FIRE GROWS HOTTER

There came an emergency, an alarming one—namely, Governor Lord Dunmore's threats and April 1775 order to seize gunpowder stored in Williamsburg, denying the citizen militia access. The militia, including Hugh Mercer, mustered, prepared for an assault on Williamsburg. According to George Weedon:

> *He faced a man [Mercer] he had never seen before. For the first time [Weedon] saw in Mercer another personality that had been hidden away. He saw Mercer's eyes become pools of fire as he strode in a military tread. The voice, usually so calm and measured, became sharp and crisp, like the crack of a whip.*[29]

In September 1775, Mercer became the colonel for one of Virginia's sixteen district militias (Spotsylvania, Caroline, Stafford, and King George Counties).[30] He became a member of the region's Committee of Safety.[31]

CHAPTER NINE

"Give Me Liberty or Give Me Death"

FROM MERCER'S REVOLUTIONARY WAR EXPERIENCE, A PORTRAIT OF THE HISTORI-cal figure emerges. Mercer was a middle-aged man whom Ron Chernow (in his biography *George Washington*) described as "the dapper, handsome Mercer."[1] "He was always valuable and dependable," wrote Colonel Robert Byrd of Mercer's militia service. "Every man was glad to know him. . . . [C]olonel Mercer was a conscientious officer, loyal to his superiors, undaunted by any emergency."[2] The summation of the regard for Mercer was "of universal approbation throughout his career." He was "always courteous [but] did not incur the jealousy that often crops out in any organization where ambitious men endeavor."[3] He was brave, ready to face danger and, if necessary, death, as his final actions and death at Princeton demonstrate. His adventurous past had color and flair.

In January 1776, the successor to the colonial House of Burgesses, which colonial Governor Dunmore had dissolved, was the Virginia Convention. The Second Convention created six new Virginia Continental Line Regiments. Old line Virginians objected to Mercer as a commander because he was a "northerner"—that is, a Scot rather than an Englishman, and a Presbyterian rather than an Anglican.[4] With those objections put aside, Hugh Mercer won election as commander of the 3rd Virginia, accompanied by George Weedon as lieutenant colonel and Thomas Marshall (father of future Chief Justice John Marshall) as major.[5] The regiment also included a young James Monroe and John Marshall.[6]

Mercer, as ordered, took his 3rd Virginia (605 men) north to Dumfries, on the Potomac south of Mount Vernon. Fretting that the British might enter Virginia from the north (which in the ensuing seven years never occurred), higher command assigned the 3rd Virginia to guard the Potomac's upper reaches. There it was that Washington reassigned General Mercer, with George Weedon taking command of the 3rd, replacing Mercer.

General Hugh Mercer and the Flying Camp

In 1890, Navy Captain Alfred Thayer Mahan wrote *The Influence of Sea Power upon History: 1660–1783*, an influential military tract that navy midshipmen continue to study and that remains relevant today.[7] A century earlier, George Washington had had an intuitive feel for concepts Mahan articulated. Based on the Royal Navy's strength, Washington foresaw a vulnerability along the Atlantic seacoast, as, with their powerful navy, the British could land, protect, and supply forces landing from sea. From Sandy Hook in the north to Cape May in the south, the New Jersey coast stretched 115 miles—a considerable distance in a time when defense forces could march only 14 or 15 miles per day. Washington did not have forces to garrison coastal points where the Royal Navy could land an invading force.

Accordingly, Washington conceived of "the flying camp," which the Continental Congress authorized in June 1776, the same month in which the Congress promoted Hugh Mercer to brigadier. Washington ordered Mercer to assume command of a force that would contain ten thousand troops, a force that was mobile, unencumbered, and able to respond on short notice, flying to points along the eastern coast. In actuality, the force never reached its authorized size, varying from three thousand to eighty-five hundred men.

The reasons for the ebb and flow? First, militia units made up a good portion of the force. As Mercer wrote to Washington, "It is essential that no cause of complaint be given to the troops. This is especially true for militia, who are always eager to return to their homes and quick to find any reason to do so."[8] Second, in his defense of Long Island and Manhattan, General Washington was wont to poach troops from the flying camp.[9] Third, threats to the coast never materialized, with the flying camp units distributed in the north, around New York Harbor: Paulus Hook, Bergen Town, Perth Amboy, Woodbridge, Elizabeth, and Fort Lee.

Mercer oversaw the building of Fort Lee, an earthen redoubt, on the Hudson New Jersey shore, opposite Fort Washington on the New York side, roughly the end points of the George Washington Bridge today. The colonials abandoned Fort Lee on November 20, 1776, four days following the surrender of Fort Washington.[10] The British captured the entire Fort Washington garrison, 2,837 troops.[11] The flying camp atomized, and General Mercer complained that the "militia [acted] in a scandalous manner . . . running off from their posts."[12] The war's low point had been reached.

The Long Retreat

Tails between their legs, the defeated patriots marched diagonally across New Jersey, traversing seventy miles and crossing the Delaware River into Pennsylvania, with Lord Cornwallis in pursuit.[13] Based on his prior service, Mercer had gathered powerful adherents. For instance, on December 21, 1776, Dr. Benjamin Rush of Philadelphia, the surgeon general, wrote Congressman Richard Henry Lee, "Mercer must not be neglected. He has the confidence of the troops."[14]

There, in Pennsylvania, desperately in need of a boost to the fledging country's morale, Washington prepared for a daring recrossing of the Delaware and an assault on Trenton. General Mercer's orders to his regimental commanders for Christmas Day 1776 read:

> *You are to see that your men have three days' rations ready cooked before 12 o'clock this forenoon. . . . [They are] to parade precisely at four in the afternoon, with their arms, accoutrements, and ammunition in the best order. . . . [E]ach officer is to provide himself with a piece of white paper stuck in his hat as a field mark. You will order your men to assemble . . . over the hill on the back of McConkey's Ferry, there to await further orders—a profound silence is to be observed.*[15]

CHRISTMAS NIGHT 1776

The weather was atrocious. Colonel John Patterson wrote, "[I]t rained, snowed, and froze, at the same time blowing a perfect hurricane. During the whole night it alternatively hailed, rained, snowed, and blew tremendously."[16] With 2,460 troops, eighteen cannons, horses, and supplies, Washington led his force across the ice flow–congested Delaware River. The frozen men marched nine miles south to Trenton, arriving late, at 8:00 a.m. the following day, nonetheless surprising the fourteen hundred Hessian troops. Mercer's brigade, in Greene's division, approached Trenton upland, on the Pennington Road, while General John Sullivan's force attacked from the river road. We "went after them pell-mell," recorded an American soldier.[17]

Victory was complete, with 106 Hessians killed and 919 made prisoner. The boost to colonial morale was immense because the victory had been against feared German mercenaries. These Germans "were war-hardened and well trained in European warfare . . . rough in manners and low in morals. Warfare to them was a bloody business." They were looters, rapists, and savage opponents, "who held in contempt the rude [American] army of yokels."[18] At Trenton, the Hessian leader, Colonel Johannes Rall, boasted that "[t]hose clod-hoppers will not attack us, and if they do, we will fall upon them and rout them."[19]

An effect of the Trenton victory was to cause the British swiftly to abandon posts south of Trenton.[20] "The effect [of our expedition to Trenton] is amazing; the enemy have deserted Borden Town, Black Horse, Burlington, Mount Holly, and are fled to [the East Jersey capital] Perth Amboy; we are now in possession of all those places."[21] A further effect was to remove threats to Philadelphia, thirty miles south of Trenton, across the Delaware.

Fearing a British counterattack, Washington marched his troops back north to McKonkey's (or McConley's) Ferry, recrossing the Delaware. In Pennsylvania, he permitted his fatigued men two days' rest, December 28–29. Then Washington crossed the Delaware again, marching back to Trenton and encamping his men on the town's southeast side, protected by Assunpink Creek, which had but a single bridge spanning it.[22]

To an Athlete Dying Young

Hugh Mercer was to turn fifty-one on January 16, 1777, not so young but with a young man's fervor. In a session with other officers on January 1, 1777, Mercer stated, with great eloquence, to Dr. Benjamin Rush, "My views in this contest are confined to a single object, that is, the success of the war, and God can witness how cheerful I would lay down my life to secure it."[23] The following night, as he dined with General St. Clair and Rush, Mercer said "that he would not be conquered, but that he would cross the mountains and live with the Indians rather than submit to the power of Great Britain in any of the civilized states."

There followed the Battle of Princeton, in which Hugh Mercer's imaginings became reality. To avenge the Hessian Trenton defeat, Lord Cornwallis rushed south toward Trenton, leaving Princeton with eight thousand men. In his haste, Cornwallis failed to send skirmishers and scouts ahead and on the wings of the projected route as his force marched. "[D]uring the night, heavy rains turned the roads into mud so that the movement of the British was [painfully] slow."[24] As instructed, patriot regiments under Generals Edward Hand of Pennsylvania and Charles Scott of Virginia fought a strategic retreat, slowing the British. These factors aided Washington in his plan to keep campfires burning while circling around the British left wing and marching toward Princeton in a midnight sojourn leaving his force unopposed. General Hugh Mercer and his brigade, decimated by enlistments that had expired January 1, thus reduced to no more than 350 men, participated in the end-run nighttime march.

Beginning of the End

Just after sunrise, Washington sent Mercer and his men to investigate a lone British rider on a hill in the west, about a mile from the American force. As Mercer's party approached, the horseman turned, riding back over the hill's crest to British Lieutenant Colonel Mawhood's force, a detachment screened from view, larger than the Americans anticipated, consisting of the 17th and 55th Regiments of Foot, plus a hundred 16th Light Dragoons. Cresting the hill, the patriots ran into the British

The death of Hugh Mercer
COURTESY OF YALE ART MUSEUM

advance for the main British column. "The British deployed along a fence at the edge of William Clark's orchard and waited."[25] A pitched battle followed. Some of "Mercer's men, dreading the English bayonet, broke from their positions," retreating toward Trenton. "Mercer, raging at them, rode his horse to an orchard in front of the position. A bullet shattered his horse's leg, and it fell." A British soldier knocked Mercer to the ground, striking Mercer's head with the muzzle of a musket.[26]

Other British surrounded Mercer, lying on the ground, yelling, "Surrender you rebel." Mercer made a movement with his sword. "'I am no rebel,' cried Mercer indignantly, while a half dozen bayonets were at his breast: and, instead of asking for quarter, [Mercer] determined to die fighting."[27] The surrounding British bayoneted Mercer at least five times. Mercer suffered a "merciless drubbing."[28] "[E]ven with a bayonet stuck in him," he did not wish to leave his men. He ordered them to prop him up against a white oak's trunk so he could rest, his men standing guard. The tree became known as "the Mercer Oak."[29]

AFTERMATH AND DEATH

Mercer's wounds were not immediately fatal. General Washington rode up to where Mercer lay, bringing reinforcements and rallying Mercer's troops. The Americans turned the tide, driving the British back and going on to rout two British regiments at Nassau Hall, a building of the College of New Jersey (which became Princeton University). American Major John Armstrong found Mercer lying on the ground in the lee of the American advance, unconscious and cold but alive. Armstrong took Mercer south about a half mile, to Thomas Clark's house. There Quaker inhabitants cared for Mercer.

Mercer subsequently revived. Lord Cornwallis's surgeon and Dr. Benjamin Rush visited, examining Mercer. They both proclaimed that he would live. Mercer disagreed, pointing to the smallest of his wounds, a slit under his arm, and predicting that it would prove fatal. Dr. Rush's notes were that Mercer "received seven wounds to the body and two to his head, was much bruised. . . . His life was yesterday almost despaired of." The following day, Rush was optimistic: "I found General Mercer much relieved, and some of the most dangerous complaints removed, so that I still have hopes of his recovery, and of his being again restored to the arms of his grateful country."[30]

Mercer was able to explain the manner of his wounding. Lying on the ground, surrounded, "I determined to die as I had lived, an honored soldier in a just and righteous cause, without begging or making reply. I lunged with my sword at the nearest man. They then bayoneted and left me."[31]

Mercer's biographer Joseph Waterman concluded, "There was no surrender in his nature. There never had been."[32] Yet his wounds were too serious. "He died the 12th of January 1777, of the Wounds He Received on the 3rd of the Same Month, near Princeton, in New Jersey, Bravely Defending the Liberties of America."[33] Brigadier Hugh Mercer, in his "steadiness, sagacity, and competence, and in commanding the respect and trust of all his associates, had many of the qualities of George Washington . . . that only needed a cause to call [them] forth," wrote Barbara Tuchman in extolling the qualities of another military leader.[34]

Chapter Ten

A Philanderer?

"IN APPEARANCE, HE WAS TALL AND HAD A SCAR ON HIS NOSE AND A GREAT MANE of auburn hair. As a revolutionary general, he had a striking military bearing."[1] He was of English stock from a prominent coastal family, the Howes, who in America dropped the "s" from the family name. David Wilson described Robert Howe as a "wealthy North Carolinian who had been educated in Europe."[2] As a young man, "[Howe] was brash, coddled, and insufferably spoiled by a family that that possessed wealth and position. He developed tastes for good literature, fine wine, art, music, and an expensive lifestyle."[3]

Howe's principal failings were two in nature. First, although the most senior of the North Carolina generals, he accomplished little in leading troops. In *The Road to Guilford Courthouse*, John Buchanan ventured that "Congress had chosen Howe [promoting him] beyond his abilities."[4] Howe's political connections and prominent family background propelled his rise. "Howe lobbied congressional allies to use their influence to get Congress to promote him.... Howe's efforts eventually paid off"[5] at first but ultimately contributed to his demotion. "[Q]uestions about his competency and character, and personality conflicts with civilian officials, hindered his efforts" in the field.[6] As a result, as a senior officer Howe was far from a success.

Second, leading to his slide downward was his continuous womanizing, seducing the fairer sex wherever he went. Euphemistic accounts labeled Howe's proclivity as "rumor," as in "[r]umor had it that Howe was a philanderer who abused the women with whom he had gotten involved."[7] Or, softer, "he had a reputation for being a ladies' man."[8] An unidentified loyalist female attributed his reputation to a laudable quality: "He has a general polite gallantry which every man of good breeding should have."[9] "[C]ontemporary accounts portrayed Howe as a man of charm [and] sophistication ... [who] loved to dance and was most impressive [i]n the midst of social activities."[10]

Other historians were more assertive. For example, "[h]is home life had been a disaster." In 1772, Sarah Howe, his wife of nineteen years, obtained a legal separation—a rare event in those times—attributed to his failure to reform his philandering ways.[11] Allegations of philandering and hard treatment of women "alarmed local officials to lobby Congress to remove Howe from his post. Congress complied on 25 September [1778]," removing Howe as commanding officer of the Southern Department.[12]

Howe thus had a rapid rise, to commanding officer of the 2nd North Carolina, to commander of all North Carolina Continentals, and to brigadier general, followed by major general before succeeding Charles Lee as Southern Department commanding officer. Howe's rise was followed by a long slide into limbo, if not purgatory. In the end, his twin sins—ineptness as a battlefield commander and incessant womanizing—caused a downward spiral.

A CAROLINA ARISTOCRAT

General Howe's great-grandfather, Job Howe(s), emigrated from England to Charles Town in 1680. Robert was born in 1732, the oldest son of another Job, a wealthy landowner whose plantation, Mount Mercy, was on the lower Cape Fear River's south side, then as now in Brunswick County, North Carolina. At age twenty-one Robert returned from schooling in England and married Sarah Grange. Not until 1770 did he come into ownership of the plantation associated with him in ensuing years, Kendal, a four-hundred-acre property on Cape Fear. He had previously inherited from his own father the one-thousand-acre Mount Mercy planation where he had been raised.[13]

Beginning in 1764, Howe represented Bladen County in the North Carolina Assembly. In the same year, William Tryon became North Carolina's colonial governor. Tryon and Howe became friends. Reposing trust in Howe even though Howe had no military experience, Tryon put him in command of Fort Johnston below Wilmington, on the Cape Fear estuary, Wilmington's primary defensive fortification. Fort Johnston was a "small, poorly constructed, rectangular fort. Passers-by ridiculed it as 'timber bush' . . . with guns sticking [through] the sticks."[14] Howe's command there was his first position of authority with the colonial militia.

THE BATTLE OF ALAMANCE

Governor Tryon called on Howe once more as he assembled a force of over one thousand to meet a ragtag, poorly armed band of two thousand Regulators twenty miles west of Hillsborough on May 16, 1771. The one-sided victory for the governor's forces signaled the Regulator movement's demise.

In some ways, the 1760s Regulator movement resembled the "Don't Tread on Me" advocacy of today's politics. Officials' corruption (sheriffs, tax collectors, registrars, clerks of court, judges, land agents) in the 1760s colonial governments, and indifference or neglect by eastern Carolina interests, including the governor at New Bern, were motivating factors for the movement.[15] More galling, the corruption was open and prominent, to the distinct disadvantage of settlers on the piedmont (known then as the backcountry) and on the frontier.[16]

North Carolina citizens felt that local officials cheated them and that eastern-dominated legislatures would do nothing about it.[17] A succinct definition was David Lee Russell's "Regulator Movement" as a "term for the attempts of western people to take control of their affairs," against the background of their grievances, such as severe underrepresentation in the government and significant corruption by local officials, including "misappropriation of collected taxes, fraudulent handling of foreclosure activities, and excessive [filing fees] and penalties."[18]

Colonial Governor William Tryon attempted a settlement with the Regulators, albeit on harsh terms. If the Regulators agreed "to lay down and deliver up their Arms," agreed to pay back taxes, and surrendered several of their leaders to Governor Tryon, he would pardon the insurgents. Unwilling to accept the governor's terms, the Regulators did not answer, "simply disappearing into the night."[19]

The final straw came in 1771. A Regulator mob announced a plan to march on New Bern (then the capital city) in time for a General Assembly.[20] In April 1771, with a force of 1,068 militiamen, Governor Tryon journeyed northwest to Hillsborough, arriving there on May 9, prepared to meet the Regulator threat.

On May 16, the royal colonial battle group—increased to thirteen hundred men—met a force of two thousand Regulators near Alamance Creek. Governor Tryon fired the first shot, killing the man at whom he had aimed the borrowed musket. In the battle, various Regulator groups' partial and then total retreat from the field induced panic. "The ill-prepared Regulators were routed."[21] Fatalities were minimal, as they often were in those days of highly inaccurate musket fire: "Estimates of the dead and wounded vary, possibly as many as 20 Regulators killed, 9 militiamen. Altogether, more than 150 men (on both sides) were wounded, many seriously."[22] The governor's troops captured fifteen of the enemy. Tryon ordered six or seven of those to be executed. One, James Few, was twice offered a pardon if he would repent. After Few refused, Governor Tryon ordered him hanged immediately, on the battlefield, as an example to deter other would-be rebels.[23] Today little is remembered of royal governors except for William Tryon, Robert Howe's patron, who is often regarded in a favorable light.[24]

EDGING TOWARD REVOLUTION

By early 1775, Howe had, depending on one's point of view (British or American), become a rebel and traitor or a dedicated patriot. He was training militia in Brunswick. Colonial Governor Josiah Martin, who had succeeded William Tryon, several times "identified Howe as one of the colony's most dangerous men." In July 1775, Martin requested of the British colonial secretary, the Earl of Dartmouth, that Robert Howe, John Ashe, Cornelius Harnett, and Abner Nash be prosecuted for "their unremitted labours to promote sedition and rebellion . . . [because] they stand foremost among the patrons of revolt and anarchy."[25]

At Hillsborough, the Third North Carolina Provincial Congress convened on August 20, 1775, with Howe in attendance. There, his political career wound down, and the military one began in earnest. The Congress created two North Carolina regiments, with James Moore and Robert Howe as colonels, in command of the 1st and 2nd North Carolina. In November, the Continental Congress took the two regiments into the Continental Line while also fixing a quota of six additional regiments for the colony.[26]

Around that time, Virginia Colonial Governor Dunmore had fled down the James River peninsula, deserting the capital at Williamsburg. At the tip of the peninsula, Dunmore and his family boarded British warships moored in Hampton Roads. With his small force of redcoats, navvies, and runaway slaves to whom Dunmore promised emancipation, Dunmore commenced his own conflict, the war within the war, a prelude to the larger revolution.

Dunmore's force had constructed a stockade at Great Bridge, some distance away, fifteen miles southeast of Portsmouth and twelve miles directly south of Norfolk, Virginia. There a series of wooden bridges spanned the Elizabeth River's south branch via two small islands in the river. For the Americans, sealing off escape routes to the south from Norfolk was vital because North Carolina, a short distance south of Great Bridge, had a significant Tory population with whom Lord Dunmore could attempt rendezvous. An advance party under American Lieutenant Charles Scott constructed a breastwork at the southern end of the causeway, in advance of Great Bridge village.[27] They also removed much of the planking from the bridge, greasing the long, arched trusses on which the planks had rested.

In early December, Colonel William Woodford (chapter 27) and the remainder of the 2nd Virginia arrived at Great Bridge. On December 9, the Dunmore force, led by 120 British grenadiers, mounted a suicidal attack on the Americans. In December 1775, the stage was set for the first real conflict in the south, "a second Bunker Hill, in miniature."[28]

British Captain (later General) Phillip Leslie and a force of 350 relaid some bridge planking. Woodford and the Americans waited at the southern terminus. The British advanced, six abreast, with bayonets fixed, true to the British convention of frontal assaults, designed to spread shock and awe among opponents. Confined as they were to the narrow bridge, however, Dunmore's force had no access to cover and nowhere to scatter. The only alternatives were to continue marching ahead or retreat.

The Americans decimated the advancing force, killing or wounding fifty before the British abandoned the assault.[29]

OCCUPATION OF NORFOLK

Howe and the 2nd North Carolina journeyed north to buttress Great Bridge's defense, the first installment arriving on December 10 and Howe arriving on December 15 with 320 additional men. It was the troops' first foray outside North Carolina.[30] The North Carolinians missed the battle, arriving late. Howe continued north for a more active mission. With 1,364 Virginia and North Carolina troops, as senior commander present, Howe was to command an occupation of Norfolk that endured a prolonged British naval bombardment and a disastrous fire. Occupation's dangers were multiplied further because Norfolk (then Virginia's largest city) was decidedly pro-British, "a town apart from the rest of Virginia." In *The American Revolution in the Southern Colonies*, David Russell continued his analysis: "Norfolk citizens lacked the philosophical view and political life that had come from the plantation environment. They were merchants, not farmers."[31] In 1660, the colonial governor strengthened the merchants' hand, decreeing that Virginia planters could no longer ship directly but had to move all goods and crops through Norfolk's port. With Britain and British possessions their primary markets, Colonel Robert Howe was "doubtful that Norfolk merchants could feel any strong prepossession in favor of America, or its cause, suspicious friends at best."[32]

The North Carolinians' mission continued into early February, when Dunmore and his small fleet withdrew from Chesapeake Bay.[33] Leaving Norfolk, their presence no longer needed, the North Carolinians went south, stopping only briefly before marching through North Carolina to Charles Town in South Carolina. There they were to assist in repelling the British attack that was to materialize in June 1776. Shortly after they departed Virginia, the Congress promoted Robert Howe to brigadier.[34]

ON TO SOUTH CAROLINA

Howe commanded fourteen hundred North Carolina officers and men in the defense of Charles Town, South Carolina's largest city, known as the Pearl of the South. As commander of the Southern Department, on paper the eccentric Major General Charles Lee superintended defense. In actuality, the defense's success was wholly attributable to South Carolina's William Moultrie and the palmetto log fortress that he and his men had constructed on Sullivan's Island at the entrance to Charles Town harbor. With only twenty-five cannons, the Americans withstood a ten-hour, 270-gun naval bombardment, turning back British General Henry Clinton, forty-five hundred redcoats, and fifty-six Royal Navy ships.[35]

Alexander Garden compared the stand of "Moultrie and his South Carolinians on Sullivan's Island," forestalling British entry into Charles Town's harbor, "to Leonidas and the Spartans at Thermopylae."[36] Author C. L. Bragg's Moultrie biography adds, "Hyperbole aside, the battle now known as the Battle of Fort Moultrie was the first absolute American victory and ranks with the three most decisive victories of the Revolutionary War."[37]

South Carolina soon thereafter adopted Moultrie's blue ensign with a white star in the upper left corner as the state's flag, with one addition. At the center of the blue field, the state added a stylized rendering of a palmetto palm. South Carolina became the "Palmetto State."[38]

Would it were otherwise, but, alas, Robert Howe and his men, while standing in reserve, did not play any noteworthy part in Charles Town's stirring 1776 defense. Howe did, however, come face to face with Southern Department Commanding General Charles Lee, whose next stratagem after Charles Town was a planned expedition south through hot, swampy Georgia to attack the British in East Florida and St. Augustine. Lee, however, suffered none of the consequences of his decision, as in August Congress ordered him north. It then fell to Lee's second-in-command, Robert Howe, to become hopelessly entangled in the ill-fated expedition and, worse yet, in Georgia politics.

CHAPTER ELEVEN

Howe's Downward Spiral

As late as 1780, a disgusted Southern Department commander, Major General Benjamin Lincoln, himself a New Englander, remarked of Georgians, "Good God, will the Malice of these people [southerners] never be at an end," having witnessed several years of Georgia politics.[1] In a book on Georgia Brigadier Lachlan McIntosh, biographer Harvey Jackson titled a chapter "Implacable Mallice [sic] of Implacable Enemies."[2]

North Carolinian Robert Howe entered the maelstrom the minute he crossed the Savannah River from South Carolina into Georgia. In Georgia, "Howe's most aggravating problem was not the British in East Florida but rather civil authorities who interfered extensively in his efforts to maintain and direct his small army."[3] By and large, in the other colonies the cause was liberty—freedom from taxation without representation, freedom from the king, his ministers, and parliament in Britain—and, finally, to achieve liberty through independence. By contrast, in Georgia "governors refused to relinquish command to the militia during military engagements. . . . Allured by the glory of military conquest the governors . . . determined to command." In opposition, "Howe insisted that a single military command was vital to an effective operation."[4] Georgia's leaders were fixated on invading East Florida and capturing St. Augustine, which eclipsed all other sentiments. Georgia looked south, and only south, rather than east or north.

1776's Aborted Mission

British forces at St. Augustine, in East Florida, were conducting raids over the border into Georgia. Fearing British raids farther north, Savannah citizens agitated for protection. Major General Charles Lee, when commanding the Southern Department, heeded their calls, dispatching the Virginia 8th and Howe with his North Carolina regulars. The Virginia and North Carolina regiments arrived in Savannah on August 17 and at Sunbury, south of the city, on August 22, where they camped. The weather was hot and muggy; men became ill with tropical afflictions. Then, without warning, General Washington recalled Lee. In September, General William Moultrie from South Carolina, now in charge, canceled the Florida expedition. Brigadier Peter Muhlenberg led the Virginia troops, hobbled by sickness and fatigue, slowly northward, reaching northern Virginia only on December 20.[5] Howe's force returned to North Carolina.

Again, in May 1777 General Howe bowed to Georgia politicians' exhortations, preparing another southern excursion, although he and Georgia Brigadier Lachlan McIntosh had misgivings. Both men favored erecting forts on the more northerly rivers such as Georgia's Altamaha and the Satilla. Further, they urged relocation of livestock and crops away from Georgia's coastal islands, making the islands less vulnerable to British raids from seaward. Howe and McIntosh noted both logistical and geographical obstacles in southeast Georgia—swamps and broad rivers to cross (Medway, Altamaha, Satilla, St. Mary's, St. Johns)—with foot soldiers rather than mounted forces, hot weather, tropical diseases, heavy wool uniforms, lack of supplies, government interference, and, indeed, hostility—militating against an expedition to Florida.[6] Their arguments failed to sway the nascent colony's political leaders.

The Second Attempt at an Invasion of Florida

In early May 1777, the expedition got underway, departing the Medway estuary and Sunbury. Though the expedition had gone only a few miles, desertion became a factor with which Howe had to reckon. On May 18, a sergeant and another who had encouraged desertion were charged with mutiny. A court found the men guilty; commanding General Howe affirmed the result. On May 21, the two men were executed. The following day eight more men were convicted of desertion and also ordered executed. All told, sixteen deserters were executed.

Despite the many travails, Howe's little army finally was across the Great Satilla River, "within striking distance" of the British Fort Tonyn on the St. Mary's, the river that defined and still constitutes the boundary between Georgia and Florida. Then ever-present political hostility entered the picture. Georgia's governor arrived with 550 militiamen on June 28, making camp within a few miles of Howe's Continentals. Hostility between the two camps descended like a summer storm. Governor John Houstoun refused to dispatch militia light cavalry, as Howe had requested, to assist the Continentals. Next, "[t]he governor ordered the Continental Army's guides, who were Georgia residents, to leave the Continental camp."[7] Governor Houstoun refused to attend a council of war. Howe's force gave up any idea of cooperation, pushing on to the British Fort Tonyn. There, in Georgia's far south, Howe and his men found an abandoned installation.

Howe now had fewer than four hundred effectives. The "chaos of command" continued. Even though Governor Houstoun had 550 men rather than the 1,300 of which he had bragged, he refused to join his undermanned force with Howe's undermanned force. "[F]riction and open hostility invariably resulted."[8] On July 14, Howe's detachment withdrew from southern Georgia. The expedition was described as a "another disastrous undertaking for Howe."[9]

PROMOTION AND THE PINNACLE

In April 1777, North Carolina General James Moore died from an undefined illness labeled "gout of the stomach." Howe had become Carolina's senior general, succeeding to Moore's post as commanding officer of all North Carolina Continentals.[10] In August 1777, despite the failed South Georgia mission, Congress promoted Robert Howe to major general in the Continental Army.[11]

Once again, for the third time, political interests in Georgia urged a military conquest of East Florida but declined to support any mission logistically. The Georgia Legislature declined to provide the foodstuffs, utensils, ammunition, weapons, medical supplies, clothing, tents, and blankets a well-supported excursion needed. The politicians did this even though other colonies' legislatures were expected to and did equip, as best they could, the Continentals from their jurisdictions.[12] In Georgia,

Robert Howe
COURTESY OF NC DIGITAL
ARCHIVES & RECORDS

at every request from the Continentals, the governor and his supporters claimed to see another attempt to have military command supersede civilian authority. As 1778 passed, the situation did not improve. Howe was ill part of the time. The expedition to invade Florida fell short again, ending in frustration with political interference, poor logistical support, and a split command.

In September 1778, Congress removed Robert Howe from command of the army's Southern Department, replacing him with Massachusetts General Benjamin Lincoln.[13]

Howe's Lament and the Causes of His Demotion

"How Sir have I deserved this disgrace?" Howe wrote to South Carolina's Henry Laurens, president of the Continental Congress, during 1778.[14] In part, Howe's deserts resulted from his lackluster performance as a military leader. David Lee Russell attributed his dismissal "to the ill-fated 1778 campaign."[15] Southerners spoke poorly of Howe.[16] He could be impolitic, even abrasive, in dealing with local authorities. Critics portrayed him as impervious to argument. Others viewed Howe's scowling countenance when in command as promoting an attitude that if he could not be loved, he could at least be feared.

Allegedly, Howe's attitude with attractive women was the opposite: he fervently wanted to be loved. It was his womanizing, or reputation for womanizing, that did him in. "Howe's womanizing finally caught up with him," is how David Wilson's *Southern Strategy* characterizes Howe's relief from command.[17] In those times, accounts of womanizing and sexual harassment were filled with euphemisms, avoiding the salacious details that media outlets would feature today. So the repeated accusations of "womanizing" throughout Howe's career may have been a cypher for more damning underlying facts. Contemporaneous accounts only scratch the surface. One more explicit account, as recorded by Richard Rankin, tells of a woman who wrote that Howe "is deemed a horrid animal, a sort of womaneater that devours everything that comes his way. . . . [N]o woman can withstand him."[18]

A few accounts traced Howe's damaged reputation to a single incident. According to Congressman Cornelius Harnett, a former Howe neighbor, the removal "resulted from an encounter between Howe and a female in [Charles Town] . . . the incident caused the South Carolina and Georgia [Continental Congress] delegates to be greatly incensed against Howe."[19] One unidentified congressman later "explained that Congress recalled Howe because of 'a ridiculous little matter he has been concerned with . . . with regard to a female [that] has induced the delegates of Georgia and South Carolina to request his recall.'"[20]

During this time other voices came forward, calling Howe "a playboy" and "a ladies' man."[21] Persistent accounts imply that more than one incident was involved, phrasing the cause of his dismissal as his "philandering ways."[22] After reciting several incidents, Howe's biography sums up as follows: "Howe was continually celebrated as the most notorious womanizer imaginable."[23] Historians such as Professor Stephen Taaffe ascribed Howe's fate to military failures as well: "Howe's lackluster record . . . as well as his womanizing reputation followed him north" when George Washington transferred Howe to the Hudson Highlands soon after one more debacle followed in the south.[24]

THE DEBACLE: A SOUTHERNER FALLS FROM GRACE IN THE SOUTH

Although in September Congress had relieved him as Southern Department commander, Howe was held over until Benjamin Lincoln could arrive in late November or December.[25] Accordingly, Howe was in charge of the Savannah garrison when a British fleet carrying four thousand soldiers anchored in the Savannah River estuary, south of the small city itself. Howe's numbers were "anemic," numbering 854 by one count and fewer than 700 by another.[26] Savannah residents, though, "argued that if Savannah could be defended for a few days, General Lincoln might arrive to relieve the town." Lincoln had indeed arrived in Charles Town, South Carolina, eighty-three miles to the north. "Howe found [the Savanah citizens'] argument compelling. He resolved to attempt a defense of Savannah."[27]

On December 29, 1778, the British landed thirty-five hundred men, with artillery, at Girardeau's plantation southeast of the city. Between the landing and the town was a steep bluff (Brewton's Bluff). Howe made the strategic decision not to base his primary defense there, on the bluff above the redcoats. He did order deployment of a fair-sized defensive line. The deployment seemed a tenable position, as the Americans' left flank was anchored in a swamp that continued down to the riverbank. The British would have to take the bluff head on, or so Howe and his officers thought.

The British, however, found a slave who led them on a path through the swamp. Coming as a surprise, from the northwest the British were able to flank the Americans, rolling up their line, charging with fixed bayonets. The Americans abandoned the position. Soon their "orderly retreat turned into a rout." Witnessing the heedless rout, other pockets of American troops also broke and ran. Howe lost 547 men (453 captured), while the British losses were limited to 24 casualties.[28] Then further tragedy ensued. The retreating Americans came to Yamacraw Creek, which they had to cross to make good their escape. "Tossing their weapons aside, soldiers and officers alike leaped into the water." In those times and until well into the twentieth century, few persons could swim, an assessment doubly true of Continental soldiers. "[An estimated] 30 men died trying to cross."[29]

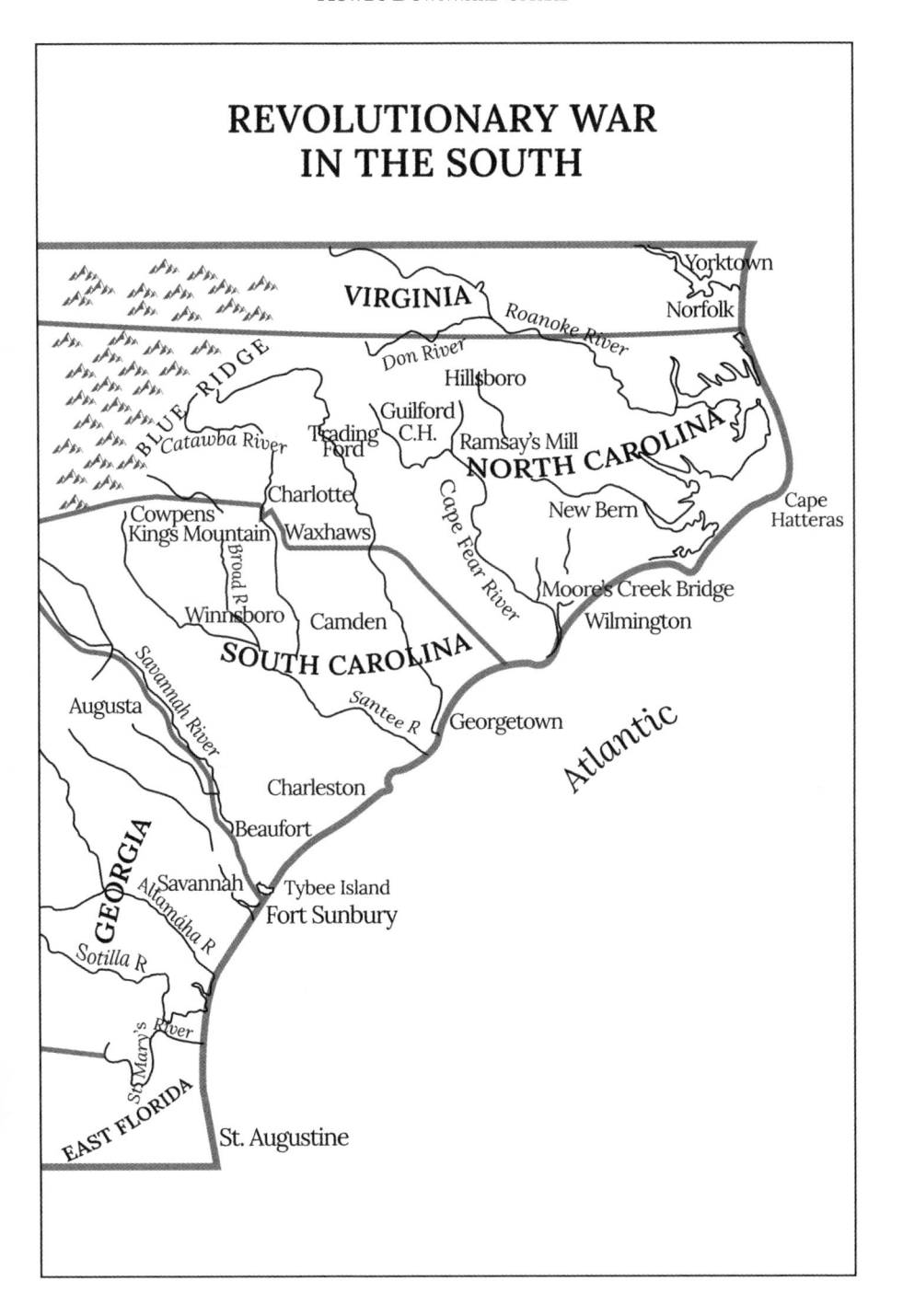

REVOLUTIONARY WAR IN THE SOUTH

General William Moultrie of South Carolina "held Howe personally responsible for the defeat. . . . [H]e never should have attempted to stand in defense against [Archibald] Campbell's larger, seasoned army."[30] Howe's loss of a regiment-sized group of men—who would have been available to General Lincoln—resulted from Howe's foolhardy attempt to defend the town. Howe was later court-martialed for his conduct of the battle, the prosecution contending that he should have made an all-or-none stand atop Brewton Bluff. The court took mercy on Howe, acquitting him of the charges.

LASTING FALLOUT

Subsequently, historians have shown Howe less mercy. David Wilson in *The Southern Strategy* adopted a harsh tone but set forth an accurate analysis of Howe's conduct that day: "Ultimately, the cause of the American defeat was not the choice of battlefield. [It was] Howe's failure to gather adequate battlefield intelligence and to anticipate enemy actions." Wilson juxtaposed Howe's failings with the British commander's efforts: "In contrast to Howe, [Colonel Archibald Campbell] scouted the terrain, interview[ed] the locals, and even climbed a tree to get a better look at 'rebel' troop positions."[31]

General Lincoln did indeed come south with fifteen hundred men. On January 3, 1779, Howe formally turned Southern Department command over to Lincoln. General Washington had ordered Howe, once relieved, to leave the south, reporting to the Middle Department's headquarters in Middlebrook, New Jersey, "without delay."[32] Howe's tenure as a southern battlefield commander was finished.

CHAPTER TWELVE

Partial Redemption

ONCE IN UPSTATE NEW YORK, WHERE HOWE REJOINED THE MAIN ARMY AND THE commander in chief, he was injured, presumably in a fall from a horse. The general was on crutches, hobbling about. Further, he had come north with the background of serious lapses in his performance as a general, a ship whose hull was fouled by barnacles. When Howe recovered maneuverability, General Washington assigned him to command American forces in western Connecticut, a backwater at the time.

Washington, however, "was concerned that a British attack up the Hudson was imminent."[1] Responding to a possible threat of General Henry Clinton coming north from New York, Washington ordered Howe to lead two brigades (commanded by Brigadiers John Nixon and John Patterson) from West Point downriver to Verplanck's Point, about fifteen miles south and on the opposite (east) shore from West Point. Sited high above the Hudson, West Point was the Gibraltar of the Hudson, able to command passage on the river.[2] Washington thought the security of West Point vital to the American cause.

ANOTHER DISAPPOINTING BATTLEFIELD COMMAND

When Howe, Nixon, Patterson, and their brigades arrived at Verplanck's Point, they found that General Alexander McDougall, the West Point commandant, had failed to provide tools for erecting batteries, cannons for the emplacements, provisions for the men, horses and horseback riders for communication, and the like. Rather than subsisting until supplies could arrive, Howe ordered a hurried withdrawal from Verplanck's Point, back toward West Point. Contemporaries faulted Howe for beating a hasty retreat, accusing him of "finding many supposed obstructions" to erecting a defensive position.[3] Throughout the war, American commanders frequently accomplished missions with spotty or nonexistent logistical support.

Through the remainder of 1779, in the region north of New York City and south of West Point, both sides sought to strike minor blows through raids, ambuscades, and surreptitious enterprises, but no major engagements materialized. Washington, however, demonstrated a continuing faith in Howe. He appointed Howe president of a court-martial convened to hear charges against General Benedict Arnold concerning Arnold's conduct as military commander of Philadelphia (June 1778 to March 1779). The initial session was at Howe's headquarters in Middleton, Connecticut, on June 1, 1779 (Arnold did not defect until September 1780).[4] General Henry Clinton's attacks up the Hudson, capturing Stony Point and Verplanck's Point on opposite Hudson shores, forced the proceedings' postponement.

General Howe then attempted to beg off the assignment to the court, claiming that he was needed to command troops if a British assault farther up the Hudson materialized. In no uncertain terms, Washington decreed that "the court martial will resume at Morristown, New Jersey, on 20 December, and . . . Howe, as president, 'will not fail to attend.'" On January 26, the court rendered its verdict, finding one minor breach of the articles of war (allowing a vessel from an enemy port into an American one) and dismissing all other charges against Arnold.[5]

THE HUDSON HIGHLANDS COMMAND

Behind and to the southwest of West Point are the Hudson Highlands—high hills, low mountains, and moderately steep valleys—a terrain difficult to patrol or defend. Schunemunk Mountain, twelve miles west, is 1,664 feet (507 meters) in elevation; Woodcock Mountain is 1,030 feet high. In 1780, General Washington appointed Howe the successor of Massachusetts Major General William Heath, who was retiring due to ill health, as Hudson Highlands force commander.[6] Washington had six generals available for the post (De Kalb, Greene, Howe, St. Clair, Stirling, and Steuben). Again, exhibiting his sometimes-mysterious faith in the North Carolinian, Washington chose Howe for the post, "although Howe had hardly shone as an American General."[7]

Under Heath, "discipline had been lax causing Howe to take a stern and unyielding stand on enforcement." As a result, Howe, regarded as a bit of a martinet in past commands, became an unpopular commanding officer.[8] Yet again, though, Washington exhibited trust in Howe. He named Howe a member of the court that was trying British Major John André, who had acted as the go-between when Benedict Arnold betrayed his West Point command to the British in New York.[9] The court found André guilty, condemning him to death, a sentence Washington affirmed, ordering it to be carried out a few days later, on October 2, 1780, at Tappan, New York.[10]

PARTIAL REDEMPTIONS: QUELLING THE MUTINIES

In January 1781, the Pennsylvania Continental Line committed mutiny. Some twenty-four hundred Pennsylvania soldiers quit their quarters, seized arms, fired on officers, and marched off toward Philadelphia, the seat of government for the new nation. From Washington, Howe "received the appointment to command a detachment . . . of the best-clothed and best-fed men" (1,150 in total) to march south to quell the rebellion.[11] Howe was able to avoid an armed confrontation, a negotiated settlement being successful. The settlement dismissed half of the Pennsylvania Line from further service while furloughing the remainder of Pennsylvania troops until March 15, 1781. "In reality, the entire [Pennsylvania] line was disbanded."[12]

Following Howe's success in quelling the mutiny, Washington sent him south once more to quell New Jersey troops' uprising. "Not only did [Washington] order Howe to gain the unconditional surrender of the mutineers, but Washington also directed him to 'execute a few of the most active and most incendiary leaders.'"[13] Howe headed south with detachments of Massachusetts, Connecticut, and New Hampshire men of the Continental Line. In the night of January 26, 1781, Howe had his men and artillery encircle the Pompton, New Jersey, camp where the mutineers lay sleeping. Howe then allowed the insurgents five minutes to signal submission. From the surrendering three New Jersey regiments, Howe selected three ringleaders. He convened an immediate court-martial, which, finding the defendants guilty, condemned them to death. A firing squad chosen from the mutineers themselves executed two of them; Howe pardoned the third. The outcome may have seemed harsh, but "the mutiny by 2,400 Pennsylvania troops occurred about twenty miles away from Pompton, [which] intensified the Jersey soldiers' discontent."[14]

On January 19, 1781, General Washington wrote to New York Governor George Clinton, "indeed the entire detachment under General Howe deserves infinite credit."[15]

Disappointment Nonetheless

In 1781, when the Middle Department forces prepared to move south for Yorktown, sidelined generals (Arthur St. Clair and Robert Howe among them) implored Washington to give them commands in the expedition.[16] Washington declined to do so, selecting from among his major generals only Benjamin Lincoln.

This was just as well. In the fall of 1781, when the Americans were laying siege to the British Yorktown bivouac, Howe was a facing a different and unwelcome fate. Continental Congress members demanded a court of inquiry or other proceeding into Howe's conduct during the British capture of Savannah nearly three years earlier, in December 1778. In September, the Congress ordered George Washington to convene a court-martial, which was to take place in Philadelphia beginning December 7, 1781. Howe relocated to Philadelphia to prepare his defense.[17] The court-martial proceeding dragged on, with weak and sometimes contradictory prosecution presentations. In his defense, Howe portrayed himself as being confronted by overwhelming odds, "with little cooperation from a recalcitrant [Georgia] state government." He argued that the proceeding, coming as it did three years after the event in question, was instead a search for a scapegoat. The court acquitted Howe, bestowing on him "the highest honors."[18]

The more lasting effect of his court-martial and his Philadelphia stay were to leave Howe destitute, as he personally had to underwrite his defense costs, including boarding in Philadelphia for three months. He was unable to cover the debts and thus could not depart Philadelphia. By February 10, 1782, he was able to borrow funds with which he could gain temporary surcease from creditors. He returned to the Hudson Highlands.

THE DOWNWARD SPIRAL

For Howe, seemingly, it never ended. On October 28, 1781, now retired Major General William Heath lodged with General Washington allegations that Howe had abandoned his division, being absent without leave for two days. The allegations proceeded no further than Washington. The accusation stung Howe nonetheless.

Despite the allegations, in June 1783, headquartered at Newburgh, New York, Washington turned to Howe once more. Howe was to go to Pennsylvania to quell another rebellion. A group of four hundred Pennsylvania ex-soldiers had begun a march to Philadelphia from Lancaster, sixty miles distant; once in Philadelphia, they would petition Congress "for redress of their grievances," including the lack of pay. The marchers reached Independence Hall, then also the Pennsylvania Statehouse. The Continental Congress answered the demonstrators' demands in three ways. First, through a committee chaired by Alexander Hamilton, the Congress agreed to meet with the uprising's leaders. Second, somewhat inconsistently, and to no avail, the Congress asked the Pennsylvania Council for protection from the demonstrations. Third, and of the most important consequence, Congress left Philadelphia for Princeton, New Jersey; went thence to Annapolis, Maryland; went north again, to Trenton, New Jersey; and finally went to New York City. Philadelphia was never again to be the seat of government.[19]

In the military response to the rebellion, Howe marched a detachment of fifteen hundred troops from the Hudson Highlands to the capital city. "Howe [kept] his corps light and unencumbered with baggage . . . march[ing] them rapidly via Ringwood, Brompton, Morristown, Princeton, and Trenton, and from there by water to Philadelphia."[20] In Philadelphia, Howe convened a court of inquiry and a court-martial, which found the ringleaders guilty, sentencing them to be executed. Congress reviewed the proceeding, pardoning the affair's leaders. To ensure that Howe's action would not in hindsight be criticized, on September 13, 1783, Congress passed a resolution thanking him "for the prudence and propriety with which he executed the inquiry into the late mutiny of a part of the Pennsylvania Line."[21]

AFTER THE WAR—A TIME OF MELANCHOLY

From Newburgh, Howe was present at the meeting leading to formation of the Sons of Cincinnati, the fraternal society for officers of the Continental Line, to be passed on to the officers' first-born sons and then to their first born. At Fishkill, across the Hudson from Newburgh, Howe was the second officer to sign the organic documents, after only Baron von Steuben.[22] The society's founders, including the guiding spirit General Henry Knox, named the organization after Roman General Lucias Quinctius Cincinnatus (519–430 BC), a retired general turned farmer who left his fields to lead Roman legions against an invasion. After having vanquished the threat, Cincinnatus returned to his farm. He is considered a legendary figure of Roman civic virtue, a shining example of the citizen-soldier.[23]

Formation of the society was the last high point in Robert Howe's checkered career. After the October 1783 Treaty of Paris, when by and large the Continental Army disbanded and soldiers and officers returned to their homes, Robert Howe did not. He spent the end of 1783 and 1784 traveling between Philadelphia, New York, and other locations, attempting to settle accounts. He had no home to which he could return, the British having sacked and burned Kendal plantation. Effectively, his wife had divorced him. His home life had become a disaster.

He was able to borrow against his plantation's land, executing a note secured by a mortgage for which he received £748. After having cleared his debts, Howe returned to North Carolina in the second half of 1785. In 1786, he stood for election to represent Brunswick County in the North Carolina General Assembly. General Howe was making his way to Fayetteville (formerly Cross Creek) for an assembly meeting when, stopping at a friend's home, he took ill and died on November 20, 1786.

CHAPTER THIRTEEN

Addendum: Intoxicating Beverages

AFTER THE NEW JERSEY MUTINY THAT GENERAL HOWE AND HIS MEN SUP-
pressed, the mutineers' commander reported that "many of the soldiers" who
rebelled "were much disguised by liquor."[1] Major General Adam Stephen, it was
said, drank heavily, including being intoxicated at the Battle of Germantown.
George Washington ordered Stephen cashiered from the army.[2] In correspondence
with Edward Heath, Robert Howe's recommendations made clear that Howe
was no stranger to alcoholic beverages.[3] "Lord Stirling [William Alexander of
Maryland] was gradually marginalized due to ill health and alcoholism."[4] Further,
Stirling's 1783 death was ascribed to alcoholism. In 1777, one congressman "was
already impugning the character of [several] generals as alcoholics" (Stephen, Sullivan, Maxwell, and Stirling were mentioned).[5]

DRINK IN THE MILITARY

Imbibing alcohol, often to excess, has a long association with the military, for several
reasons. First, in revolutionary times a reason to partake was for warmth; alcohol
was thought especially comforting on autumn and winter evenings, spent in out-
of-doors encampments, frequently after a long day's march. Second was availability.
The custom—indeed, a term of many enlistments—was the provision each day to
each soldier of a gill, five fluid ounces, of rum, whiskey, or sometimes apple brandy
("applejack," or distilled hard cider).[6] In addition, at the Battle of Saratoga, Commanding General Horatio Gates issued "a standing order for a half gill of rum for
every man first thing in the morning . . . [as] another remedy for their stiff joints."[7]
Returning in midwinter from Indian country in Ohio, General Lachlan McIntosh, "[a]s a mark of satisfaction with the behavior of [the men], ordered a pint of
whiskey each man."[8] Whether or not enlistments required dispensation of alcohol,
distributing it was a long-standing practice. When Ben Franklin commanded the

Pennsylvania Militia in the early 1750s, he instructed the chaplain to dole out a daily ration of rum right after services: "Never were prayers more generally and punctually attended."[9] On occasion, battlefield commanders shorted soldiers on the daily rum ration, with disastrous results.[10] In addition, to supplement official supplies, sutlers (purveyors of various goods) followed army units, on payment of several pence standing ready to augment the military's daily whiskey or rum allowance.[11] Imbibing was essential to military culture.

Third, in revolutionary times the waters from springs, streams, and shallow wells in bivouac areas often were polluted, a health hazard causing sickness, with the water foul to the taste. A widely held belief was that alcohol was both a substitute and a palliative for ingestion of bad water. Indeed, this rationale and equivalent rates of consumption prevailed in much of eighteenth-century American society. Describing the late eighteenth and early nineteenth centuries, Gordon Wood observed that "[a]lcohol flowed freely, and Americans were drinking more per capita than nearly all other nations."[12] The Revolutionary War military appears to have matched and at times greatly exceeded the general population's rate of consumption.

WARMTH AND LIVING ROUGH

A soldier or officer standing close to the roaring fire would feel warm facing the fire and cold on the opposite flank, the side away from the fire.[13] The same was true for Revolutionary War soldiers: at Valley Forge, for instance, "roaring fires served at least to roast the belly while the buttocks froze."[14] To fight cold, many military men would drink themselves just short of oblivion, with wine, mead, or other alcoholic drinks. In that age, people "depended on wine and beer as an essential part of [their] diet."[15]

Those practices applied to many Revolutionary War officers and troops. Major General Adam Stephen served twenty-four years in the military, from the French and Indian War beginning in 1753 to 1777. He headed up the task force to build the Forbes Road through the wilderness. He led Virginia forces in the Cherokee Wars as well as in Pontiac's War.[16] General Andrew Lewis, later to command all Virginia regiments in the Revolution, was as a young man a surveyor who laid out much of the territory in southwest Virginia, including what today is West Virginia (hence, Lewisburg in Greenbrier County, West Virginia). Generals Moultrie, Pickens, Davidson, Caswell, and others served in the Cherokee Wars in the western Carolinas. Farther north, again as a young man, George Washington surveyed and mapped the Allegheny Mountain valleys west of the Shenandoah, such as the Lost River Valley, today in West Virginia.[17] George Rogers Clark, the "Hannibal of the West," who headed up militia forces in far western Virginia (today Kentucky) and the Illinois Territory, was a surveyor from age nineteen. He surveyed lands in far western Virginia, continuing his profession for decades.[18] As surveyors, or later as officers, one of the creature comforts these men enjoyed was drink in the evenings.

PROVISION OF ALCOHOL TO OFFICERS AND SOLDIERS

In commanding his New Hampshire force, General John Stark consistently put at the head of his requisition list alcoholic beverages for his troops. The lore relating to the American victory at the Battle of Bennington (1777) has it that before the battle many of Colonel Stark's troops had fortified themselves with whiskey.[19] Part of the reason for young Colonel George Washington's 1754 surrender at Fort Necessity to the French and Indian forces was that, according to Washington, "What was worse [than a persistent downpour and being surrounded], it was no sooner dark, than one-half of our Men got drunk."[20] Twenty-five years later, in the January to March 1778 winter encampment at Valley Forge, and undoubtedly at other long winter encampments, "gambling, intoxication, and assault" permeated the army's ranks.[21] During the siege of Charles Town (April–May 1780), militia Captain Earle Hughston "had a fondness for rum and a seemingly endless supply from his tin canteen. Every day at mid-morning and again at sunset he shared the rum" with fellow officers.[22] Early in the war the spread of drunkenness among Charles Scott's troops at Suffolk, Virginia, caused Charles Scott to order "all tippling houses . . . not to sell spiritous liquors to Soldiers under pain of confinement."[23] After news of the "stupendous" October 1777 Saratoga victory reached Virginia, "[f]or the special occasion each soldier was to receive an [extra] gill of rum."[24]

Reports of alcohol abuse could fill pages. As a younger man, Revolutionary War hero Daniel Morgan was a hard drinker. Morgan "bought rum, by the pint, the quart, the half-gallon, or the gallon—and '[one] pint mugs' to drink it in."[25]

Even among New England forces, who numbered among themselves Puritan stock, ingestion of alcohol was not taboo. Historian David McCullough explained in *The Pioneers* why religious conservatives' views were not well received: "[S]tiff-necked and somber [a Puritan] was not . . . contrary to latter-day conceptions." McCullough explained that "Puritans were as capable as any mortals of exuding an affable enjoyment of life. . . . [M]any a Puritan loved good food, good wine, good stories, and good cheer."[26] Groups were labeled Puritan not because of any strict moral code but because of group members' desire to rid the Church of England ("purify it") of vestiges left from the Church of Rome.[27] The heavy drinking that dates from the earliest periods of organized militaries included soldiers of Puritan stock.[28]

British forces were not immune to excessive drink's perils. Early on, at the siege of Boston, Lieutenant Frederick MacKenzie of the 23rd Foot—the Royal Welch Fusiliers—recorded in his diary "that 'many men are intoxicated daily' and that two had died of alcohol poisoning in a single night." He added that "[w]hen the soldiers are in a state of intoxication, they are frequently induced to desert."[29] Seeking to court allies, the British (and the French before them) plied Native Americans with alcohol and did nothing to restrain private merchants: "The Indians wanted powder and lead" for hunting, "but the traders brought rum" to sell.[30]

Water Supply

In 1781, at Gloucester Point across from Yorktown, General Lafayette "[e]specially sought from [General] Weedon spiritous liquors, 'as the water of this Country is very unhealthy.'"[31] In January 1777, following the Colonial victory at the Battle of Princeton, in gratitude the Council of Safety sent General Washington's army "twenty hogshead of rum," amounting roughly to 1,280 gallons, according to the measurement of a hogshead.[32] In 1778, after his men had stood all of a cold and rainy night on alert, General Charles Scott thought his men in such a "Horred [*sic*] Condition" that he bought enough rum to give each soldier a gill. "I was obliged to pay the economic price of Twelve dollars a gallon for it, which I thought better Than letting the men Suffer."[33] Rum and whiskey were important in Revolutionary War soldiers' everyday lives.

Health Concerns

A universally held belief was that alcoholic beverages, either straight up or diluted with water, were necessary for good health. The supplies of what would have been potable water carried coliform bacteria. Then, too, knowledge of public health and sanitation was imperfect in those times. "In the unwholesome atmosphere [of military camps], smallpox, typhoid, dysentery, measles, malaria, and pneumonia flourished" even eighty years later in the War Between the States, or Civil War. Generals in that war often saw a third of their armies on the sick list, Ron Chernow recounts in his biography *Grant*.[34] Revolutionary War sick lists exceeded that figure. "[T]yphus, scurvy, pneumonia, and dysentery . . . swept patriot ranks in summer and winter."[35] Alcoholic beverage consumption was thought to be an answer to waterborne sickness.

The Generals

Nor were higher-ranking members of the Continental Army immune to drinking, possibly to excess, even surpassing the lower ranks:

- Major General John Sullivan of New Hampshire was rumored to be a hard drinker, whose performance at Brandywine was judged by some to have been deficient, influenced by alcohol.[36]

- Brigadier William Maxwell, the "Wee Scot" from New Jersey, was accused of excessive drinking and, along with Major General Adam Stephen of Virginia, was court-martialed.[37]

- After the war, in considering whom to appoint as commander to combat Indian marauders in the west, President George Washington said of Virginia's General Charles Scott, "[b]rave and means well; but . . . by report, is addicted to drinking."[38]

- The historian Harry Ward wrote that the enjoyment of spiritous drink was well known among high-ranking officers; the same "*could be said of all the generals, especially from Virginia.*" He added that at the time of Germantown, "[Adam] Stephen, however, undoubtedly was tippling a little bit more of late, fortifying his constitution wearied by the long marches and heavy responsibilities."[39]

- A French traveler who had interviewed General William Alexander, who claimed entitlement to a Scottish peerage (thus Lord Stirling), began his report, "He is accused of liking the table and the bottle."[40]

By contrast, Francis Marion, the "Swamp Fox" who in the war led the South Carolina Militia, allowed his men to drink only water (or water cut with vinegar).[41] Marion told an officer recruit, "If you served with me, you'd be as sober as a rock, day and night, or you wouldn't serve."[42]

Today, US Navy regulations forbid intoxicating beverages aboard US men-of-war. Army regulations greatly circumscribe the availability on army posts, relegating imbibing to officers' and NCOs' clubs, after working hours. To be sure, there is still excessive drinking, but off duty, away from ships, posts, and bases.[43] Another difference is that today heavy drinking appears confined to younger sailors, soldiers, and junior officers.

PART V

WILLIAM LEE DAVIDSON

Chapter Fourteen

Piedmont Partisan: Tall Tree Davidson

THE *NEW YORK TIMES*'S 1619 PROJECT AND THE CONTEMPORARY EXPLANATIONS BY author Nikole Hannah-Jones attribute societal mistreatment of African Americans to the four-century legacy of slavery.[1] Demonstrable inferior or insufficient benefits continue to exist for African Americans in housing, education, medical treatment, transportation, employment, and many other aspects of American society. Subjective attitudes and treatments persist in the majority's views of the racial minority oveall.

A corollary to Ms. Hannah-Jones's thesis is the notion that slavery and the anticipated British eradication of the slave trade (and then of slavery itself) caused opinion makers in the colonies to favor and advocate revolution, leading to independence from Britain. In support of this thesis, its advocates highlight weathly planters' dependence on slave labor to preserve their standards of living.[2] Of course, most northern colonies had a very low incidence of slaveholding.[3] Pennsylvania, being Quaker dominated as it was, not only had a low incidence of slavery but also was viewed as a refuge by escaping slaves journeying north from Maryland and Virginia.[4]

THE MIGRATION

In the 1740s and 1750s, many settlers abandoned central Pennsylvania, frightened by the prospects of Indian raids out of the Alleghenies to the west. Marauding efforts by Native American war parties, replete with kidnapping of women and children; murder of men, women, and babies; wanton destruction of houses, barns, and other buildings; and the burning of crops took place in a wide area far east of the Allegheny mountains.

Why did settlers leave their Pennsylvania farms and homes, depopulating the region? As noted in chapter 8, due to the colony's Quaker-dominated politics, Pennsylvania would not fund a military force to deter Indian raiding. "For German farmers in Pennsylvania . . . the frequent raids of the Indians devastated German settlements and forced the farmers to emigrate." Settlers in central Pennsylvania petitoned the governor "to protect them against the inroads of the Indians . . . but no help was forthcoming."[5] The Pennsylvania Assembly and the successor proprietors would not even agree to equip a volunteer force.

The migrating settlers were Quakers, Presbyterians, Lutherans, Scots, Scots-Irish, and Germans, most of whom had lived under dominant Quaker influences. A majority were not slaveholders; a larger subgroup even opposed slavery. These families, either alone or in groups, migrated down the "Great Wagon Road" stretching from the Pennsylvaina-Virginia border through the wide, flat Shenandoah Valley. In Virginia, the colonial House of Burgesses would fund weapons, militia, and other military to protect these industrious peaceful settlers, new Virginians whom the colony welcomed with open arms.

Numerous migrants journeyed beyond Virgnia's southern border, settling in the North Carolina backcountry, as central North Carolina was then known. "[The] large emigration of Germans soon spread [from Virginia] into the present states of Kentucky, Tennessee, and North Carolina."[6] These people were not the low-country, Church of England, slave-owning and prosperous planters of whom Ms. Hannah-Jones writes.[7] Rather, they were hardscrabble farmers and tradesmen.

WILLIAM LEE DAVIDSON

A true Revolutionary War hero was North Carolina's William Davidson. With his backcountry and Presbyterian background, Davidson emerged from a farming family who had migrated south from Pennsylvania.[8]

Davidson's biographer and descendent, Chalmers Gaston Davidson, envisioned his ancestor as "the lodestar of backcountry patriotism," certainly in North Carolina but also throughout the south.[9] In the north, Davidson was present at Valley Forge, where, according to Ryan Cole in *Light-Horse Harry Lee*, he and the mercurial Light-Horse Harry Lee "became comrades in arms."[10] Lee, the Virginia Tidewater aristocrat and College of New Jersey graduate, "found the backwoods Carolinian a man of popular manners, pleasing address, active and indefatigable."[11] On the opposite end of the spectrum from the sophisticated Lee, a rough-hewn backcountry patriot such as Virginia's Daniel Morgan also found Davidson "a close friend . . . since their days at Valley Forge."[12] Davidson, a thin, wiry man (like many backcountry settlers), had a pleasing countenance, a thin smile often on his lips, compared to the grim physiognomy so common in those parts, engendered by years of hard labor in near wildness.

In 1837, North Carolina Presbyterians named their institution Davidson College, to memorialize the North Carolina brigadier who died at Cowan's Ford, in the Revolutionary War's last principal year.[13] However, other than this college, Davidson is now largely forgotten.[14]

It was only after the "guerilla war that [had] begun" against the British, following South Carolina's 1780 Battle of Camden, that William Lee Davidson merited mention in the historical record.[15]

DAVIDSON FAMILY MIGRATION SOUTH

William's father George Davidson emigrated from Northern Ireland in 1740 or 1741 (like half the population of Ireland, a victim of the 1740s potato famine), settling in central Pennsylvania. In 1746, George's youngest son, William Lee Davidson, was born a few years after his parents had settled in Pennsylvania.

As noted earlier, "the hostile Indians and French traders made the Pennsylvania frontier a precarious place in which to nurture progeny, and the Quaker aristocracy of Philadelphia was not disposed to bestir itself on behalf of the westerners."[16] The Quaker-dominated assembly would not provide funds for armaments. Neither the proprietor nor his successors, Thomas Penn and John Penn, would permit taxation of the vast Penn landholdings, even replacing any royal governor who indicated willingness to entertain taxation proposals.[17]

The Davidsons (George and his brother John, with their families) made the 435-mile trip on the Great Wagon Road through Virginia's Shenandoah Valley, continuing on the Catawba Trading Path through central North Carolina and settling west of Salisbury, North Carolina.

Later, in 1755, British General Edward Braddock suffered a devasting defeat in western Pennsylvania.[18] That summer, "[w]ord of Braddock's defeat by the French and Indians in Pennsylvania reached the Carolina Piedmont. . . . [Additional] refugees from Pennsylvania began to appear in Rowan County [North Carolina]."[19] Unfortunately, even in North Carolina, Indian raids continued to plague the settlers. "[The] Cherokees lurked in the Blue Ridge. . . . The Catawbas stole and the Cherokees scalped. A frontier family in an isolated [North Carolina] cabin expected no mercy when the savages took to the war path." Chalmers Davidson described his ancestor's time: "[C]harred timbers and mutilated bodies alone remained to tell the tale of Cherokee marauders."[20] Settlers built a stockade near Salisbury in which they could shelter, christening Fort Dobbs after royal colonial Governor Arthur Dobbs.

EARLY MILITARY EXPLOITS

Davidson's first military exploit was escort duty in 1767 when, at age twenty-one, he accompanied colonial Governor William Tryon, whose palace dominated what was then North Carolina's capital, New Bern. Governor Tryon ventured into southwestern Carolina, where the boundaries between Cherokee hunting grounds and land grants to white settlers remained unestablished, creating sources of friction. "His excellency liked the plain people of the frontier," Tryon wrote to the Earl of Shelburne. "I found on those hilly back settlements a race of people, slight, active, and laborious, and loyal subjects of his Majesty."[21]

In December 1767, Davidson married Mary Breyard before a justice of the peace. In the colonies, dissenters' (Presbyterians, Catholics, Puritans) clergy were not permitted to officiate at the rites of matrimony, a heavy-handed restriction the British enforced pursuant to the Act of Conformity.[22] In fact, in accordance with the Church of England edict, "marriages, baptisms, communions, and burial services performed by Presbyterian clergy were illegal. . . . [C]lergymen could be arrested if they tried to administer those rights."[23] Britain subjected colonists to "unending burdens" directly, through enactments such as the Stamp Act and the Townshend duties, as well as indirectly, as in "delegation of power to the Anglican Church to further subjugate the Presbyterians," who predominated in the backcountry.[24]

THE PRESBYTERIANS VERSUS THE GOVERNMENT

North Carolinians came to minimize east versus west, coast versus backcountry tensions.[25] Before the war, in 1771, North Carolina Governor Tryon and the militia met a large, armed mob of western Carolinians, aggrieved at colonial officials' alleged overcharges and arrogant behaviors. At the Battle of Alamance, the militia defeated the Regulators' mob, but ensuing government reforms eased tensions in North Carolina.[26] The Regulator movement symbolized the east-west, coastal-backcountry divide. Presbyterianism and patriotism also were inextricably interwoven: Earlier, "'[P]resbyterian' and 'Episcopalian' were frequently used as synonyms for 'rebel' and 'loyalist.'"[27]

RUMBLINGS AND THE EARLY WAR YEARS

By 1775, at age nineteen, William Davidson was captain of the Rowan County Militia. In September of that year, the Continental Congress authorized two North Carolina regiments, with James Moore and Robert Howe as colonels.[28] Colonel (later General) Griffin Rutherford commanded the North Carolina Militia in the backcountry. Rutherford made Captain Davidson adjutant of the western Minutemen.

Near the North Carolina coast, Scottish Highlanders settled in the southeast, where Fayetteville (then Cross Creek) stands today. Unlike the Scots-Irish of the backcountry, the newly arrived Scots were loyalists.[29] The Crown had granted them land after they had taken an oath of allegiance following their defeat in the Jacobite Rebellion of 1747.[30] Fourteen hundred Cross Creek Scots marched southeast to join the British troops expected to invade: "A number [of Scots] were armed [only] with Claymores, traditional Highland swords."[31] Eighteen miles upriver from Wilmington, North Carolina, militia forces vanquished the loyalists.[32] Colonel Rutherford led his troops east to help, but he, Davidson, and the force arrived too late to participate.

In April 1776, the Continental Congress authorized six additional North Carolina regiments, commanded by Francis Nash, Alexander Martin, Jethro Sumner, Thomas Polk, Edward Buncombe, and Alexander Lillington. William Davidson became major (third in command), 4th North Carolina Regiment.[33]

A False Alarm, a Leave, and a Journey North

The false alarm came in spring 1776. Two British fleets with armies aboard sailed into the Cape Fear estuary, downriver from Wilmington, North Carolina's principal port.[34] After Moore's Creek, the British declined to disembark, soon departing. Meanwhile, however, the Continental Congress had ordered the six additional North Carolina regiments, including Major Davidson's, to converge on Wilmington.[35] The British departure averted the specter of a cataclysmic battle.

In 1776, Davidson's Continental regiment released him to participate with militia Colonel Griffith Rutherford in another campaign against the Cherokees, who were raiding, marauding, scalping, and killing settlers again in the state's western reaches.[36] Rutherford led two thousand militiamen, with temporary soldiers from North Carolina, Virginia, South Carolina, and Georgia serving under him.[37] The force "burned at least thirty-six Cherokee towns."[38] As Chalmers Davidson recounted, "The Indians had their villages burned [and] their cornfields leveled. . . . Rutherford left in his wake only the ashes of wigwams and the stubble of maize fields. The Cherokees were never again a serious menace to Carolinians."[39] The excursion complete, Major Davidson returned to service with the 4th North Carolina.

In April 1777, following General James Moore's death, Francis Nash, promoted to brigadier some months earlier, headed the North Carolina forces. The Continental Congress created the 7th, 8th, and 9th North Carolina Regiments, to be commanded by Colonels James Hogun, James Armstrong, and John Williams. Congress followed with another directive, ordering all nine North Carolina regiments north to the Middle Department. Brigadier Nash, later killed at Germantown, led the Carolina contingent. Once in the north, Washington kept the North Carolina regiments in reserve, the Carolinians being "virtual spectators" at Brandywine on September 11, 1777. With the rest of the army, the Carolina regiments marched and countermarched. It was at Germantown a few weeks later (on October 4, 1777) that the North Carolina contingent lost its second commanding general. "Francis Nash fell in action and died a few days later."[40]

Much Ado about Nothing: Service with the Middle Department

In December 1777, George Washington took his army, crestfallen after Brandywine and Germantown but heartened by the October Saratoga victory in the north, into the

Valley Forge encampment. Davidson endured the winter without major incident. As aforesaid, Davidson became friendly with famous Virginians Harry Light-Horse Lee and Daniel Morgan.[41] About to break camp, George Washington reorganized his army into three divisions under Major Generals Charles Lee, Adam Stephen, and Nathanael Greene. As part of the preparations, Congress collapsed nine North Carolina regiments into three. Lt. Colonel Davidson became second-in-command of the 3rd North Carolina, under Colonel Jethro Sumner. In June 1778, Sumner, Davidson, and their troops formed the Philadelphia garrison after the British had vacated the city.[42]

RETURN HOME

After two years in the north, Davidson returned to North Carolina, taking leave to visit his family. On May 1, 1780, Davidson left his family and the backcountry, journeying from central North Carolina to join his regiment on the coast, at Charles Town, South Carolina. In South Carolina, Davidson could not penetrate the British blockade. Charles Town surrendered a few weeks later (on May 12, 1780). "The fall of Charleston . . . released many 'Huzza for King George' from long repressed Tories. Loyalists in western North Carolina [included] the peace-loving Germans who were grateful to the British government for a haven from strife . . . and a remnant of the Regulators . . . who felt bound by the oaths of allegiance which Governor Tryon had exacted for forgiving their rebellious past."[43] However, differences thought to have dissipated had not done so completely.

Deprived of his Continental command because of his regiment's capture at Charles Town, Davidson returned to the backcountry, accepting a militia command. In early July, Davidson was shot in the stomach while leading two hundred troops at Colson's Mill near where the Yadkin River joins the Pee Dee, southeast of Salisbury.[44]

On August 31, the North Carolina Legislature decreed General Davidson commander, Western Carolina Militia, replacing General Griffin Rutherford, whom the British had captured at Camden. Although "Davidson held a Continental Commission and was a veteran of Washington's army," he now commanded militia.[45]

The defeat of the American forces at Camden, South Carolina, on August 16, 1780, "so soon after Charleston's fall turned doubtful Whigs into triumphant Tories." As Chalmers Davidson wrote, "[t]he counties east of Mecklenburg [Charlotte] and Rowan [Salisbury] had shown themselves as yet unweaned from King George. . . . [I]n all sections there was disaffection."[46] Yet, as Professor Davidson noted, "To frontier Scots England had been an invader for generations. [Scots] detested her religion, despised her dukes and earls, and considered her Redcoats the private prey of any sharpshooter."[47]

On August 31, 1780, Congress promoted William Lee Davidson to brigadier general.

Chapter Fifteen

Cowan's Ford

The events that set the stage for Wiliam Davidson's heroism and death began with defeat of Britsh troops, including Colonel Banastre Tarleton and his famed and ruthless mounted British Legion. The "Old Waggoner"—the rough-hewn Bridgadier Daniel Morgan—and his men had worked a devastating defeat of British at Cowpens, in South Carolina, a short distance below the North Carolina line.[1] Forty or so minutes after the battle, Morgan's men broke camp, prefatory to a hasty and long retreat. Coming up on the opposite east side of the Broad River from Cowpens, Lord Cornwallis, with 2,200 men, plus armed Tory loyalists, learned of the defeat. Outraged and seeking vengeance, Cornwallis and his troops burned their baggage. Armed with weapons, ammunition, and a few rations, the British set out at a fast (and then faster) pace to catch Morgan, who was retreating diagonally across North Carolina toward a point north of the Dan River, east of Virginia's Danville, two hundred miles northeast. Southern Department Commading General Nathanael Greene met with Brigadier Davidson. Greene charged Davidson and his 800–1,100-strong militia with their mission—namely, to delay, not defeat, the hellbent British force by guarding a dozen or more fords across the near flood stage Catawba River. The Catawba flows southeast from north of Charlotte. In their pursuit of Morgan, Cornwallis and his men would have to cross the Catawba.[2]

The Larger Framework

With the May 1780 fall of Charles Town, the British now imagined that a southern strategy was the pathway to victory.[3] The northern strategy had come to naught with Saratoga, the 1778 defeat of Burgoyne coming down from Canada. In the Middle Department, despite numerous losses (Brooklyn, White Plains, Brandywine, Germantown) and smaller successes (Trenton, Princeton, the draw at Monmouth Courthouse), the Americans had done enough in the mid-Atlantic to preserve the quest for independence. Middle Department strategy thus represented a draw, the equivalent of patriot success.

So now the British command initiated a third focus, to the south, early on achieving successes at Savannah, Charles Town, Waxhaw, and then Camden. But the British force's peregrinations lengthened supply lines, entered increasingly hostile territory, and suffered surprising defeats at Kings Mountain (October 1780) and Cowpens (January 1781).

In September 1780, Lord Cornwallis had come seventy miles north from Camden, South Carolina, to occupy Charlotte. In command of militia, as aforesaid, Brigadier Davidson "[f]ound himself faced with a bellicose, turbid mob of about 400 frontiersmen." These backcountry frontiersmen had "one unique advantage in arms. Hunts and Indian wars had led to the importation of the rifle . . . whereas the coastal regiments and the British began the war [and continued] with their main dependence on the smooth-bored musket."[4] With their rifled-barrel "Kentucky Rifles," Davidson's men resembled Daniel Morgan's Rifle Corps, heroes of Saratoga and Cowpens. The rifles' effective range was two hundred or more yards, as opposed to muskets' fifty- to sixty-yard field of fire, inaccurate even at that range.

Cornwallis came north from Camden with more than two thousand British regulars and probably half as many loyalists. As he came north, Cornwallis sent a large party, a few regulars combined with armed Tories, under Colonel Patrick Ferguson, to the west. Several things occurred. First, Davidson and his men's increasing hit-and-run tactics against Cornwallis and Charlotte plagued the British to no end. Second, on October 7, 1780, American militia, commanded by Virginian William Campbell, defeated Colonel Ferguson and his now party of eleven hundred men at Kings Mountain, southwest of Charlotte, a few miles below the North Carolina border.[5] Although not present at Kings Mountain, Brigadier Davidson passed on news of the victory to his superiors, writing Horatio Gates, "[British] Colonel Ferguson fell in the action besides 150 of his men—810 were made prisoners . . . 1,500 Stands of arms fell into our Hands. . . . We lost about 20 men. . . . The Blow is great and I give you Joy upon the Occasion."[6] If only temporarily, the tide had turned. After embarrassing losses at Charles Town and Camden, at Kings Mountain the Americans had achieved a measure of redemption.[7]

"Meanwhile, Cornwallis was finding Charlotte an inhospitable hostess. Every able-bodied Whig in the vicinity did his bit to make his lordship uncomfortable." Fifty horses were rustled from Tory camps; over twenty-five barrels of gunpowder were taken from a British depot; a supply train coming up from Camden was stopped in its tracks and raided; and an estimated fifty messengers to Cornwallis were fired on, wounded, or killed before reaching British headquarters. Davidson's militia "[m]ade life miserable for the British soldiers." Harassed, nervous British

Charles Cornwallis
COURTESY OF
UK PORTRAIT GELLERY

sentries fired at the smallest sound. British foraging parties sent out to collect food were ambushed, attacked by small patriot groups. Detachments of British troops sent to guard grist mills were harassed. Snipers hid in the trees, picking off careless British soldiers. According to Hugh Rankin, bright red coats made good targets.[8] "The bushwhacking proclivities of the backwoods-men were beating down the morale of the [supposed] conquerors."[9]

Forage for both men and horses was not to be had in what was then the village of Charlotte and its surrounding area. Ferguson's defeat at Kings Mountain resulted in Cornwallis's left flank being unprotected. On October 12, 1780, the British began leaving Charlotte, bound for South Carolina.

CONTEST WITH CORNWALLIS

Lord Cornwallis retreated slowly. Fall rains impeded the British withdrawal; the baggage train moved with difficulty. "Rain fell for several days without intermission"; the rivers and streams were swollen, the red clay roads turned into quagmires.[10] "The laboring and lumbering [British] column was harassed almost continuously by little groups under colonels [William] Davie and Davidson."[11] By the end of October, Cornwallis and his "bedraggled" force reached Winnsboro, a South Carolina village seventy miles south of Charlotte. There, Cornwallis took his army into winter quarters. On the American side, on December 2, 1780, Major General Nathanael Greene arrived in Charlotte, relieving the disgraced General Horatio Gates (see chapter 20).

The British still mistakenly believed that once they entered North Carolina, "a large number of North Carolina Loyalists would flock to their standard," as groups of loyalists had previously done in South Carolina. The British began their second trek north in mid-January 1781.

Cornwallis sent ahead his prized British Legion, commanded by the dashing, give-no-quarter Colonel Banastre Tarleton. On January 17, General Daniel Morgan and his men administered "a devil of a whipping" at Cowpens, as Lawrence Babbits titled his historical account. Rather than keeping militia in the rear, in reserve—the unvarying patriot practice—General Morgan placed militia in the first of three lines. He requested that his militia fire two or three rounds and then retreat to the rear via openings in the crescent-shaped regulars' formation. Thinking he had the colonials on the run, Tarleton and his men ran pell-mell ("As always, speed was Tarleton's measure of imminent victory")[12] into a double envelopment. The result was the most

Banastre Tarleton
COURTESY OF NATIONAL PORTRAIT GALLERY

lopsided American victory of the war, with 120 British killed, 229 wounded, and 702 captured, out of a 1,200-man British brigade. American losses were negligible.[13]

Davidson missed the opportunity of participating at Cowpens. After the battle, Davidson gave Morgan wholehearted applause, writing, "You have in my opinion paved the way for the Salvation of this Country."[14]

Back in the Carolina backcountry, General Davidson "was using all his powers of persuasion to bring in the militia. This, in the piedmont [the high wide plateau before the foothills and then mountains farther in the west], was the time that tried men's souls."[15] Cornwallis and the British were coming with a vengeance. Americans suffered war fatigue as the seventh anniversary of Lexington and Concord (April 1774 to April 1781) approached.

DAVIDSON'S FINAL CHAPTER: THE CROSSING AT COWAN'S FORD

Triply chagrined at the utter defeat of his crack troops at Cowpens, Lord Cornwallis pursued Morgan at more than a double-quick march, seeking to overtake them, intending revenge. After a feint toward Charlotte, Morgan and his men veered to the northeast, in the direction of Hillsboro, near the Virginia border and then perhaps across Virginia's Dan River. In Morgan's wake, the Catawba River, above present-day Charlotte, and the Yadkin River, west of Salisbury, approached flood stage. The swirling waters made crossing difficult, if not impossible. Cornwallis and his men found it necessary to pause until rains eased and fast-flowing rivers became fordable.

It was Commander Nathanael Greene's opinion that the enemy would attempt to cross the rivers, "probably sending their cavalry at night by some private ford," rather than crossing on a well-used route.[16] Lord Cornwallis also might attempt a diversion, sending units toward various river fords. Davidson had about eight to eleven hundred militiamen under his immediate command, including Graham's cavalry, who rode plow horses rather than sleek steeds.[17] General Greene "assigned Davidson and his North Carolina militiamen the unenviable task of contesting the [pursuing] British at the fords of the Catawba."[18]

General Davidson distributed his force along the east banks of the Catawba, guarding private fords. At Cowan's Ford, however, there were two fords, a wagon ford and a horse ford (today under the large, artificial Lake Norman, north of Charlotte). The latter option was shallower, going straight across the river. The wagon ford started at the same point on the right bank but proceeded diagonally, probably because wagons were less able to take the river current nearly head on. The wagon ford reached the left (east) bank a quarter mile below the horse ford's terminus. Davidson himself "paraded at the horse ford," where he placed a contingent of troops. Later, at the sounding of the alarm, he rode to the wagon ford, lightly guarded because Davidson and his officers had not believed the British would attempt to cross there.[19] "General

Davidson, a confident thirty-five-year-old of Continental experience at Germantown, awaited the redcoat advance. . . . Davidson coolly awaited the enemy as if he still led a Continental regiment."[20]

Lord Cornwallis himself led the Brigade of Guards, the Royal Welch Fusiliers, and the Hessian von Bose Regiment into the river. On the opposite shore, upriver Davidson sat his mount, having just arrived to rally the wagon ford sentries and a contingent of militia calvary, such as they were, on the crest of the hill behind him. "The [river's] waters were swift and the sentries soon heard the splashing of water as the British struggled along, trying to maintain their footing. . . . Out on the river, the British were experiencing rough going . . . roped together to prevent being swept away by the current."[21] Several British drowned; foot soldiers crossed the swirling waters with great difficulty. A patriot shot hit Lord Cornwallis's horse. For the British, "[s]ome men and horse had been swept away by river current, and some had been killed or wounded by the first [American] volley. [British infantry] were up to their breasts in the rapid stream."[22]

On the American-held riverbank, an officer with General Davidson, colonial Colonel William Polk, shouted, "Fire away boys. There is help at hand!" For a moment, having arrived at the wagon ford terminus, reining in from a gallop, "Davidson stared in the direction of the man with the smoking gun. Then, without a sound, he fell from his horse." "Davidson was hit by a musket ball in the chest. . . . [H]e died instantly. Without their leader the patriots ran."[23] Davidson lay dead of a wound near the nipple of his left breast. The musket ball had pierced his heart.[24] General Davidson's battlefield death set off "a confused and precipitous Colonial retreat."[25] "[T]he death of General Davidson was [a] catastrophe, creating panic among his followers, who fled in wild disorder, all thought of further resistance disappearing."[26]

A Partisan's Contribution

"Measured by the contemporary criterion of a great soldier, Davidson fails to qualify." He neither commanded nor participated in any critical encounter throughout the Revolution. Measured by subjective criteria, however, "[t]here was no more completely adored soldier in North Carolina."[27] In the backcountry, "[t]he militia of the Salisbury District would do for him what they would do for no other man." Davidson was a rough-hewn senior officer, "[a] backwoodsman who won the allegiance of such ambitious and self-assured Princetonians as Harry Lee, William Davie, and Waightstill Avery. . . . It was, however, [Davidson's] hold on the plain men of dirt farms . . . that made him important."[28]

PART VI
CHARLES LEE

Chapter Sixteen

Professional Soldier Lee

General Charles Lee was not true-blue American. He emigrated from England, hoping to win a high rank in the American army. Many of the other revolutionary generals were immigrants of long-standing residence, permanent citizens before whiffs of revolution filled the air.[1] For instance, Hugh Mercer (chapter 8) emigrated from Scotland in the 1740s, Andrew Lewis's parents emigrated from Ireland to Virginia several decades before the war, and Richard Caswell's parents emigrated from England to Maryland in 1712. By contrast, until before the war commenced, Charles Lee and Horatio Gates had been British army officers. Both resigned, selling their commissions (sales of rank were customary in the British army) and coming to America in the mid-1770s, Lee by way of several years' service in the Portuguese, Polish, and Turkish armies.[2]

Artistic renderings of Lee—caricatures, really—show him as thin, chinless, and worm-like in profile. He was usually pictured surrounded by dogs; his favorite dog, a Pomeranian named Spada (Italian for sword), he carried everywhere, in his lap when he rode horseback. Lee was said to be so thin that he appeared to lack shoulders. With a high forehead, small hands, deep-set eyes, and a large nose, he even appeared eccentric. Stephen Taaffe augmented the picture: "Tall, slender, and with a nose so large that soldiers made fun of it, Lee was the Continental army's most eccentric officer. . . . He was so outspoken, sardonic, critical, contemptuous, and quarrelsome." Far from flattering, Taaffe's description continued: "Lee was well-known for his blasphemousness and slovenliness. He rarely smiled or laughed but projected a morose cynicism that sucked the energy and initiative right out of the room."[3]

As external dress, Lee often wore a Polish cavalry officer's dress uniform, black with silver buttons, epaulettes, and decorations, garnished with a fox pelt and strapped-on holsters containing gold-inlaid steel pistols. On horseback, Lee rode wearing green sherryvallies, heavy cloth protective leggings, with leather stripes

Charles Lee
ALAMY.COM

down each side. On other occasions, Lee wore his bone-white Polish general's uniform, festooned with red ribbons, giving prominence to his enameled Polish decoration, Star of the Order of Saint Stanislaus.

Beginning and Ending of Lee's Service

Congress bestowed the second major generalship of the four it initially awarded on Charles Lee.[4] American politicians and military leaders considered this strange man a military genius, by far the most experienced military man on America's shores, and a possible successor or alternative to George Washington as commanding general. Lee obtained his commission, beginning his Continental Army service in June

1775. In the Continental Army, Lee "maintained," and bolstered, "his reputation as a skilled and experienced general." Stephen Taaffe also wrote that Lee "had assisted Washington in organizing the army overlooking Boston and then oversaw the defense of Rhode Island and New York City." From the very beginning, some of it was bluster. "Self-assuredness was never a problem with Lee, so his advice and orders seemed authoritative to amateur local military authorities." The Continental Congress also saw Lee in a very favorable light. "Benedict Arnold," a colonel at the time, "told Washington that he would welcome [Major General] Lee as his commander."[5]

Serving in various roles, Lee had no permanent abode until late 1779, after a court-martial followed by his congressional dismissal from the Continental Army.[6] He returned to Prado Rio, his Virginia estate, where he became a hermit. He settled in Berkeley County, "[m]ore eccentric than ever, preferring the companionship of dogs rather than humans."[7] Not long thereafter, Lee began spending time in Philadelphia, where he died on October 2, 1782, age fifty. Lee's permanent domicile in the United States amounted to less than three years.

CHARLES LEE IN HISTORY BOOKS

Several Charles Lee biographies exist, some favorable.[8] Others treat Lee as though he were a share of stock: buy Lee, sell Lee, sell Lee short, and so on. Lee was, according to biographer Paul Burrow, "[o]ne of the most enigmatic military leaders of the American Revolution . . . erratic and talented." Burrows continues, finding that Lee's "brash and often abrasive attitude earned him enemies that prevented his advancement to the level he felt he deserved."[9] George Washington deemed Lee "the first officer in military knowledge and experience [although] fickle and violent, I fear, in his temper."[10] Author Rick Atkinson finds that "Lee's increasingly erratic, bickering behavior [even as of 1776] had been growing nettlesome," and his incessant self-promotion soon became insufferable. "His habit of carrying Thucydides in the original Greek burnished his [self-]image as a military thinker . . . 'learned, judicious, and penetrating.'"[11] David Wilson concludes that "Lee's only true loyalty was to himself," that he "was seen as egotistical and arrogant by all who met him, and the two dogs he kept constantly at his side annoyed many."[12] Even then, the general American view was that English nobility's (including Lee's) preferential treatment of pet dogs was bizarre.[13]

CONTRARY VIEWS

"John Adams adored him." A contemporary newspaper declared Lee "the greatest military character of the present age." Historian Richard Alden saw Lee "as a remarkable personality who should not be denied a place among the great leaders of the American Revolution."[14] John Burrow concludes that Lee's "contributions [and] patriotism . . . place him as one of the founders of the fight for independence."[15]

In truth, Lee's military accomplishments seem to have been overstated, not really having amounted to much. He commanded the American left wing at Bunker Hill, but accounts do not single Lee out in any particular. Later, Washington and the Congress sent Lee south to superintend the defense of Charles Town against the first British siege, in June 1776. After the fact, he was dubbed "the hero of Charleston" (Charles Town in those times).[16]

In truth, the defense of Charles Town succeeded not because of Lee's efforts but despite them, as he repeatedly urged abandonment of the fort on Sullivan's Island, the barrier island that guarded the entrance to Charles Town's harbor. In defiance of General Lee, defense of the fort, which Lee had termed "a slaughter pen," became a rallying cry for the troops and Charles Town's citizens, the key to a hoped-for American victory. In June 1778, at Monmouth Courthouse, Lee ordered a retreat instead of an attack, resulting in Washington relieving Lee of command, ordering Lee to the rear, and convening Lee's subsequent court-martial. For the heart of the war, from December 1776 to mid-May 1778, Lee was on the sidelines, not participating in the conflict at all.

THE HIATUS

After the 1776 defeats at Brooklyn and White Plains, and the improvident abandonment and surrender at Forts Washington and Lee, Washington and his bedraggled army retreated across New Jersey. "With each backward step the army sloughed off men, weapons, and equipment; [the men] who remained were dispirited, hungry, ragged and dirty."[17] Washington left Lee, who had arrived from the south too late to be at the Battle of Long Island (Battle of Brooklyn), and a sizable contingent of troops behind to protect against the British cutting New England off from the other colonies. With twenty-seven hundred men under his command, Lee proceeded independently of Washington. "[F]eeling slighted that the less experienced Washington had been given command of the Continental Army, [Lee] showed no inclination to rush." He lingered near northern New Jersey's Morristown for three days. An after-the-fact explanation Lee gave others was that he purposely dragged his feet so that if Lord Cornwallis attacked Washington's colonials from the rear, Lee would then be able to attack Cornwallis's rear.[18] Finally, prodded by General Washington, Lee forsook his intentional foot-dragging, beginning to take his army south.

At Basking Ridge, New Jersey, the British took Lee prisoner on December 12, as he and his army meandered behind the retreating Washington. Lee, however, separated himself from his troops, sheltering in an inn three miles away from the force's encampment, with minimum security. Allegedly, Lee was visiting a prostitute.[19] A detachment of British dragoons captured Lee at Widow White's tavern, with one version being that Lee emerged in a "dirty nightdress."[20] Other versions are no less uncomplimentary: "Lee stepped through the [tavern's] front door, bareheaded and disheveled, a blanket draped over his dingy white shirt."[21]

For this escapade, Lee had with him an aide and fifteen bodyguards. On the morning of the December 13, thirty of the 16th Queen's Light Horse under Colonel William Harcourt surrounded the inn, capturing Lee. Lee remained a British prisoner for seventeen months, until May 1778.

The British cavalry who captured Lee regarded him not as a prisoner of war but as British and a traitor, tying Lee's hands behind his back and forcing him, clad only in his nightshirt, aboard a horse, according him none of the respect due a major general's rank.[22] The effect of Lee's capture on morale, already at a low point, was demonstrated by Dr. Benjamin Rush's letter to Congressman Richard Henry Lee: "Since the captivity of General Lee, a distrust has crept in among the troops of the abilities of some of our general officers in high command."[23]

THE PRODIGAL RETURNS

The British held Lee captive during 1777. When the British released Lee in mid-May 1778, he returned to the Continental Army bivouac, where George Washington welcomed him. Behind General Washington's back, however, to others Lee asserted "[t]hat he found the army in a worse situation than he expected and that General Washington was not fit to command a sergeant's guard."[24]

Before his capture in fall 1776, Lee had written a letter to General Joseph Reed, Washington's adjutant, who was traveling at the time and unable to receive the letter. Instead, General Washington received the letter, opening it by mistake. Lee had written in the letter unfaithful, self-serving lines that became ammunition for a future cabal: "Oh . . . an indecisive mind [Washington's] is one of the greatest misfortunes that can befall an army. How often have I lamented it in this campaign. . . . I think yourself & some others should go to Congress & form the plan of the new army," one that Lee strongly intimated he would lead.[25]

Chapter Seventeen

Lee's Privileged Background

Charles's father, John Lee, was a British army major general. As a younger man, Colonel John Lee married Isabella Bunbury, daughter of a peer, Baronet Lord Banbury. Charles Lee, Isabella and John's son, attended a grammar school in Bury St. Edmunds, Suffolk, going on to school in Switzerland.[1] In 1747, when Charles was fifteen, as was done in that day, his father purchased for Charles a commission in the 55th Foot. For several hundred pounds then, Charles became an ensign in his father's regiment, later renumbered the 44th.[2]

Having disposable funds of his own, Charles purchased a lieutenant's commission in 1751. His captain's commission, purchased in 1756, cost him £900. Similarly, on purchasing another commission, Lee went up the ladder to the rank of major. In 1754, at age twenty-four and as a lieutenant, Lee had gone to North America in service as an aide to Edward Cornwallis, Charles Lord Cornwallis's older brother. Lee served in General Edward Braddock's 1755 ill-fated campaign to oust the French from the Forks of the Ohio. Lee saw service in several British campaigns, including the siege of Louisbourg, Nova Scotia; the capture of Fort Niagara in New York; and the failed British attempt to wrest Fort Ticonderoga from the French. At the cessation of the French and Indian War, Lee returned to England.

A Career as a Mercenary

On his return to Britain, Lee began acquiring the disloyal, or at least fluid, mindset that surfaced later in the American army. In England, the War Ministry dissolved Lee's regiment; Lee retired on half-pay. At that point, he was thirty-one. Seeking to advance his military career, he sold his services to various bidders. He served as a lieutenant colonel in the Portuguese army, fighting the Spanish. In 1765, Lee hired out to Poland, as aide-de-camp to King Stanislaw II. He served with forces allied with the Turkish army in the Russo-Turkish War. In the interim, he returned to England; then, after again not finding a billet with a British regiment, he returned to Poland to serve once more in Stanislaw's military. Those shifting alliances inculcated in Lee a vacillating and illusory notion of loyalty. He had "a reputation as a soldier of fortune."[3]

INCREASING ECCENTRICITY

As Lee grew older, he preferred the company of dogs to humans. He took his meals with two or three of his dogs seated alongside. Earlier on, when he still had feelings toward humans, while serving in North America, Lee married Seneca Chief White Thunder's daughter. He was accepted into the Mohawks' Bear Tribe. Prompted by Lee's argumentative and sometimes truculent behavior, the tribe bestowed on Lee the name Quewaterika ("boiling water"). Lee lived with the Mohawks in upstate New York. His Native American wife bore him twin boys.[4] After Lee returned to England, neither wife nor sons were mentioned again. Lee abandoned them.

Lee "was habitually unkempt and reputedly owned but three shirts, each in such disrepair that he named them Rag, Tag, and Bobtail."[5] Rick Atkinson concluded that in uniform, and contrary to Lee's wearing a dirty nightdress or ragged shirts, "[n]o more flamboyant figure ever served the American cause."[6]

INCREASING DISLOYALTY

Charles Lee befriended George Washington when the two served in the French and Indian War, Lee as a British officer, Washington commanding the contingent. When Lee expressed interest in immigrating to the colonies, Washington urged him to come to Virginia.[7] Two decades later, after Lee had immigrated and the Revolution was about to begin, Lee made a six-day visit to Mount Vernon and George Washington in December 1774. "Haughty, imperious, and overflowing with opinions, Lee seldom had a kind word for anyone's military talents but his own," Ron Chernow summarized. Lee intimated to Washington a desire to volunteer for Continental Army service. Washington responded positively, although again, by Washington biographer Chernow's lights, Lee "had a razor-sharp wit [that] must have made Washington feel a bit insular by comparison."[8]

Not so secretly, Charles Lee wished to be America's commander in chief. The Continental Congress, however, sensed that although Lee was the most experienced candidate, the position called for a native-born person.[9] Ron Chernow wrote that "[w]hen comparing Washington with the rivals for the top spot—especially Charles Lee and Horatio Gates—one sees that [Washington] had superior presence, infinitely better judgment, more political cunning, and unmatched gravitas. With nothing arrogant or bombastic in his nature, he had the perfect temperament for leadership." Moreover, Washington "was also born in North America," "which was considered essential."[10]

Cartoon lampooning General Lee

In June 1775, Congress appointed George Washington. Lee then angled for the number two slot, with only George Washington his superior, as commander in chief. Instead, Congress awarded second-in-command to Artemas Ward of Massachusetts, who commanded the American siege of British-occupied Boston. Undaunted, in early summer 1776, General Lee reacquainted himself with George Washington, then still at Mount Vernon. Lee and Washington rode together from Virginia to Boston, where, after Lexington and Concord (April 1775), the siege of Boston had begun.

During the ensuing months at Boston, Lee set to work undermining Major General Ward. "Artemas Ward," Lee not so quietly confided, "is a fat old gentleman who has been a popular church warden but who had no acquaintance with military affairs."[11] On the contrary, Artemas Ward served in the French and Indian War as colonel of the Third Massachusetts Militia Regiment. In June 1775, Ward was at Bunker Hill, and in 1776 he was at the Battle of Long Island. After two years' service, Ward resigned due to ill health, returning to Massachusetts. John Adams described Ward as "universally esteemed, beloved, confided in by his army and his country."[12] To the scheming Lee, Ward seemed to be a roadblock to his hoped-for upward progress.

Disloyal and Conniving

The Ward episode is one demonstration of Lee's manipulative inclinations. Another was the Conway cabal in 1778. Charles Lee had a "resentment of Washington as Commander-in-Chief [that] would [grow] and continue to surface throughout the war." In "efforts to undermine George Washington," in 1776 Lee wrote a congressman, "Had I the powers"—that is, were he commander in chief—"I could do you much good."[13] He grumbled about "Washington and his puppies," referring to Washington's subordinate officers, who Lee felt "were incompetent."[14]

The Conway cabal was an attempt to replace Washington with Major General Horatio Gates, the alleged "Hero of Saratoga." The ringleader was Thomas Conway (see chapter 29), an Irishman who had come to America after heading the French army's Irish Brigade. From the Continental Congress, Conway received a major general appointment, leapfrogging over a promotion list of twenty-seven brigadiers. Despite the snap promotion, led by the still unsatisfied Conway, "army officers and congressmen began to plot Washington's replacement. . . . Benjamin Rush, Samuel Adams, Thomas Mifflin, and Richard Henry Lee were the leading congressional instigators," according to Andrew Zambone.[15] Historians disagree on whether an actual plot took place or grumbling merely occurred about George Washington's competence.[16] Groups of malcontents exchanged these views after the 1777 Brandywine and Germantown defeats, but whether there was grumbling or an actual conspiracy, Charles Lee was at the center.[17]

A testament to the character of the "arrogant, irascible Charles Lee" was his treatment of men under him. Confirming his arrogance, "Charles Lee [also] couldn't control his temper."[18] One soldier recorded an instance in his diary, an example that David McCullough utilized: "We was ordered to form a hollow square. General Lee came in and the first words were, 'Men, I do not know what to call you; [you] are the worst of all creatures,' and he cursed and swore at us."[19]

ILLUSORY COMBAT EXPERIENCES

Accounts hail Lee as the "hero of Charleston," the most experienced, a brilliant strategist. As has been seen, the evidence for those propositions is countered by considerable evidence to the contrary.

In February 1776, Congress created the Southern Army, on February 29 putting the British soldier of fortune Charles Lee as major general in command. Congress charged Lee with setting up defenses along the mid-Atlantic and southern colonies' coastlines, with their many bays, inlets, and estuaries. Soon thereafter, Lee wrote Washington, "I feel like a dog in a dancing school. I know not where to turn myself, where to fix myself. . . . The uncertainty of the enemy's designs and motives, who can fly in an instant to any spot they choose."[20] Rick Atkinson records that Lee first spent six weeks along the Virginia coast, "with his dogs, his gaudy sherryvallies, and his draconian military philosophy."[21] Then word came that a combined naval-land force under British General Henry Clinton was sailing toward Charles Town, South Carolina (the 1776 siege of Charles Town). Lee led two thousand Virginia and North Carolina Continentals south to Charles Town, augmenting the four thousand troops already in or arriving in the city. Lee set about improving the city's defenses, riding to and fro with his beloved dog Spada accompanying him. "Nothing worried Lee more than the vulnerability of Fort Sullivan," on the three-mile-long barrier island north of the harbor entrance, on which Lee "considered a flimsy palmetto fort [to be] a 'slaughter pen' for its defenders."[22]

A thousand men manned the fort, a square-sided fortress with diamond-shaped bastions at its corners. To militia General William Moultrie, after whom the fort was later renamed, Lee voiced doomsday sentiments. "Sir, when those [British] ships come to lay alongside your fort, they will knock it down in half an hour," Lee preached to the South Carolinian.[23] Incessantly, Lee advocated that the locals abandon the fort. "When Lee came to Sullivan's Island, he did not like the post at all. . . . [T]he garrison would be sacrificed . . . and [Lee] wished to withdraw the garrison and give up the post," William Moultrie remembered.[24]

The opposite occurred. Rather than undergoing destructive enemy fire, "[t]o everyone's surprise, the soft palmetto logs (backed by sixteen feet of earth) easily

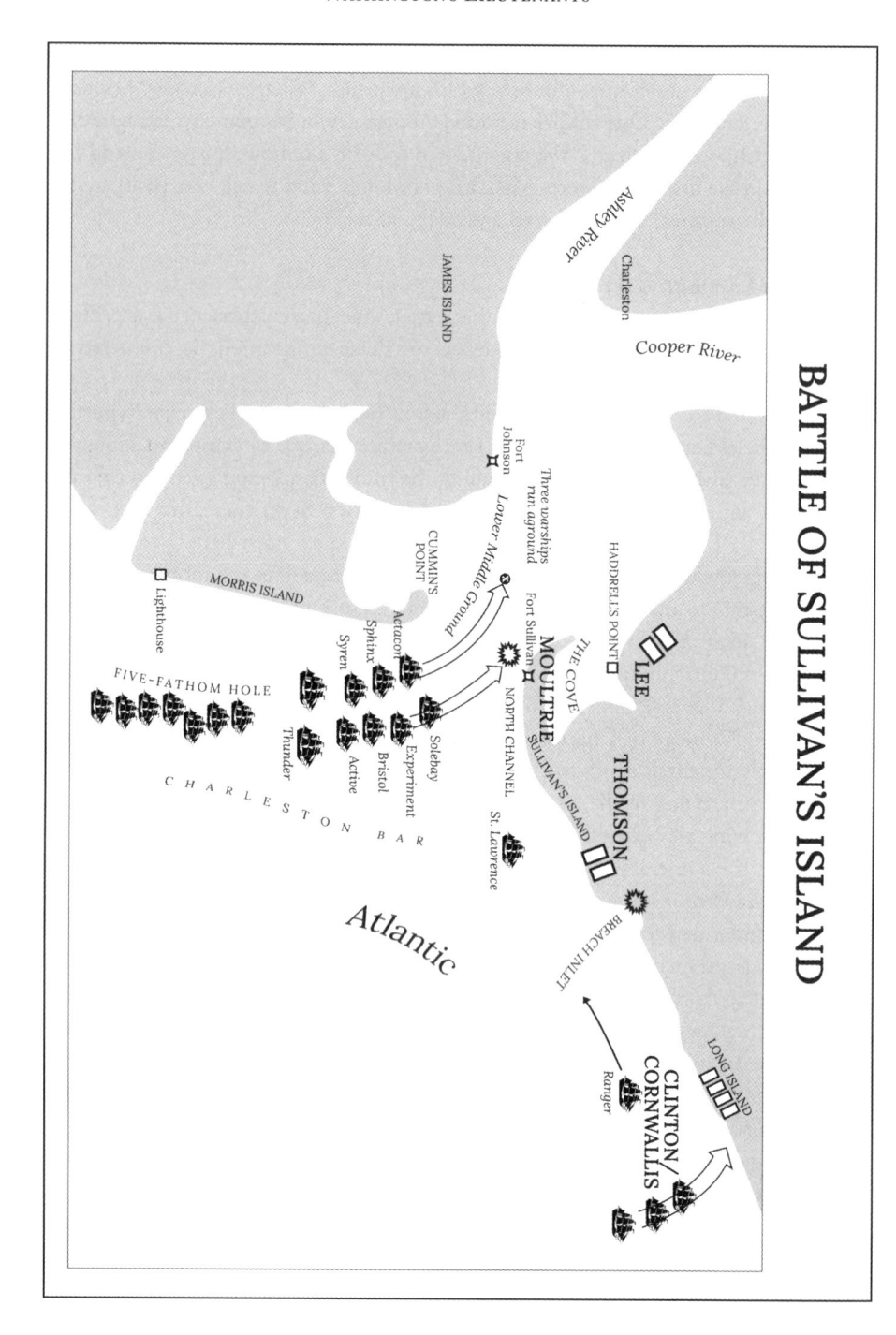

BATTLE OF SULLIVAN'S ISLAND

absorbed or deflected the heavy [British] cannonballs."[25] The fort held through a fourteen-hour seige.

Faced with the American force's defense of Fort Sullivan and their defeat despite all-around British superiority, the British reboarded their ground troops onto transports, hoisted the sails of their sizable fleet, sailed seaward, turned north, and made for New York.[26] Charles Town had defeated the British. South Carolina became the Palmetto State; Moultrie's battle ensign with a white star in the corner of a blue field became the state flag, with one addition—an artist's rendering of a palmetto palm in the center of the field.

Again, though, history is much like cement.[27] Quickly a mythical account replaces reality. Thereafter, "[n]o amount of archeology can shake the fairy dust from [the myth's] heels."[28] The cement—the mythical account—was that Charles Lee's efforts, not those of South Carolinians such as William Moultrie, President John Rutledge, the palmetto palm, and militia forces, saved Charles Town.[29]

CHAPTER EIGHTEEN

Lee's Fall from Grace

LEE HAD SEVERAL FALLS FROM GRACE. THE FIRST FALL OCCURRED IN LATE 1776 when he bivouacked in a central Jersey tavern (chapter 16). He spent the night several miles from his men, thereby letting his guard down, allowing a British cavalry unit to capture him. Lee spent seventeen months as a British prisoner.

The second noteworthy fall, which turned out to be lasting, resulted from Lee's actions at the Battle of Monmouth Courthouse. As usual, thinking he knew better than anyone else, including Commander in Chief George Washington, Lee ordered the troops to retreat rather than pressing their advantage. Lee's actions infuriated Washington. They marked the beginning of the end for Charles Lee's military career.

Charles Lee always thought he knew better. He was a tireless advocate of defensive tactics and small group guerrilla warfare, as opposed to cataclysmic confrontations of major army groups. On one occasion, Lee stated that "[h]e would erect a bridge of gold for the enemy," meaning that he would give up Manhattan to the British rather than turn and fight.[1] Of course, under Washington at Kip's Bay and at Harlem Heights, the retreating Americans did the opposite, resisting the attackers.

MONMOUTH AND ITS PREQUEL

In early summer 1778, the Americans left Valley Forge, site of the army's infamous winter of death and discontent. About the same time, twenty miles to the southeast, the British abandoned Philadelphia to make their way slowly across New Jersey toward New York. General Washington convened several successive councils of war between June 16 and June 18, 1778, on how best to meet these circumstances. At first, ten general officers (Brigadier "Mad" Anthony Wayne dissenting) supported Charles Lee, who spearheaded the movement not to attack the retreating British.[2] Washington accepted the council's judgment, fearing that "provoking a major battle might lead to another Brandywine."[3]

A few days later, however, the tide turned, with all the senior officers now advocating an attack on or harassment of some sort—that is, "more aggressive action" against the British.[4] Having been persuaded, General Washington reversed himself, sending Virginia's General Charles Scott with a fifteen-hundred-man light infantry force across the Delaware River to harass the British until the main American army could mobilize and catch up—that is, to attack the British column from behind. General Washington then ordered Marquis de Lafayette to catch up with Scott's force with another one thousand troops.[5] By the time General Lee rode up to General Washington and the main American force, Scott's advance force contained fifty-two hundred men,[6] four thousand select regulars and Colonel John Cadwallader's twelve-hundred-man Pennsylvania Militia. "Discovering that the forward units amounted to half the army," in a fit of pique, Lee "asserted his right to command by virtue of the fact that he was the senior major general," senior to Major General Marquis de Lafayette.[7] Washington conceded the point, compromising a bit by stating that Lee would replace Lafayette when Lee arrived at the front. Lee arrived and took command but neither by himself nor in conjunction with his generals formulated any battle plan.

Washington was coming up toward central New Jersey's Monmouth Courthouse with the remainder of the army's main force. Behind the American advanced troops, Washington met General Lee a second time, Lee now riding away from the front at the head of a column. "Tradition has it," wrote Harry Ward, "that the commander in chief . . . was so chagrined that he used intemperate language toward Lee."[8] He loudly burst out, "Damn your multiplying eyes, General Lee! Go to the front or go to hell. I care little which.'"[9] Then, negating any intent to give Lee a choice, Washington sent him to the rear, relieving him of command on the spot. General Charles Scott, who was present, painted a picture of General Washington's vehemence: "Even the leaves shook on the trees."[10]

Denying Responsibility

Lee answered Washington's irate query by blaming everything and everybody but himself: "contradictory intelligence, battlefield confusion, superior British cavalry, and insubordination by junior officers" were among his explanations.[11] In particular, he singled out Brigadier General Charles Scott, whose brigade constituted the American left wing. Scott, too, had ordered his soldiers to conduct an orderly retreat. Lee "singled out Scott in particular for condemnation."[12]

Lee admitted that he had ordered troops to pull back. Indeed, he never denied it. He stated that he saw artillery men toward the center hurriedly going toward the rear. He mistakenly interpreted the movement as a retreat, when in truth the gunners were returning to their limbers for more ammunition. Lee maintained that his intention was to pull the troops back, reform, and advance as a whole rather than piecemeal. According to Lee, "[h]is gallant delaying action allowed Washington the time to form the main army."[13] Author Andrew Zambone has expressed doubt about this claim. "The advance force at Monmouth," according to Zambone, "was a compromised force, led by a man [Charles Lee] who opposed the attack" in the first place.[14] He also was a man who was disrespectful of his commander in chief, having said, in a thinly veiled reference to George Washington, "I lament that fatal indecision of mind which in war is a much greater disqualification than stupidity."[15]

Lee commenced to dig himself a deeper hole. "What you sow, you reap" proved true in Lee's case. After the battle, the brotherhood of generals came out squarely against Lee, "who had shown himself as less than infallible in combat." Fellow officers "emerged from the woodwork to condemn" Lee. "The consensus the officer corps forged . . . was that Lee's timidity, selfishness, inability to control his troops, and failure to carry out Washington's orders" had prevented the Americans from achieving a clear-cut victory.[16]

DENOUEMENT

Washington had never been one to carry a grudge or to scapegoat generals. Lee, however, wrote an impassioned letter to the Congress in which he made numerous allegations against George Washington, reminiscent of the letter another major general, Adam Stephen (chapter 7), sent to Congress after his court-martial for actions at Germantown.[17] Washington became convinced that "Lee was more trouble than he was worth." Lee had asked for "an immediate court martial which Washington granted straightaway."[18] Attempting to rally fellow British veteran Horatio Gates, Lee warned that Washington was out to get Gates as well: "For God's sake, watch yourself. . . . [T]here is a mine laid under your feet."[19]

The court-martial took place in December 1778, trying Lee on three charges: disobedience, directing retreat of his force contrary to orders, and disrespect of a senior officer; he was found guilty of all three offenses. Congress approved a one-year suspension from the Continental Army. Lee's colleagues urged him to moderation. "They advised him not to force Congress to choose between himself and the commander in chief." As Mark Lender observed in *Cabal*, "[S]uch advice was foreign to Lee's combative nature."[20]

Not content with a slap on the wrist, Lee wrote another scathing letter to the Congress, filled with additional attacks on General Washington. Around the same time, in another missive to Horatio Gates, Lee characterized Washington as a "dark designing sordid ambitious vain proud arrogant and vindictive knave."[21] He further denigrated Washington's role at Monmouth. After his letters sealed his fate, Lee was cashiered from the army.

Lee took up residence on his recently acquired estate in Berkeley County, Virginia, becoming a hermit. He became increasingly eccentric. With his dogs, he lived in a barn-like structure with no interior walls.[22] In 1782, Lee moved permanently to Philadelphia. He died there in October of that year.

Beyond Disobedience—Treasonous?

Not until the late 1850s did a historian, George Henry Moore, discover the depth of Lee's disloyalty to the American cause, "evidence of [Lee's] even greater betrayal."[23] During 1776–1777, while the British held Lee in captivity, he had written a lengthy letter to General William Howe, the North American British commander, detailing the means by which the British could defeat the American rebellion. In 1860, George Moore digested the contents of the 1777 letter, which had never before surfaced. Moore published a volume, *Mr. Lee's Plan . . . the Treason of Charles Lee*, detailing his findings.[24] No other interpretation, it seems, could be placed on Charles Lee's offer to the British. While holding the highest rank—major general—Charles Lee was disloyal to the American cause to the point of treason.

Apologists

At times, history also resembles a pool hall scoring rack: points for one, points to another. There are Revolutionary War historians who view Charles Lee favorably. They include John Alden, who in 1951 called George Moore's work "permeated by strong prejudice against its subject," contending that the book was "filled with distortions of fact, baseless charges, and unsupported insinuations."[25] Mr. Alden contended that Lee "was a remarkable personality and should not be denied a place among the leaders of the American Revolution."

In his 1976 book *The Making of a Scapegoat*, Theodore Thayer's premise was that political and not military factors motivated Lee's court-martial and dismissal. After Washington's confrontation with Lee on the Monmouth battlefield, Washington did not bring Lee up on charges until, in his letter, General Lee demanded reparations for Washington's "cruel injustice" to him. Mr. Thayer concluded that Washington was not so much critical of Lee's battlefield actions as he was intent on using Lee as a scapegoat to maintain and enhance the positive favorable public and congressional views of Washington.[26]

Thereafter Lee apologists delved into psychoanalysis. In 2013, Professor Dominick Mazzagetti theorized that Congress, in refusing to grant Lee an audience in 1776, near the beginning of the war, left Lee feeling "marginalized and frustrated."

The congressional slight and the feelings it produced justified Lee's later letter, written as a prisoner of war, to the enemy General William Howe. Lee's betrayal and resulting treason were, in Professor Mazzagetti's opinion, excusable, considering Congress's earlier refusal to hear Lee.[27] Of course, Lee's missive to the enemy's commanding general may well have traced its source to a conviction that he, Charles Lee, not George Washington, should have been commanding general of American forces.

Last of all, in his 2014 biography of Lee, Phillip Pappas hypothesizes that General Lee suffered from "bipolar disorder and manic depression." Thus, psychological motives rather than any baser cause or political motivation led to Lee's subversion of Washington, his actions at Monmouth, and his letters to Howe and to Congress. Lee's psychological deficits therefore excuse altogether his actions in 1775–1778.[28]

Part VII

Horatio Gates

Chapter Nineteen

Genuine Battle Experience?

ANOTHER BRITISH ARMY OFFICER WHO SOLD HIS COMMISSION AND THEN IMMI-grated to America was Horatio Gates. Like Charles Lee, after selling his commission, Gates came to America to obtain a Continental Army commission as a major general. Later, in command of the army's Northern Department, Gates achieved fame as the "Hero of Saratoga."

Saratoga's two conflicts (the Battles of Freeman's Farm on September 25, 1777, and Bemis Heights on October 7, 1777) offered Horatio Gates opportunities to prove himself a battlefield commander. He availed himself of neither opportunity. At Freeman's Farm, he stayed in farmhouse headquarters far in the rear. His timidity became evident as he failed to supply sufficient reinforcements, despite entreaties from his staff and requests from the field. Reserve forces, if committed, would have enabled the Americans to convincingly carry the day. Twelve days later, in the second conflict, Gates reprised his nonperformance. Only upon urging by subordinates did he utter, "Well, let Morgan begin the game." That was the sum of Gates's meaningful activity: no battle plans, no orders of battle, no shuffling and reshuffling deployment of combat units and reserves, nothing.

The Battle of Saratoga was the war's greatest American victory, stopping cold British General Burgoyne's descent from Canada, by which the British attempted to cut the putative new nation in two. After the conflicts, General Gates and his officer corps accepted the surrender of the entire British force. America's victory proved its bona fides, convincing France to supply forces to the Continental Line and to enter the war on the American side.[1]

THE FIRST CONFLICT: BATTLE AT FREEMAN'S FARM

The losses were three hundred American casualties and six hundred British casualties. Impressive as those results may have been, the Americans could have achieved more,

Horatio Gates
FINE ART AMERICA

a decisive victory, one for the ages. However, Gates, as commanding general, was far in the rear at Wordsworth Farm, less able to judge the battle's progression, and there he adamantly refused to commit additional troops. Eventually Gates committed one-fourth of the available Americans, doing so in dribs and drabs throughout the afternoon, while his primary focus continued to be on the wrong, illogical place, adjacent to the Hudson. As a result, effectively the Battle of Freeman's Farm was a draw.

"Gates was inclined to fight defensively, waiting for the enemy to attack him."[2] He conceived of his mission as delaying Burgoyne rather than defeating him—even though as of early September Gates had nine thousand troops compared to Burgoyne's decimated force of fifty-five hundred.[3] Dean Snow, in *1777: Tipping Point at Saratoga*, concluded that Gates was "nervous . . . cautious to a fault." On September 16 and in the ensuing days before the battle, worrying about a British attack, Gates had the troops turn out at 4:00 a.m. On later days, he commanded 5:00 a.m. callouts. His orders for each day "were fuzzy and probably unnecessary. Gates was . . . nervous . . . like an expectant father." As evidence of this, Snow described how *ad infinitum* Gates had "troops constructing earthen breastworks . . . felling trees for abatis defenses ahead of the Americans' defensive lines."[4]

In addition to his unvarying insistence on defense, Gates's focus on the potential field of combat was wrong. He believed that enemy attack would come along the Hudson, on the narrow plain along the river. At Bemis Tavern, the plain was 450 feet wide.[5] Gates added troops there when it was evident to all that if the British were to attack along the river, their assault would be suicidal. Gate's second-in-command, General Benedict Arnold, the officer in charge of the American left wing, a mile inland from the river, implored Gates to concentrate his efforts there and to take the offensive. Gates still wanted to fight a defensive battle, from behind the abatis, trenches, and breastworks that protected the American position, holding ground rather than thumping the enemy. Moreover, Gates actively disliked Arnold, going so far as to give Arnold a pass so he could go through American lines, returning to Albany. Arnold stayed, three years before his legendary treason, in 1777 becoming one of the true heroes of Saratoga.

The "Game" Begins

Out on the left, the day of the first battle, Americans counted eight opposing regiments of General Simon Fraser's Light Infantry taking the open field at John Freeman's farm. The British intention was clear: They were attempting to turn the American left flank. Colonel Daniel Morgan's Rifle Corps and Major Henry Dearborn's New Hampshire Regiment not only resisted but also prevailed, the riflemen first picking off British officers and artillery men, the two elements the most difficult for the British to replace. Dearborn's men repelled British ground troops. Later in the day, General Enoch Poor came to the rescue, committing large portions of his New Hampshire Brigade. But "Gates still refused to commit more units," coming as they would from the American right down along the river. The right wing, of course, idle by the riverside, was under Horatio Gates's direct command, rendered useless by its leader.

Entreaties did cause Gates to bend—a bit. Out on the left, "Dearborn could only hope that Gates would send more forces forward soon, or both he and Morgan would have to fall all the way back."[6] Dearborn's messengers carrying requests noted that "[t]he other officers around [Gates] were staring at him, as the message was clear." Finally, General Gates relented: "You shall have them."[7] He ordered the remainder of Poor's Brigade into the fray as well as New York and Connecticut regiments but refused to commit any of General Ebenezer Learned's Brigade.[8]

Gates "had been clear about forbidding deployment of regiments from Learned's Brigade." The ever-aggressive Benedict Arnold, however, discerned that

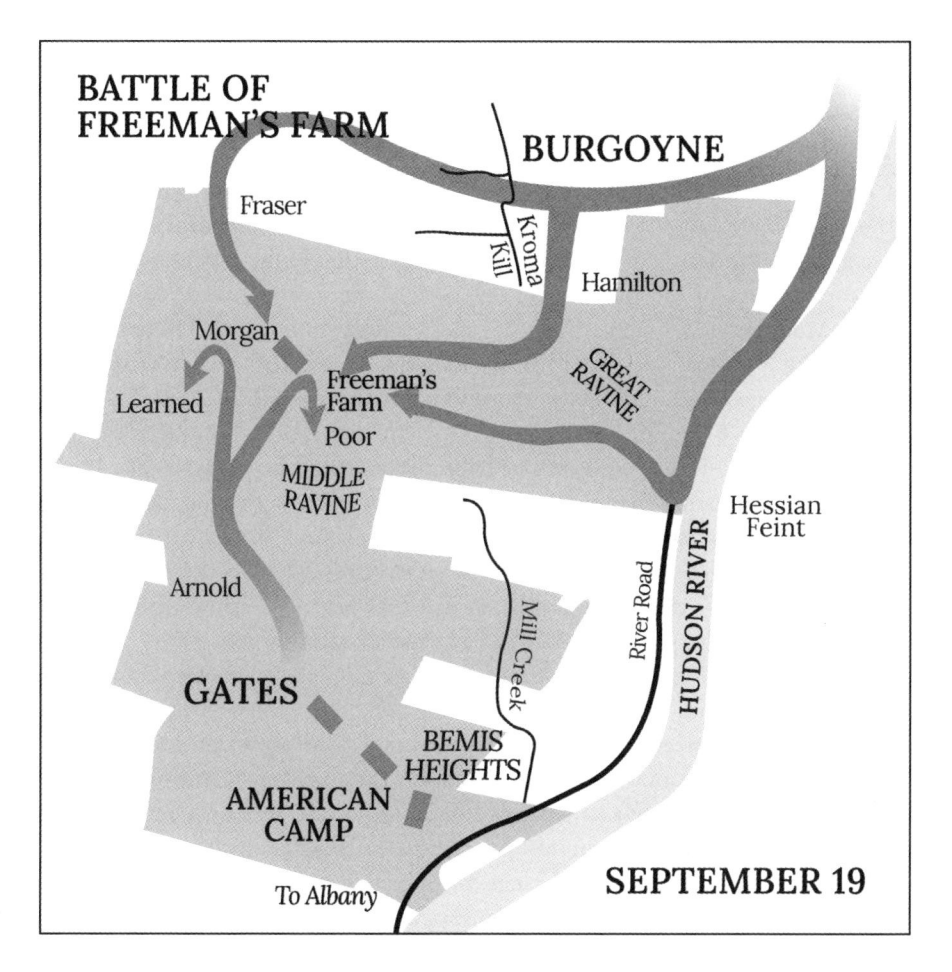

Gates had not precluded recruitment of volunteers, effectively reading between the lines of Gates's order. Arnold raised regiments of volunteers who, late in the day, came into the fight on the American left.

Arnold's badgering of Gates for more troops was a source of additional friction between Gates and Arnold. "Gates was exasperated. Nearly half [a quarter?] of his army was committed to fight a mile north [and west] of where he intended them to be."[9] Even late in the day, according to Snow, Gates thought "he could still pull back into his line and wait to fight a defensive battle."[10] After the conflict, the consensus among American officers was that "[h]ad Gates known of [the British] disposition," which he failed to grasp, being so far in the rear, "he would have ordered out a great part of the army, which probably would have defeated Burgoyne" decisively, then and there.[11] Events at Freeman's Farm had overtaken him, but Horatio Gates did not realize it, continuing with the characteristic uncertainty he had exhibited all day.

Real Heroes of Saratoga

So the Freeman's Farm engagement's true heroes were Daniel Morgan, Benedict Arnold, and Henry Dearborn, not Horatio Gates. "If a man ever landed in the right place at the right time," however, "it was Horatio Gates. [T]he two best American field commanders of the war were on his side . . . the peerless field commanders, Daniel Morgan and Benedict Arnold," and in large part Henry Dearborn, too. Author John Buchanan concluded, "It was well that [Gates] remained in camp while the fighting raged, because leading troops in battle was not his forte and . . . by his record, not to his liking."[12]

Daniel Morgan's sharpshooters had Kentucky rifles (also called Pennsylvania rifles), with rifled barrels that increased their effective range to two hundred yards or more, as opposed to highly inaccurate smooth-bored muskets. Brown Besses, as muskets were known, had a range of only fifty to sixty yards. Morgan also deployed his corps in a shallow U-shaped formation, so that they began the battle with a partial envelopment. His sharpshooters thus had an expanded field of fire.

The weapons Morgan's men used were not the rifles of the nineteenth or twentieth centuries. Kentucky rifles were still single-shot weapons, as were muskets. Rifles also were not breech loading, as are modern weapons; rather, they were muzzle loaders, again, as were muskets. The eighteenth-century rifleman had to ram shot, powder, and wadding down a long barrel. Rifles then were superior weapons in range and accuracy, but equivalent in terms of leading and reloading, with one exception.

Despite their vastly improved range, rifles had disadvantages. The rifled barrel made the hunting rifle demanding in terms of cleaning the grooves of debris. They thus were slow loaders, or slower loaders, as their barrels and grooves had to be absolutely clean. Their genesis as hunting implements also meant that the sharpshooters were not capable of fixing bayonets. As a result, the riflemen would be at a great disadvantage if it became necessary to fight redcoats hand to hand. The favorite British infantry tactic consisted of an eighteenth-century version of "shock and awe" that was consummated in a furious bayonet charge.

Morgan solved the trade-offs—that is, mitigated the riflemen's disadvantages—by coordination with traditional infantry. His sharpshooters would be in the trees or on slightly higher ground than the infantry. From there the riflemen would fire two or three rounds, climbing down and taking cover to clean their weapons, reload, and reposition. In the meantime, Colonel Henry Dearborn's men would keep up musket fire and, if necessary, fix bayonets.

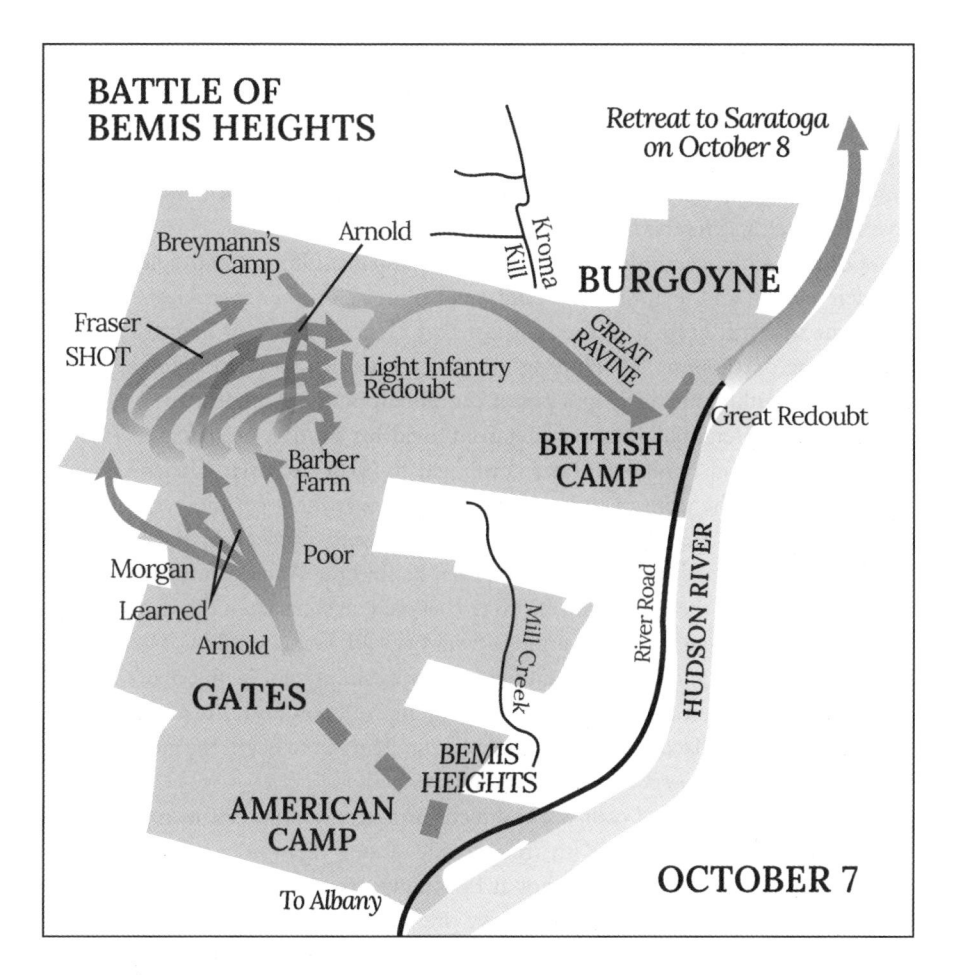

Morgan's ingenuity and his means of warfare contributed mightily to the American success at the Battle of Freeman's Farm. Close coordination of sharpshooters and infantry, U-shaped deployments, and Daniel Morgan's leadership produced another major victory at Cowpens, South Carolina, in January 1781.[13]

CONCLUSION OF THE BATTLE: BEMIS HEIGHTS ON OCTOBER 7

Saratoga was not over after the Battle of Freeman's Farm. Horatio Gates would have a second opportunity. In the lull between major confrontations, Gates's army strengthened. General Benjamin Lincoln arrived with two thousand troops. New York and Massachusetts militia arrived in dribs and drabs. Over a several-day period, the American force grew by three thousand men.[14]

The interval between the two battles was like a shoving match before an outright brawl. "The Americans were becoming bolder. There was gunfire every night."[15] American raiding parties, often in force, and snipers, particularly those from Daniel Morgan's Rifle Corps, picked off sentries, challenged British foraging parties, and forced on those in the British camp the necessity to always seek cover, escalating levels of stress and foreboding.

On the American side, speculation ran rampant. Officers and soldiers alike wondered when and if Burgoyne would make a move. Further speculation was that Burgoyne was still hewing to the prospect that General Howe or General Clinton would come north along the Hudson with a large British reinforcing force, joining Burgoyne's southbound army in a pincer movement on the Americans.

At Bemis Heights, Horatio Gates continued his fixation on defense. "Despite great superiority in numbers, Gates continued to favor defensive tactics." Among the makeweights he utilized to justify his attitude was the great mass of militia in camp. He worried that "[i]f undisciplined militia were repulsed in the open field . . . it would be difficult to re-form them, even behind the American breastworks."[16]

On October 7, the Americans heard two signal gun shots from the British camp. The game was on again. Despite urgings from his staff, Gates would not order units to meet Burgoyne's men in the open fields. "It was simply not in the man's nature." In fact, Gates did nothing at all. Entreated by his adjutant and other staff officers, Gates replied with a laconic, "Well, then, order on Morgan to begin the game."[17] That was it for the American force's commanding general.

Bemis Heights was, of course, a complete American victory. The intrepid British General Simon Fraser, rallying his troops, rode among them on a great gray steed. One of Morgan's riflemen took a shot at Fraser, even though at three hundred yards the British general was beyond a Kentucky rifle's serviceable range. The shot pierced Fraser's breast, a grave wound that led to his death and a blow to British spunk and morale from which the redcoats never recovered. The defeat at Bemis Heights led to General Burgoyne's surrender, at the village of Saratoga, on October 17, 1777.

The analysis here, though, is about the general, and only secondarily about the battles, Freeman's Farm and Bemis Heights. In reality, the "Hero of Saratoga" did little at Freeman's Farm and Bemis Heights. Gates spent both days in farmhouses far to the rear.[18] One possible explanation for his terse Bemis Heights command "let Morgan begin" was that Gates had gained confidence in Morgan and associated forces based on their actions at Freeman's Farm. At Saratoga, Jim Piecuch wrote, "Gates left tactical matters to his capable subordinates, Daniel Morgan and Benedict Arnold."[19] The opposite view was that Gates had no experience as a battlefield commander, did not know how to devise a battle plan, and did not even know that a battle plan was highly

Simon Fraser burial
COURTESY OF NATIONAL ARMY MUSEUM, LONDON

recommended. His later actions at Camden, in South Carolina in August 1780, reinforced the view that Gates was clueless as a battlefield commander.

REVOLUTIONARY ERA SQUINTING

Although Gates had little to do with the Saratoga victory, his congressional supporters (Gates was a persistent lobbyist) as well as the press hailed him as the "Hero of Saratoga." Hyperbole ratcheted Gates's alias up to "Gates, the mighty Caesar of the North, Hero of Saratoga."[20] Late in 1777, Congress created the War Board, appointing Pennsylvania's Thomas Mifflin (chapters 24–26) the first member, three weeks later adding Horatio Gates as the board's president.[21] Influential members of the Continental Congress narrowed their gaze, seeing only that Horatio Gates had been a victorious commander.

CHAPTER TWENTY

Gates's Cowardice at Camden

IN MAY 1780, MAJOR GENERAL BENJAMIN LINCOLN, THE SOUTHERN ARMY'S commander, surrendered six thousand troops to the British. General Lincoln became a prisoner of war. Squinting again, congressmen looked for a battle-hardened leader to assume Lincoln's post. Into their line of sight came Major General Horatio Gates, by reputation but not in reality such a leader.[1] In June 1780, Congress appointed Gates the Southern Army commander, of what was left of the Southern Army after the Charles Town capitulation and the imprisonment of six thousand Americans.[2]

BEFORE THE NEW COMMAND—THE CONWAY CABAL

After Saratoga, during the War Board period, the aforementioned Conway cabal, in which the ever-conniving Horatio Gates figured prominently, took place.[3] Led by an Irish-born American general, Thomas Conway (chapter 29), and joined by several other generals and supported by certain politicians, they formed a cabal aiming to replace George Washington, with Horatio Gates slated to become the American army's commanding general. Among others, future President John Adams and the acclaimed physician Benjamin Rush saw Horatio Gates as a possible replacement for George Washington. "Privately, John Adams questioned Washington's leadership." After British defeats of the American army at Brandywine and Germantown, Adams stated, "The Virginian has been 'out-generaled' again."[4] Congressman Jonathan Dickinson Sergeant wrote, "We want a general; thousands of lives and millions in property are yearly sacrificed to the insufficiency of our commander-in-chief. Two battles he [Washington] had lost for us by such blunders as might have disgraced a soldier of three months' standing."[5]

In turn, Washington, although at first having a favorable opinion of Gates, wrote, "I discovered very early in the war symptoms of coldness and constraint in General Gates' behavior toward me. These increased as [Gates] rose into greater consequence."[6]

According to another version, the alleged "cabal" was nothing more than an armful of complaining letters written by disgruntled officers and certain congressmen, the most prominent being Dr. Benjamin Rush. After an extensive review of the evidence, Stephen Taaffe concludes, "The truth of the matter was that there was no conspiracy . . . [P]eople griped about Washington's recent lack of success . . . but there was no secret, coordinated plan . . . to remove [Washington] from office."[7] Or, as Chalmers Davidson characterized the Conway cabal, it was "a whispering campaign to oust [Washington]."[8] Further, no evidence exists that Horatio Gates was an active participant, although his megalomania undoubtedly made him at least a sideline rooter.[9] For example, Professor Kenneth Rossman, in his biography of Thomas Mifflin, concluded that although "[i]t was Gates who was the one to be elevated upon Washington's ruin . . . it cannot be established that he actively joined in any such plot."[10] Realizing, however, that to fatten his résumé he needed another battlefield command to demonstrate his military credentials, Gates lobbied for such a command and received one—namely, command of the Southern Department.

THE SOUTHERN ARMY AND CAMDEN

After the cabal was quashed, "Washington indicated that he remained suspicious despite Gates's protestations of innocence."[11] Little did Washington's suspicion of Gates matter to Congress and Gates's supporters. On June 13, 1780, without consulting the commander in chief, Congress selected Gates as the Southern Army commander.[12] Gates had a new stage on which to perform. On July 25, 1780, he arrived in Hillsborough, North Carolina, where the Southern Army's remnants had sheltered, 230 miles north of Charles Town. Hillsborough, seat of Orange County, lay approximately 135 miles southwest of Richmond, Virginia, not far below the Virginia–North Carolina line.

Two days after arriving, Gates marched his army toward Camden, South Carolina, 152 miles southwest of Hillsborough. The march was no easy one; the route of travel crossed harsh countryside. In the words of Colonel Ortho Holland Williams, the land "was by nature barren, abounding with sandy plains, intersected by swamps and thinly populated, the people there mostly hostile to the American cause."[13] Owing to their hasty departure, little in the way of provisions was available. The troops nourished themselves by picking and eating green apples and unripe peaches along the route of the march.

Before the battle, lacking spirits (the usual daily ration was rum; see chapter 11), Gates's commissary dispensed to each man a gill of molasses. The result was an army unfit for duty, enfeebled as most soldiers were by diarrhea, bought on by the combination of molasses with unripe fruit. Colonel Ortho Holland Williams wrote,

"[I]t was unluckily conceived that molasses would be an acceptable substitute [for rum.] . . . [M]olasses . . . operated so carthartically as to disorder the men, who were breaking ranks all night [with diarrhea attacks] . . . certainly much debilitated before the action commenced."[14]

To further complicate matters, and greatly to do with his sense of urgency, in the rush Gates operated with little or no intelligence. First, Commanding General Gates thought he had an army of seven thousand men, recently reinforced by General Richard Caswell's fifteen hundred North Carolina and General Edward Stevens's seven hundred Virginia militiamen. In truth, the head count was no more than thirty-two hundred effectives.[15] Second, Gates thought he would oppose only a seven-hundred-person British force under Lieutenant Colonel Lord Francis Rawdon, left in central South Carolina after a raid on the American supply depot at Camden. In fact, marching up from Charles Town, General Lord Charles Cornwallis was about to reinforce Rawdon with 2,239 men, "all of them a tough, tenacious breed." John Buchanan summarized the approaching British force: "[Cornwallis] had a good army. It was small but very professional."[16] The British force consisted of Rawdon's Irish Volunteers, the Royal North Carolina Regiment, the 33rd Regiment of Foot (West Ridings), the 23rd Regiment of Foot (Welch Fusiliers), and Fraser's kilt-clad Highlanders.

The British army, including its mercenary Hessian and Brunswicker colleagues, was well known for its mistreatment of American prisoners, whom the British regarded as criminals rather than prisoners of war.[17] From time immemorial, too, the British army had engaged in unsurpassed marauding, including rapes, murders, looting, and destruction to crops, over a wide swath of the country through which the army passed.[18]

Little evidence exists that those abhorrent behaviors characterized the Cornwallis expedition. First, the British felt they knew the Carolinas as hotbeds of loyalist sentiment, which by reprehensible behavior the redcoats could render into patriots. So Cornwallis's men restrained themselves. Second, Lord Cornwallis ran a tight ship, including having a low tolerance for looting and marauding. Third, the fast pace at which Cornwallis's army moved did not permit the kind of extracurricular activity for which the British army was known.[19]

On the American side, marching south, fifteen miles north of Camden Gates called his procession to a halt along the north-south Waxhaw Road. The British troops were a bit north of Camden themselves, along the same road. On August 15, Gates ordered a night march straight south by his emaciated forces, including the untrained militia. The orders filled Gates's officers "with consternation": "[H]ow could an army of untrained militia who had never before done it do a night march?" author Buchanan asked.[20]

ARRIVAL AT THE FIELD OF BATTLE

By coincidence, Cornwallis ordered a night march north as well. The American and British forces met on August 16 near Ramsour's Mill on the Waxhaw Road, at two o'clock in the morning. Limited skirmishing and pickets' exchanges of gunfire filled the time until sunrise, which occurred at 4:20 that August morning.

Informed that the British were nearby, sometime before sunrise Gates called a council of war, exclaiming, "Gentlemen, what is to be done?" As was typical of the Gates style, nothing—no battle plan, no order of battle—had been done. Only Virginia Militia General Edward Stevens answered: "[I]t is too late now to do anything but fight!"[21] So still no battle plan evolved. "There was no indication that Gates had a plan or had put his mind seriously to work."[22] In addition, the order of battle Gates handed down—if it could have been termed as such—was seriously flawed, lopsided, with all the militia on one side of the road, the American left and center, and on the other side of the road the American right, the battle-tested Delaware and Maryland troops. The latter were under the capable leadership of General Baron Johann De Kalb, assisted by Maryland General Mordecai Gist. Similar to what had occurred at Saratoga, Gates stationed himself far in the rear, too far distant to observe events or to intervene as the battle unfolded. Gates was even to the rear of the American reserve force, General William Smallwood's four hundred regulars.

On the American left, untrained American militia faced the Royal Welch Fusiliers under one of Britain's most able battlefield commanders, Lieutenant Colonel James Webster. Crossing the creek, the fusiliers displayed to the right and to the left—that is, formed a double line across the field of battle, with eighteen-inch bayonets fixed on four-and-one-half-foot muskets. "The sight of a line of disciplined British infantry . . . muskets leveled and protruding from them some eighteen inches of cold steel . . . was known to turn American militia bowels to jelly and heels to quicksilver," Buchanan noted, describing what frequently occurred in Revolutionary War battles.[23] Before the British line even reached them, two thousand American militiamen dropped their weapons and ran, not stopping until they reached Hillsborough, 150 miles away. Moving through the abandoned American left wing's former position, British Colonel Webster wheeled his line to the left, flanking the American right wing, in position to "roll up" De Kalb's line. The Americans fought valiantly, but, "being greatly out flanked and challenged by superior numbers, [the American right] was obliged to give way."[24]

A CONTINUING DISGRACE: FLIGHT OF THE COWARDLY GENERAL

Camden was an overwhelming, devastating American defeat. Of 3,052 effectives at the battle's onset, the Americans suffered 1,050 casualties (250 killed). The British suffered 300 casualties (68 killed). But the worst followed. Seeing the militia drop

Johann De Kalb
COURTESY OF THE
LIBRARY OF CONGRESS

their arms and run, General Horatio Gates mounted his horse and rode toward Charlotte, North Carolina, sixty miles away. Among others, Gates left behind General De Kalb, wounded several times by sword, musket ball, and bayonet, who nevertheless fought on.

In a report to Congress, Gates greatly exaggerated or fabricated his actions: "I ordered the left [all militia] to advance and attack the enemy. . . . [North Carolina Militia] General Caswell and myself did all in our power to rally the broken troops."[25] Eyewitnesses contradicted Gates's version. Garrett Watts of the Carolina Militia recalled, "There was no effort to rally, no encouragement to fight."[26]

Two points may be made on the pro-Gates side. First, Gates maintained that he rode so quickly and so hard because he knew he needed to reach Hillsborough in advance of his retreating troops so as to arrange accommodations and supplies.[27]

Second, at Saratoga he had had no battle plans and yet still achieved noteworthy victories with reliance on Morgan, Dearborn, Poor, Learned, Arnold, and other battlefield commanders. Gates was entitled to similar reliance on his subordinates at Camden and justified in his rationalization that no plan of battle was needed. Neither excuse by Gates for his cowardice had even a glimmer of truth or plausibility.

As the militia at Camden dropped their weapons, sprinted rearward, and disappeared into the woods, General Gates likewise turned rearward. Not stopping, he rode 180 miles to Hillsborough via Charlotte, in an amazing time of three days. Meanwhile, on the army's right wing at Camden, General De Kalb suffered more than eight wounds. Again, it took General Gates "three days to reach Hillsborough. It took De Kalb three days to die."[28] De Kalb's dying words were "I die the death I always prayed for—the death of a soldier fighting for the rights of man."[29]

GENERAL GATES'S LEAVINGS

For a time after Camden, Gates continued as Southern Army commander. In early December 1780, at Charlotte, Nathanael Greene relieved Gates. Gates traveled quietly northward to his plantation, Traveller's Rest, in northern Virginia, where he remained until 1782. "He never again commanded in the field."[30] In addition, after his flight from Camden, "Horatio Gates never recovered his reputation or standing."[31]

With the passage of months after Camden, "public anger against Gates cooled."[32] Make no mistake, however—Gates had "lost his reputation," due to "withering criticism of his generalship. . . . American generals . . . had lost battles, but Gates's flight from the field before the fighting ended put him in a different, odious league."[33] Gates squirmed under the criticism. He tried to assert that it had been the "North Carolina militia most responsible" for the defeat. He "claimed that the disaster had prodded North Carolina and Virginia to invest more energy into the war," urging that the lopsided loss's outcome had a silver lining.[34]

At Gates's request, the Continental Congress ordered an inquiry into the general's conduct. In October 1780, the Congress suspended Gates from duty. Months passed, with the inquiry never materializing. In August 1782, Congress rescinded its resolution for an inquiry.[35] Limpet-like, Gates was able to cling to his commission and rank. He reported to General Washington for assignment. Historian John Buchanan's epitaph for Horatio Gates rings true:

> *One hesitates to call any man a coward. . . . But we are entitled to expect of officers that they never shirk, never run. In an age when generals commonly exposed themselves to inspire their men and often paid with their lives, Major General Horatio Gates was conspicuously absent from the battles of Saratoga and rode far and fast from Camden's terrible field.*[36]

Chapter Twenty-One

A Gates Roadmap of What Not to Do

Horatio Gates's sins at Camden, distilled down to cowardice in the face of battle, outrank Washington's other major generals' malfeasance. Arthur St. Clair and his three thousand men abandoned Fort Ticonderoga without firing a shot. Adam Stephen was drunk and derelict in leading a column at Germantown, resulting in commands that snatched defeat from the jaws of victory. Too many pretty heads turned Robert Howe's, leading to appraisal of Howe as a "womanizer," his behavior fueled by excessive alcohol consumption. General Thomas Mifflin's lackadaisical service as quartermaster for the American army (chapter 25) contributed to the misery at Valley Forge, including two thousand deaths that exposed Mifflin as a wolf in sheep's clothing. Bizarre and haughty, Charles Lee's downfall came at Monmouth Courthouse, where he openly defied George Washington.

Horatio Gates outdid them all. John Dickinson, a delegate to the Continental Congress, criticized Commanding General George Washington as having no more miliary prowess than a newly recruited soldier. Even were that true, in his ineptness Horatio Gates outdid any recruit of any stripe. Gates's behaviors constitute a roadmap—more accurately, a reverse roadmap—for what a military commander should do in the face of battle.

Gates's Demotion and Partial Resurrection after Camden

Leapfrogging over analysis of Gates's behavior at Camden (a subject this chapter revisits later), what happened to Horatio Gates after Camden?

In 1782, in an act of forgiveness, George Washington summoned General Gates from Virginia to Newburgh, New York, on the Hudson's western shore, fifty-two miles north of Manhattan. At Newburgh, Washington made his headquarters in the last years of the war, a time of vigilance and skirmishes but no major engagements. The war had not ended with Yorktown in October 1781.

After Yorktown, General Washington removed the army northward, to Newburgh, Fishkill, and Peekskill. To the south, New York remained the British army's American headquarters. American leaders still worried that a British force could descend from Canada, as General Johnny Burgoyne's had in 1777, linking up with a British force coming north from New York. The combined British contingent could, belatedly, again attempt to split the fledging nation in two. As Walter Isaacson observed, "[u]ntil the present [British] ministry resigned, there was always the chance that Britain would," in that manner, "renew the struggle."[1]

A British do-over never occurred. No major battles took place. The American military, though, engaged in skirmishes with British troops, garrisoned outposts serving as pickets for the major American camps, and patrolled the territory.[2] The war had not ended, despite British Prime Minister Lord North's remark after Yorktown, "Oh, God! It's all over."[3]

GATES AND THE NEWBURGH CONSPIRACY

American camps along the Hudson, however, were not beehives of activity. Days of idleness facilitated lengthy discussion, grumbling, and a variety of overtures and proposals, in which Gates was a shadow figure, emerging in plain sight as the machinations crescendoed. Two major outgrowths were the Newburgh Addresses and the Society of the Cincinnati.

The shadowy Newburgh conspiracy consisted of a movement and then putative rebellion against the government by Continental officers who had not been paid since 1781. The ever-conniving Gates was involved, his aides-de-camp participating, but the movement was short lived. On March 15, 1783, General Washington quelled the incipient revolt by reaffirming the civil authority's primacy.

In March 1783, disgruntled American officers circulated two draft letters (the Newburgh Addresses) intimating that they would invoke military force should Congress continue to ignore back pay requests and demands. The letters called for a meeting on March 10, 1783.[4] George Washington learned of the proposed meeting and banned it.[5] He shared the grumbling officers' sentiments but summoned the officer corps before him for an alternate meeting on March 13, at the cavernous Newburgh Temple of Virtue. In no uncertain terms, the commanding general set down the superiority of civilian government over the military, the government for which the officers and soldiers had fought long and hard.[6] Author John Fitzpatrick described Washington, normally a paragon of self-control, as "sensibly agitated."[7]

"How unmilitary! How subversive of all order and discipline!" General Washington condemned "the blackest designs" and "most insidious purposes behind the cabal" of his officers. Acting against the government of the United States would "cast a shade over that glory which has been so justly acquired, and tarnish [the] reputation of the army."[8]

"George Washington rarely addressed his officers as a group, but he showed himself a natural at it," biographer Ron Chernow found. Washington pulled from his pocket a letter from a congressional representative who expressed sympathy for the officers' plight. As Washington began to read the letter, he stopped, pulling his glasses from his pocket. "Gentlemen, you will permit me to put on my spectacles, for I have grown not only gray, but almost blind, in the service of my country." Washington's performance drew tears from those present.[9] The Newburgh conspiracy dissipated, "averted," according to historian Chernow, "by Washington's succinct but brilliant, well-timed oratory."[10]

Writing in *The First Inauguration: George Washington and the Invention of the Republic*, history professor Stephen Browne singles out President George Washington's 1789 inauguration address: "That Americans have been spared the trauma of the military coup d'etat is owing in no small measure to a general [George Washington] insistent on the privilege of civil authority." Professor Browne asks, "Can there be any stronger proof than the Inauguration Day of Washington's continued relevance?"[11] Well, yes, there may be: General Washington's decisive action in quashing the Newburgh conspiracy, firmly asserting the superior authority of civilian rule.[12]

GATES AND THE SOCIETY OF THE CINCINNATI

For his part, still feeling a need to conspire, Horatio Gates shifted to involvement in the Society of the Cincinnati's formation, with actions at Fishkill and Peekskill, across the Hudson from Newburgh.

Once more, after the 1783 Treaty of Paris, Gates returned to Virginia. Shortly after his arrival, Gates's wife Elizabeth died. Gates remarried, to a wealthy younger woman, Mary Vallance. Gates sold his rural holdings and moved to New York where he and Mary lived comfortably for two decades. He died in 1806, his remains being interred in the churchyard of Trinity Church, at the foot of Wall Street, on Broadway.

RETURN TO A REVERSE ROADMAP OF GATES'S CONDUCT AT CAMDEN

After the Camden disaster, Gates lied, stating that his "efforts to rally [the fleeing troops] failed and he had been swept along in their flight to Charlotte."[13] Eyewitness accounts described Gates hurriedly departing as the militia's line crumbled, without attempting at all to rally the men. Gates led rather than followed the wholesale flight. One after another, like dominoes, Gates's earlier errors compounded, culminating in the defeat and Gates's shameful abandonment of the scene:

1. Insistence on immediate departure: Assuming Southern Army command, Horatio Gates arrived in Hillsborough, North Carolina, on July 25, 1780. Within two days he embarked his troops on a forced march. Veterans of the march "blamed Southerners," under stress to protect their homeland, "for pressing Gates to leave Hillsborough" so quickly.[14] Having joined the army only a few days earlier, "Gates was entirely unacquainted with the character of the officers or the merits of the different corps," wrote North Carolina Colonel William Davie.[15] It was, in the words of Delaware Colonel Thomas Rodney, "[t]oo hasty a pursuit."[16] Gates rejected Major General "Baron de Kalb's advice and pushed his troops through a barren and picked over region."[17]

2. Departure without adequate provisions: Had the Southern Army waited, the column would have received foodstuffs for the march. "Lacking supplies, the troops ate green corn . . . and green peaches they gathered along the route," leading to gastrointestinal upheavals and diarrhea.[18] In *The Road to Guilford Courthouse*, John Buchanan raised the point, "If Gates had only waited a few days."

3. A forced march: It "was a long and fatiguing march," Sergeant William Seymour recalled, leaving the troops worn out by the time the expedition reached Rugeley's Mill, a dozen miles north of Camden.[19]

4. Dismissal of cavalry: Even though that region of South Carolina consisted of piney woods and open spaces, "some of the world's best cavalry country," from Hillsborough Gates sent Colonel William Washington's mounted regiment "packing."[20] Before the days of aircraft and mechanized vehicles, cavalry functioned as an army's eyes and ears. Cavalry patrols may well have reported back the size and progress of Lord Cornwallis's reinforcements heading for Camden.

5. Further detachment of available American forces: With one thousand troops, South Carolina's Militia General Thomas Sumter, the "Gamecock," was attempting to interdict the British supply route from Charles Town to Camden. The British relief column would provide additional clothing, ammunition, arms, and other supplies for the Camden British force.[21] Gates dispatched American Lieutenant Colonel Thomas Woolford with an additional four hundred troops (one hundred regulars, three hundred militia), along with several cannons, to Sumter. Richard Henry Lee pounced on Gates's shortcoming: "Gates weakened his army . . . by detaching to Sumter four hundred men."[22] Compounding Gates's error, the British defeated the Woolford detachment and Sumter-led militia at Fishing Creek on August 18, 1781.

6. Operating with faulty and misleading intelligence: Gates stated that he hurried the Hillsborough departure because he believed that Camden represented "easy pickings." Gates believed that Colonel Francis Lord Rawdon had only 700 British troops (the Irish Brigade) there, blissfully unaware that on August 14 Lord Cornwallis had arrived from Charles Town with 2,239 additional troops. When Gates learned of the late arrival, "[t]he general's astonishment could not be concealed."[23]

An excuse for his rashness is that Gates had no intention of engaging in an immediate battle. As Gates wrote to the Continental Congress, "I resolved to march at 10 at night [August 15], to take a post in an Advantageous Position, with a Deep Creek [Sander's Creek] on front, seven miles from Camden."[24]

7. A patently lopsided order of battle: On the left and in the center, Gates placed fifteen hundred North Carolina and seven hundred Virginia militiamen, untrained. Further, "[t]hey were fatigued. The August weather was excessively warm. The men had been fed a short time previously on molasses entirely," explained North Carolina Militia Captain William Gipson.[25] Alexander Hamilton, an experienced officer himself, later wrote to James Duane:

> [D]id one ever hear of such a disposition [of troops] or such a flight? His best troops placed on the side strongest . . . his worst on the side weakest. . . . 'Tis impossible to give a more complete picture of military absurdity. It is equally against the maxims of war, and common sense.[26]

The result was the militia's wholesale retreat, termed by Maryland Brigadier Mordecai Gist "the most scandalous conduct of the militia." An intermixture of regular troops would have strengthened the militia's backbone. Colonel William Davie was less judgmental and more factual: "The center and left of the front line were composed of militia. . . . [T]he consequence was that this flank was turned."[27] A follow-on effect was that the American right-wing troops were, according to the 5th Maryland's Lieutenant Colonel Benjamin Ford, "outnumbered and outflanked," resulting in great losses and a complete British victory.[28]

8. Absence of any battle plan: The only battle plan was made by the Virginia Militia's Edward Stevens, who said it was too late to do anything but fight.[29] Fighting an army, though, requires a plan or schematic. As at Freeman's Farm and at Bemis Heights, Gates put none forward. He "seemed disposed to events—he gave no orders."[30]

9. Lack of direction during the engagement: Gates stationed himself two hundred yards or more in the rear. He was not able to readjust if crises arose or answer questions posed by line officers. At Saratoga, General Gates had stayed well behind the lines, far from the battle, and he did the same at Camden. The only difference was that at Camden Gates was mounted on a horse and outdoors, conducive to a quick getaway.[31]

10. Abandonment of his men in the midst of the battle: On August 20, Gates wrote to the Continental Congress, "By the time the militia had taken to the Woods. . . . I concluded with General Caswell [North Carolina Militia commander, later North Carolina governor] to retire towards Charlotte. I got there late at night."[32] The commanding general left the field of battle while the action still raged. The following day, he rode on from Charlotte to Hillsborough, in upper North Carolina, again a 180-mile retreat from the battle at Camden, South Carolina.

    The North Carolina attorney general, John Iredell, offered a damning criticism, albeit one expressed benignly: "General Gates's conduct is much censured. . . . The report is that upon the Militia giving way, he immediately fled, without sending any orders to the Continental troops. . . . [I]t is said, that if he had given them timely orders to retreat, they would have done so in good order."[33] Alexander Hamilton was more condemnatory when he asked his correspondent, "[W]as there ever an instance of a General running away as Gates had done from his whole army? . . . It disgraces the General and the soldiers."[34] Colonel Ortho Holland Williams saw the effect on morale: "General Gates used the utmost expedition in getting from the lost Field. . . . An unfortunate [General] looses [sic—loses] the Confidence of his Army, and this is much the case" with the Southern Army.[35] More explicit condemnations were that Gates fled the field out of cowardness, or feebleness, or a combination of the two.

APOLOGISTS FOR HORATIO GATES'S CONDUCT

One excuse was that General Gates never expected a battle at all. As future South Carolina Governor Thomas Pinckney wrote, "The movement on the night of the 15th of August was not made with the intention of attacking the enemy, but for the purpose of occupying a strong position."[36] Others blamed the militia, excusing General Gates. Lieutenant Christopher Richmond wrote to Maryland Governor Thomas Sim Lee, "[O]ur fair Hopes, Wishes, and Confidence were withered and blasted by the uncommon, and most unheard of, Cowardice of the Militia."[37] Others adopted a wait-and-see posture. Dr. James Thacher voiced an opinion that "[t]ime and investigation must decide how far he has been guilty of any culpable error."[38]

The most ill-informed and galling remark came ten days after Gates's shameful retreat. On August 25, 1780, influential Congressman Dr. Benjamin Rush wrote to future president John Adams, "General Gates who you know is doing wonders in the Southern States."[39]

Indeed, based solely on his behavior in the southern colonies, Horatio Gates ranks at or in a tie for bottom of the generals' list, the most inept and cowardly of all those who served, brigadiers as well as major generals.

Part VIII

Peter Gabriel Muhlenberg

CHAPTER TWENTY-TWO

Another Tall Tree:
Fighting Parson Muhlenberg

THE US CAPITOL HOUSES STATUARY HALL. IN 1864, CONGRESS ORDERED THAT each state choose two statues of famous, courageous, or accomplished citizens to represent it. Pennsylvania has chosen Robert Fulton, inventor of the steamboat, and Revolutionary War Brigadier Peter Gabriel Muhlenberg.[1] Twenty-five of the Capitol statues represent the thirteen original colonies.[2] Fourteen of the twenty-five statues are of politicans. Four are likenesses of Revolutionary War generals: John Stark (New Hampshhire), Nathanael Greene (Rhode Island), George Washington (Virginia), and Peter Muhenberg, who, although pastor of a Woodstock, Virginia, parish and commander of the 8th Virginia Regiment (the "German Regiment"), had been raised in and, several years after the war, returned to Pensylvania. For more than a decade, though, Peter Muhlenberg was a Virginian. After he had relocated back to Pennsylvania, Muhlenberg was elected to the House of Representatives, served briefly in the Senate, and was appointed to a high government post.

HIS MIGRATION

Woodstock, Virginia, was the oldest town in the northern reaches of the Shenandoah Valley, seat of Frederick County (until 1772, then Dunmore County, and finally, in 1777, Shenandoah County). In 1771, Woodstock's James Woods recruited Muhlenberg to relocate there. As a Lutheran minister, Muhlenberg could conduct a Lutheran service for the German settlers. "For some years, the German inhabitants of [Pennsylvania] commenced emigrating in considerable numbers to Virginia, settling principally in the valley.... German settlements gradually became quite large."[3] As has been seen,[4] Germans fled Pennsylvania because the Quaker-dominated legislature took no steps to protect settlements from Indian raids.[5] In turn, Virginia welcomed and protected

Peter Gabriel Muhlenberg
GILBERT STUART DIGITAL HISTORIC
TRAPPE MUSEUM

them: "They were precisely the lowly, hardworking, ethical Protestants that Virginia visionaries had long sought to populate Virginia. . . . [S]omething that generations of British settlement had not hitherto demonstrated."[6] As an ordained Episcopal priest, Muhlenberg also could conduct services for Church of England worshipers.

At the Revolution's outset, the Virginia Convention conceived the newly created 8th Virginia Regiment primarily to be comprised of Germans from the lower Shenandoah Valley (the Valley).[7] "The colonel the Convention chose to lead the 8th was the Woodstock parson Peter Muhlenberg."[8] The Convention chose Muhlenberg for the same reasons that James Woods recruited him. No sacristy-bound minister, Muhlenberg loved to fish, hunt, and be outdoors. He was well traveled, having been to England and Germany. Most of all, since immigrating to Virginia, Muhlenberg had proven himself an integral part of the Woodstock community, a strong leader who could garner adherents who trusted his leadership.

NORTHWESTERN VIRGINIA
The Shenandoah is a wide, flat, long valley between the Blue Ridge to the east and the Alleghenies thirty or thirty-five miles to the west. As celebrated Civil War historian Bruce Catton wrote, "There may be a lovelier country somewhere . . . but when the sunlight lies upon it and the wind puts white clouds to racing their shadows, the Shenandoah Valley is as good as anything America can show."[9]

In this great valley, Muhlenberg, also an ordained Church of England cleric, could conduct a Woodstock service in accordance with the Anglican *Book of Common Prayer*, in English or, according to the Lutheran rite, in German. Muhlenberg also had a martial past, albeit a brief one. In 1766, young Muhlenberg had served in a German-speaking English regiment, the 50th Regiment of Foot, in Lubeck, Germany, which was later posted to North America.

THE FAMED MUHLENBERG CALL TO ARMS

In January 1776, Muhlenberg stood before his Woodstock congregation before going off to war, delivering his farewell homily:

> *"[I]n the language of Holy Writ there is a time for all things, a time to preach and a time to pray, but those times have all passed away. There is a time to fight, and that time has now come." Then, after pronouncing the benediction, he opened his clerical robe and stood before his congregation in the uniform of a Virginia colonel.*[10]

"[D]escending from the pulpit, Muhlenberg ordered the drums at the church door to beat for recruits." Nearly three hundred Woodstock men joined Virginia's 8th.[11] Few objected, or those who did soon became converts of the call to arms.[12]

In subsequent years, historians have questioned whether the farewell benediction occurred.[13] Sculptors, though, have memorialized the romantic version. Life-size bronze statues of the Muhlenberg episode exist on the town square in Woodstock; in the sculpture garden outside the Philadelphia Art Institute; on the campus of Muhlenberg College (Allentown, Pennsylvania); and in the US Capitol.[14] In these renditions, Pastor Muhlenberg, in clerical garb, opened the front to reveal a military uniform.

A CIRCUITOUS PATH TO MINISTRY

Born in 1746, Muhlenberg came from Trappe, thirty-eight miles northwest of Philadelphia, near Pottstown, Pennsylvania. Indian raids took place on Pennsylvania's frontier and eastward, including the Pottstown vicinity, resulting in destruction of homesteads, kidnapping, scalping, and savage murders.[15] In spite of the dangers, Peter's father sent him several miles distant, where "Peter Muhlenberg received valuable training in English, for German was spoken at home."[16] Young Peter's father, Henry Melchior Muhlenberg, was famous in his own right, a Lutheran minister generally credited as the founder of the Lutheran Church in America.[17] Pennylvania's excellent liberal arts college, Muhlenberg College, named itself after Henry (or Heinrich) Muhlenberg rather than after his son, Peter, a hero of the Revolution.[18]

Later, the father, Henry, wrote to the headmaster where Peter and his two brothers were being schooled:

> *My son Peter['s] . . . chief fault and bad inclination has been his fondness for hunting and fishing. But if our most reverend fathers . . . observe any tendency to vice, I would humbly beg that they send him to a well-disciplined garrison town. . . . [T]here he may obey the drum if he will not follow the spirit of God.*[19]

Young Peter was "[e]mphatically a country boy."[20]

Peter's father placed Peter for indoctrination at Swedish Lutheran churches along the Delaware River in lower Philadelphia. Swedish Lutherans preceded most German settlements, arriving with John Fenwick's 1675 expedition that had settled West Jersey.

SETTLEMENT IN THE SHENANDOAH VALLEY

Woodstock, Virginia, Justice of the Peace Wood promised Muhlenberg a £250 salary, a parsonage, and "a Farm of at least Two hundred acres of Extremely Good Land."[21] An obstacle was that to accept the ministry in Woodstock, Muhlenberg had to be ordained in the Church of England.[22] So Muhlenberg made a cross-Atlantic trip. "The Bishop of Ely [north of Cambridge] conferred deacon's orders upon Muhlenberg and [William] Braidfoot, followed by private ordination to the priesthood in April 1772, by the Bishop of London in the King's Chapel at St. James [Palace]."[23] Returning to the colonies, in Woodstock Muhlenberg conducted services. On the civic side, Pastor Muhlenberg was "[c]hosen . . . as chair of the six-person Committee of Safety and Correspondence for the county."[24] Thus, "[P]eter Muhlenberg was recognized not only as the spiritual but also the civic leader . . . of the Woodstock region."

AS THE WAR BEGINS, COLONEL MUHLENBERG SERVES

Prior Virginia colonial governors had adopted a light touch, evincing a conciliatory attitude toward those colonists who bridled under British rule. In contrast to his predecessors, John Murray, 4th Earl of Dunmore, was not conciliatory. As British colonial governor, Dunmore took great umbrage at the Second Virginia Convention's resolutions, in March 1775 calling them "'treason,' commencing revolutionary conflict in Virginia."[25] In an event presaging war, Dunmore caused to be confiscated twelve casks of gunpowder that the Williamsburg militia had stored in a church basement.

As events progressed, Dunmore rallied Tory sympathizers, along with a small force of British troops, fleeing down the James River, promising slaves emancipation, and enlisting some eight hundred African Americans in his counter-rebellion. In a prequel to the Revolutionary War—namely, "Dunmore's War"—Lord Dunmore's force boarded HMS *Fowey*, a British warship.[26] In March 1776, Muhlenberg and the 8th ("the German Regiment") marched to Southeast Virginia, at Suffolk, constituting the outer ring of the defense thrown up around Dunmore.[27] The 8th stood by while Revolutionary General Andrew Lewis's forces bombarded Dunmore's small fleet, anchored in the lee of Gwynn's Island at the tip of the James River Peninsula, site of Dunmore's last stand.

MUHLENBERG UNDER FIRE—THE FIRST SIEGE OF CHARLESTON (1776)

A short time after colonial Governor Dunmore had fled, in June 1776, with eighty-five hundred troops and fifty-six Royal Navy ships accompanying him, British General Henry Clinton arrived off Charles Town, the South's leading city, a metropolis of ten thousand.[28] American Major General Charles Lee, in command of the Southern Department, had five thousand men, including Peter Muhlenberg's regiment, who, after Dunmore's War (a sideshow), had marched south from Virginia to South Carolina.[29]

On June 23, led by the fifty-gun HMS *Bristol*, British warships bombarded a small fort on a narrow barrier island north of the Cooper River mouth, Sullivan's Island. Fourteen hours' incessant bombardment did little damage. Muhlenberg's troops, seven hundred Virginians, coming from Haddrell's Point, reinforced Colonel William Thomson's Americans defending Sullivan Island's eastern end.[30]

The British invasion attempt was a "fiasco."[31] In the fourteen-hour bombardment, the Sullivan's Island fort, built of spongy palmetto logs backed by sixteen feet of sand, repelled the British cannonballs. "General Lee was astonished by the bravery of the untrained American soldiers [Muhlenberg's regiment included], about whose valor he had hitherto held no high opinion. His reports on the engagement were full of praise for the men," Edward Hocker noted in his Muhlenberg biography, *The Fighting Parson*.[32] General Lee wrote to Congress and to the commander in chief, "I have the greatest reason to be pleased with Muhlenberg's Virginians . . . alert, zealous, and spirited."[33]

FUTILITY FOLLOWING ACTION: DUNMORE'S WAR REDUX

At the time of Dunmore's War, in another war before the larger Revolution, British forces in East Florida were conducting raids over the border into Georgia. Fearing raids farther north of Florida, Savannah citizens agitated for protection.[34] Major General Lee heeded their calls, dispatching Muhlenberg's regiment. The regiment arrived in Savannah on August 17, 1776, and at Sunbury, twelve miles south of the city, on August 22, where they camped. Due to hot and muggy weather, Muhlenberg and his heavy-wool-uniformed troops were beset by tropical afflictions. Meanwhile, Washington had recalled Charles Lee to the mid-Atlantic region. In September, South Carolina's General William Moultrie, of Sullivan's Island fame, then in charge, canceled the expedition. Muhlenberg led his Virginia troops, hobbled by sickness and fatigue, slowly northward, reaching northern Virginia only on December 20. "Muhlenberg himself suffered all his life from the consequences of disease contracted on the futile Georgia-Florida campaign."

Chapter Twenty-Three

Muhlenberg the Brigadier General

On February 21, 1777, Congress promoted Colonel Peter Muhlenberg to brigadier general.[1] As brigadier, Muhlenberg took command of half of the Virginia regiments (the 1st, 5th, 8th, and 9th) that comprised a brigade in General Nathanael Greene's division.[2] Newly arrived from the Florida expedition, though enervated from the long march and tropical afflictions, Muhlenberg and his regiments missed Washington's crossing of the Delaware as well as the late 1776 through early 1777 Second Battle of Trenton and conquest of Princeton. Later, in early summer 1777, when Muhlenberg and his charges marched and countermarched through New Jersey, Washington and his generals conjectured about the British forces' next move.

Would British General William Howe go north from New York up the Hudson Valley, linking up with General Burgoyne coming south from Canada, in an effort to bisect the colonies? Or would Howe order a march southwest from Staten Island, across Arthur Kill and New Jersey, occupying Philadelphia? Or would Howe and his force sail south from New York and then up either the Delaware River or the Chesapeake Bay? General Howe chose the latter option. In September 1777, he landed his force at Head of Elk, where the Elk River flows into the Susquehanna, in turn representing the uppermost reach of Chesapeake Bay, a site from which Howe eyed Philadelphia fifty miles away.

Brandywine

As much as any other brigade at Brandywine, Muhlenberg and his Virginians acquitted themselves with honor. Commander in Chief Washington had arrayed his troops to defend the main Philadelphia road's ford across Brandywine Creek, a stream wider than many rivers. In a major error, Washington had left his right flank to the north unprotected. British General Howe decoyed the American defenders by menacing them with Hessian mercenaries, feinting at the major ford. Meanwhile, with seven thousand men, Charles Lord Cornwallis marched several miles north, turned east, forded the creek's branches, turned to the right, and proceeded southward, intent on rolling up the patriot line. "Muhlenberg's brigade . . . rendered service of incalculable value by holding back the British advance long enough to permit the badly battered American regiments to retire from [Birmingham Meeting House Hill]," wrote Edward Hocker. Late in the day, Washington had ordered divisions under Generals Stirling, Stephen, and Sullivan north. Those divisions had been unable to counteract Cornwallis. Battered, they retired from the field. "[M]uhlenberg's men alone, after having marched four miles in forty minutes, faced all of Cornwallis's army. [T]heir commander [Muhlenberg] led them in desperate hand-to-hand bayonet fighting. The Virginians' fortitude prevented the [American] defeat from becoming a rout," concluded Hocker.[3] All accounts record that "Muhlenberg's brigade was the last to leave the field of battle."[4] One historian recorded that "the conduct of General Muhlenberg at this crisis was such as to win him the admiration and esteem of the whole army. Conspicuous at the head of his men, he braved every danger, leading the charges upon the enemy."[5]

The British took control of Philadelphia in September 1777. The Americans retreated to the northwest, passing Trappe, the Muhlenberg ancestral home. War's hardships are reflected in the September 19 journal entry of Pastor Henry Melchior Muhlenberg:

> *The American Army, four miles from us, forded the Schuykill breast-high and came [past us] upon the Philadelphia Road. . . . His Excellency, General Washington, was with the troops . . . who marched past here. . . . The procession lasted through the night [with soldiers] and officers, wet breast-high, who had to march in this condition the whole night, cold and damp as it was, and to bear hunger and thirst at the same time.[6]*

Washington marched his troops west of Trappe. Eastward, a large body of the British army remained outside Philadelphia, camping at Germantown, five miles northwest of the city. In council, Washington and his generals, seeing the British bivouac as a tempting target, decided to reverse course, attacking the foe at Germantown, sixteen miles away.

GERMANTOWN

Following a long night march, an assault on the British and Hessian position was to begin. The American attack was to be in four columns, two to three thousand men each to attempt flanking movements, left and right; another two thousand were

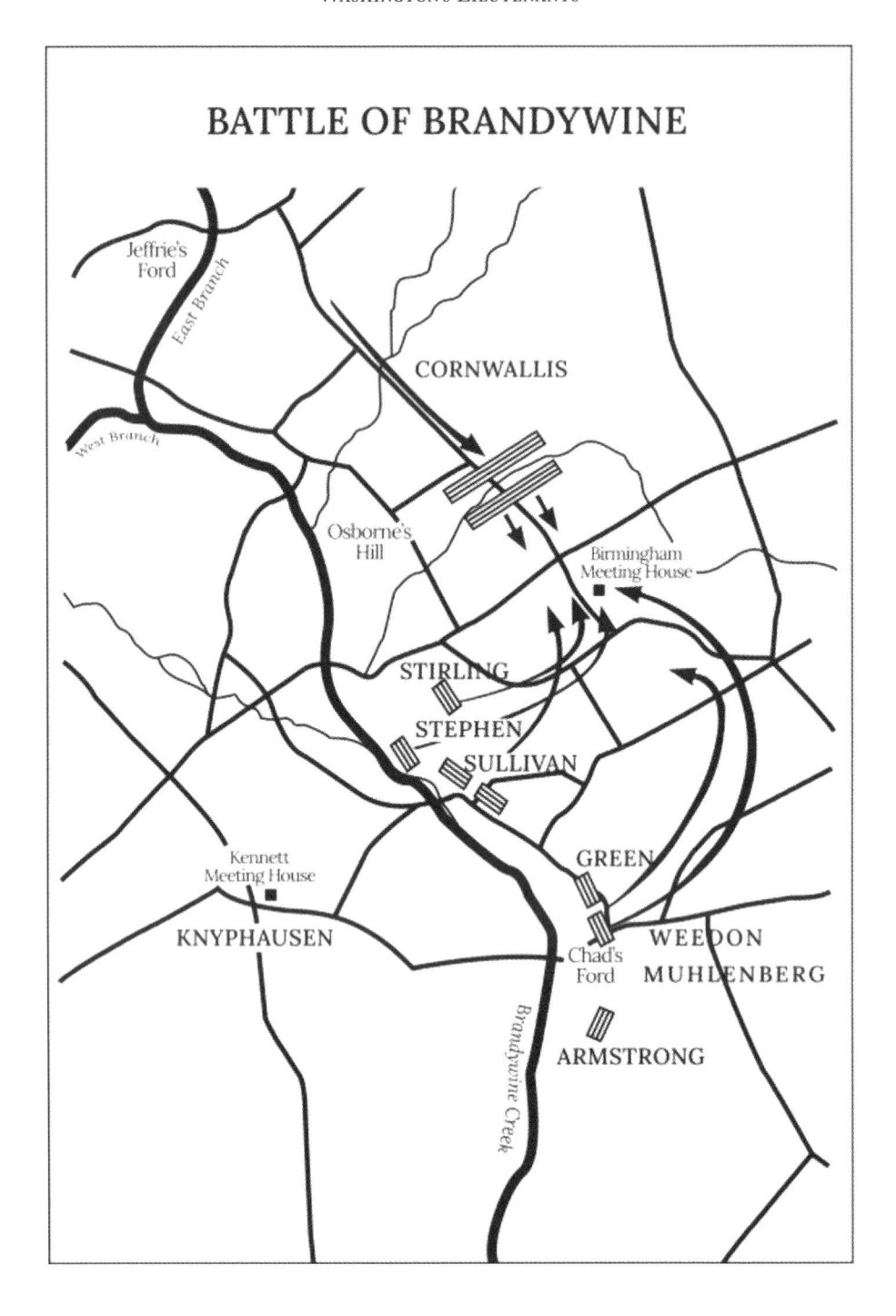

BATTLE OF BRANDYWINE

in the center under Generals Nathanael Greene and John Sullivan, with a fourth column in reserve. Muhlenberg took charge of his regiments, which, along with Adam Stephen's division, were to be a flanking detachment, moving forward on the colonials' left wing. Conway's and Sullivan's forces constituted the van of the center columns that were to proceed up the main road. Professor Harry Ward described the strategy's central aspect: "For the broad pincer movement, it was of the utmost importance that the advance be synchronized to the greatest precision so that the Americans would attack at once."[7]

According to some sugar-coated accounts, early morning fog limited visibility, greatly interfering with plans for cooperation among the American columns. A less euphemistic account was that one of the commands under Greene, that of General Adam Stephen, wandered from its intended course, moving westward until it collided with General Wayne's troops in the center. The credible explanation was that General Adam Stephen, drunk, ordered his force to turn right rather than to stay left. Coming on the American center, Stephen's troops encountered the rear of General Anthony Wayne's, opening fire on their colleagues. Wayne's men fired back. Friendly fire killed and wounded many Americans.[8]

Meanwhile, with the advantage of surprise, the other American forces had pushed the British back two miles, to the center of Germantown. Unsupported on its left flank, the colonial advance in the center created an unprotected salient. With the advantage to the Americans, the tide turned, with the advantage to the British. General Stephen, again in all probability intoxicated, had sounded a premature signal for a general retreat. British General Howe then was able to reform his men, reversing direction, from retreat to attack. The American retreat turned into a rout. The 9th Virginia, of Muhlenberg's brigade, found itself marooned at the point of the salient, soon surrounded by British, compelled to surrender. "Thus, after having marched all night, and fought for four hours, or longer, the tired troops retraced their steps . . . and then continued the retreat some miles farther," with the British in pursuit.[9]

Washington was said to have had "the mortification to assure the troops that they had fled from Victory."[10] Quelling misgivings among his generals, "Washington did not parcel out any blame on his division commanders for the defeat at Germantown. The commander in chief thought the major problem was the fog." However, "[a]s at Brandywine, [at Germantown] the Virginians had again been the heroes of the day."[11]

A LULL IN THE ACTION

In late December 1777, the American army retreated westward seven to eight miles from Whitemarsh, into winter encampment at Valley Forge, twenty-three miles northwest of Philadelphia.[12] From Valley Forge, Muhlenberg made a Christmas visit to his parents' home in Trappe. Having learned a lesson from the 1776 British Lee capture in New Jersey, General Muhlenberg took extreme measures in Pennsylvania. "[P]recautions were adopted to prevent his presence from becoming known in the [Trappe] neighborhood."[13] At night, "blankets were hung over the windows and doors to prevent his being seen by lurking spies. He himself never undressed or allowed his horse to be unsaddled [which was kept] close at hand."[14]

RANKING AND RANKLING VIRGINIA'S GENERALS

Congress and a board of officers ranked General William Woodford senior to Brigadiers George Weedon, Peter Muhlenberg, and Charles Scott. Muhlenberg and colleagues found this unfair, as they had continuous service while Woodford had resigned his commission in September 1777, returning to the army in February 1778. Further, cashiering General Adam Stephen for, inter alia, drunkenness at Germantown, had opened a major general billet that Congress bestowed on Woodford. Both Muhlenberg and General George Weedon formed the intention to resign.[15] Washington's April 1777 letter to Muhlenberg entreated him not to do so:

> *I cannot judge the feelings of others, but my own should generally be regulated by the set of opinions of a set of gentlemen [who voted to promote Woodford] who I conceive have been actuated by the purest principles of impartiality and justice. . . . I would not be thought to press on you a hasty decision upon this matter but when you consider that we are upon the verge of a campaign, you will think with me that no time is to be lost.*[16]

Washington's frank letter placated Muhlenberg, and he returned from Woodstock to Valley Forge.[17]

MONMOUTH COURTHOUSE

Emerging from Valley Forge, on June 17, 1778, a senior officers' council of war voted, "unanimously," to recommend no attack on Philadelphia, but the issue became moot.[18] The following day, the British—now under General Henry Clinton—evacuated Philadelphia, beginning a slow march to Sandy Hook, New Jersey, where they would board transports taking them into New York City. Encumbered by hundreds of wagons and thousands of camp followers who had joined the British effort in Pennsylvania, the British caravan moved at a pace less than two miles per day. The American army then set out from Valley Forge toward New Jersey in pursuit.

The Americans crossed the Delaware River, catching the British in central Jersey at Monmouth Courthouse, where on a sweltering summer's day (June 28, 1778), the sides met. Monmouth Courthouse was, as it turned out, the last major northern engagement of the war. General Muhlenberg and his men fought at Monmouth, "[doing] their duty but nothing more can be claimed."[19] The battle was a draw, in a war of attrition tantamount to an American victory.[20]

INACTION IN THE NORTH AND RETURN TO ACTION IN VIRGINIA

The Middle Department army spent the 1778 and 1779 winters at Morristown, in northern New Jersey. In December 1779, Washington detached Muhlenberg, ordering him south to lead a major portion of Virginia's defense. "Virginia was then the richest and most populous of the thirteen states, [but], so far, [the Commonwealth] had suffered comparatively little from the war."[21] Now storm clouds gathered. "[T]he enemy deemed the breaking up of Virginia a primary object."[22] A probably more accurate view was that by making necessary the defense of Tidewater Virginia, the British hoped to siphon off colonial troops that otherwise would go farther south to aid the Continentals' Southern Army, opposing Lord Cornwallis. In 1780 and early 1781, the British landed several two-thousand- to three-thousand-man raiding parties up Virginia's Tidewater rivers.[23] "Having collected 5000 men, Muhlenberg advanced with them against [British General] Leslie's army and drove in the pickets but [avoided contact with] the main force."[24] In November, the British reboarded their ships, sailing back to New York.[25] Other British raids occurred, with the troops, after completing their mischief, retreating down the James River, boarding Royal Navy ships, and sailing out to sea.[26]

AN IMPORTANT MILITARY ENGAGEMENT IN VIRGINIA

At Yorktown, on the north side of a peninsula bound on the south by the James River and on the north by the York River, Lord Cornwallis and his men built strong defenses, including fortified redoubts, for protection. There they waited for a Royal Navy fleet to board them, returning to New York and safety.

On the night of October 15, 1781, the French attacked one of the British redoubts. The Americans, under General Muhlenberg, then attacked another. "One of his aides who survived . . . was quoted as saying that General Muhlenberg led the storming party in person."[27] Current accounts credit the Marquis de Lafayette with leading the force that captured the redoubt, but it may well have been Peter Muhlenberg fronting the attack.[28] At Yorktown, Washington divided his force into three divisions, one of which Lafayette commanded. In command of half of that division, Washington placed Brigadier Muhlenberg in charge. Professor Stephen Taaffe writes in *Washington's Revolutionary War Generals*, "Washington had always respected Muhlenberg and took advantage of an open slot in Lafayette's outfit to give him an active position."[29]

MILITARY DENOUEMENT

After Yorktown, with permission duly granted, Muhlenberg returned to Woodstock. "Thereafter, General Muhlenberg's headquarters were ... in Winchester, at the foot of Shenandoah Valley ... thirty miles from his family in Woodstock." On September 30, 1783, Congress promoted General Muhlenberg to major general. The disbanding of the Revolutionary War army was ordered the following November. The same year, 1783, Muhlenberg became an original member of the Order of the Cincinnati.[30] A few years later, General Muhlenberg moved north again, to Pennsylvania.

PART IX
THOMAS MIFFLIN

Chapter Twenty-Four

A Political General

All Things Liberty ranks Thomas Mifflin seventh of the "Ten Worst Continental Army Generals." The website posits that Mifflin's "work as quartermaster general was disastrous, being in large part responsible for the suffering at Valley Forge."[1] By contrast, after the war Pennsylvania citizens elected Mifflin governor. Mifflin was Pennsylvania's first governor, serving two terms, from 1790 to 1799.[2] Previously, from November 1783 to November 1784, Mifflin had served as president—that is, elected by congressional delegates to be president of the Congress authorized under the Articles of Confederation.[3] As a politician, Mifflin was successful. In stark contrast, as a general, he was not.

In martial conflicts, there are fighting generals. In the Revolutionary War, Virginia's George Washington and Daniel Morgan, or North Carolina's Francis Nash and William Lee Davidson, were fighting generals. They fought hard, suffering myriad deprivations, with the latter two brigadiers dying in combat. At the other extreme are politicians turned general, mostly so they can wear the uniform. Outfitted, they fly a false flag of personal bravery and military prowess, impressing onlookers. In between are politicians who serve, and mostly serve well, but who flit back and forth between military and political worlds.[4] Pennsylvania's Thomas Mifflin represents the latter. Rather than pursuing roles *in seriatim*, as in politician/civilian to military to civilian again, and so on, as others had done, Mifflin served military, political, and civilian objectives simultaneously, leading to questionable performances in all three spheres.

Mifflin the Wealthy Pennsylvania Merchant

Thomas Mifflin was the third generation of a successful Philadelphia merchant family. His grandfather had emigrated from England early in the eighteenth century.[5] "In person, [Mifflin] was not tall, but he was well-formed and handsome. A man of agreeable manners and cultivated tastes, he had a lively temperament."[6]

Born in January 1744, Mifflin graduated from the College of Pennsylvania (later the University of Pennsylvania).[7]

Mifflin was through and through a blue blood. Although Episcopalian (Anglican), he mixed well with the "broad brims," as non-Quakers referred to the Friends, who dominated Pennsylvania society.[8] Following university, Mifflin's parents sent him for a year across the Atlantic. Then age twenty, he spent the time in England and France. On his return, Mifflin went into trade with his younger brother George. Mifflin also became a member of many of Philadelphia's exclusive clubs, such as the American Society, Philadelphia Hunt Club, Schuylkill Fishing Company, Philadelphia Dancing Assembly, and more. A salient characteristic was Mifflin's talent as a persuasive speaker: he had "a great talent for public speaking. . . . [H]e had all the attributes of a successful" gentleman. Again, most noteworthy was that he acted "[a]n easy and very correct speaker, very sensible and agreeable."[9] In addition to his membership in Philadelphia's exclusive clubs and an old family pedigree, Mifflin demonstrated the trappings of great success as a merchant. He had "a grand, spacious, and elegant home."[10]

First Step in a Public Life: Politics

Philadelphia citizens elected Mifflin, at age twenty-eight, representative to the Pennsylvania Assembly. While in that capacity, Mifflin did double duty. The Provisional Convention elected Mifflin delegate to the First and Second Continental Congresses.[11] In the latter capacity, on July 2, 1776, Mifflin signed the Declaration of Independence, enumerating certain "self-evident" rights over which Britain had run roughshod.[12]

Having achieved great success at an early age and having signed the Declaration of Independence, bestowing on him a touch of immortality, Mifflin had carved his niche as a gifted politician. Reliance on his loquaciousness, his ability as a gifted public speaker, and his political contacts and savvy subsequently never left him—even though these qualities did not mesh with a military career.

In the first Continental Congresses, John Adams had taken notice of Mifflin, finding him "a sprightly and spirited speaker."[13] Shortly after Lexington and Concord, in April 1775, Mifflin had addressed a town gathering of eight thousand enthusiastic Philadelphians (Philadelphia's population was forty-three thousand at the time): "Let not the patriotic feelings of today be forgotten tomorrow, not let it be said of Philadelphia, that she slept upon them and afterwards neglected them."[14] Silas Dean, who would be America's commissioner in France, called Mifflin "the soul of Philadelphia." John Adams added another compliment: "[Mifflin] ought to [be] a general for he has been the animating soul of the whole."[15] On another occasion,

Adams spoke more plainly, labeling Mifflin "the animating soul of the revolutionary movement."[16] Previously, as a colleague in the Continental Congress, John Adams had found Mifflin "a welcome addition to the house," a spirited radical even though Mifflin's background as a merchant suggested otherwise.[17]

"He had a knack for charming people, bringing them around to his perspective. . . . [H]e knew which levers to pull to get his way."[18] Physician General Dr. James Craik wrote to General Washington that Mifflin was "plausible, sensible, popular, and ambitious, takes great pains to draw over every officer he meets with his own way of thinking and is ever engaging."[19]

MILITARY LIFE COMMENCES

In spring 1775, the prominent young Pennsylvanian received a commission, entering the army as a major.[20] Later that year, after his June 15 appointment as commander in chief, Washington named Mifflin his aide-de-camp along with Joseph Reed as military secretary. Buoyed by participation with General Washington in the siege of Boston, Major Mifflin wrote to his cousin Jonathan Mifflin, "I ride Morning and Night—I never had better Health or Spirits. . . . It is a righteous cause. My whole Soul is ardently engaged in it."[21] Without evidence, such as accounts by contemporaries, Mifflin's biographer, Professor Kenneth Rossman, credited Mifflin with conceiving the idea of fortification on Dorchester Heights, allowing for cannons to be sighted over the entirety of Boston.[22] The fortification signaled the beginning of the end for British occupation.[23]

Later in summer 1775, Congress had formed the Quartermaster's Department to procure and supply the army with supplies as well as performing other services. Having discovered and seen as a natural fit Mifflin's merchant background, Washington appointed Mifflin quartermaster of the army, later changed to quartermaster general.[24] Congressional delegate Richard Henry Lee congratulated George Washington on the choice: "I think you could not possible [sic] have appointed a better Man to his Present Office than Mr. Mifflin."[25] A footnote may be that there were few takers for the office, as most Continental Line officers hoped for acclaim due to battlefield exploits. As an added inducement for accepting the position, Congress promoted Mifflin to colonel.

Thomas Mifflin was not immune to the near universal desire of officers to seek battlefield recognition and acclaim. He also aspired to be a combat leader, a seeker of battlefield glory. "[He] refused to lead from the rear [and] was present at the battles of Trenton and Princeton, and assisted in the defense of Philadelphia."[26] Having Washington's ear, at the Battle of Long Island Mifflin allegedly pointed out the vulnerability of the American Brooklyn Heights position. When the wind was right, Royal Navy ships could sail up the East River, hoving to opposite Brook-

Thomas Mifflin
FINE ART AMERICA

lyn and bombarding Washington's headquarters and surroundings to oblivion. British ships could also cut off the American avenue of retreat to Manhattan.[27] Overall, though, little evidence exists that Thomas Mifflin waded into the thick of the Battle at Brooklyn.

TROUBLE AHEAD: CONFLICTS OF INTEREST

His earlier enthusiasm aside, George Washington began to have misgivings about Mifflin, due mostly to appearances of self-dealing, related party conflicts of interest, and neglect by Mifflin of his duties as quartermaster. Mifflin was sending much of the army's business to his cousin, Jonathan Mifflin, and his firm. In correspondence, Mifflin referred to Jonathan and partner William Barret as "his lads." He directed that his name—that is, "Mifflin"—not appear on certain invoices, mostly bills for goods that would be diverted to officers in private transactions rather than to the army.[28] To another relative, Matthew Irwin, Mifflin wrote that "sales" to others "will meet with a good price." Continuing, he exhorted Irwin to "[k]eep this letter entirely to yourself, as the least Hint of what I have written many ruin your scheme of trade."[29] Early on in his office, then, Mifflin had been "double dipping," actively participating in a private business alongside his official duties.[30]

It may be that standards were different then, but today, even under promanagement business organization principles, business with a first cousin or other close relative represents a conflict of interest. Doing business with firms in which the relatives have a material interest would have a presumption against the transactions. Disinterested decision-makers would review such transactions approving or rejecting them or, better yet, directing that transactions be avoided altogether.

George Washington had more than an inkling of such considerations when he wrote to Colonel Joseph Reed, "I have taken occasion to hint to a certain gentleman [Mifflin] in this camp, without introducing any names, my apprehensions of his being concerned in trade."[31] Even Mifflin's generally positive biographer, Kenneth Rossman, wrote that Mifflin was "suspected of acquiring fortunes while in the quarter master department."[32]

Mifflin's disregard of conflicting interest transaction principles continued. In March 1776, Colonel Reed wrote to General Washington, "I ought to mention to you Continuance of one of your officers in private trade with which you [were] most dissatisfied last fall—you can be at no loss to know who I mean [Thomas Mifflin]."[33]

ADDITIONAL TROUBLE AHEAD

Then too, Mifflin had begun to neglect his office. His biographer concludes that even early on the restless Mifflin "found the duties of his office distasteful and irksome."[34] Wishful thinking for combat, however, was no excuse for Mifflin's neglect, then followed by complete abdication of his office, let alone an excuse for his conflicting interest exploits.[35]

By one account, neglect of Mifflin's quartermaster general post caused "around two thousand men [to die] that winter at Valley Forge from hunger, disease, exposure, and exhaustion."[36] At one time, earlier in the war, Mifflin had done yeoman-like service as quartermaster. At the Battle of Long Island, he oversaw "procurement of housing for officers, supplies for the men, and barracks for soldiers."[37] Washington had spoken of Mifflin as "a man of excellent talents."[38]

A preview to Mifflin's biography, though, records the allegations of Mifflin's offenses, principally absence from Valley Forge, as toppling him from lofty heights to be regarded as one of the War of Independence's worst generals: "The breakdown of supply was responsible for the sufferings of the army at Valley Forge."[39] It is a side of the Valley Forge winter, a season of adversity about which all Americans learn as schoolchildren, that few know—namely, that General Thomas Mifflin was in great part responsible for what occurred there.

CHAPTER TWENTY-FIVE

Dereliction of Duty and
Abandonment of His Post

HARSH THOUGH THE ALLEGATIONS THAT FOLLOW MAY BE, MIFFLIN'S STORY CON-
tinues. In 1777, Mifflin returned home to Philadelphia, where he was better able to
pursue his political interests. He left the army's winter headquarters in Middlebrook,
New Jersey, ten miles north of New Brunswick, never to return. Washington had
granted Mifflin a short furlough, charging the inspiring speaker, Mifflin, with Pennsylvania recruiting duties.[1] Still, in Philadelphia, in May 1777, Mifflin responded
to the commander in chief, "who had requested Mifflin's return to Middlebrook."
Mifflin informed Washington "that upon request of several members of Congress
. . . [he] thought his attendance in Philadelphia necessary . . . he must remain
there"—that is, in Philadelphia.[2]

In June, Mifflin was still in Philadelphia. Journals of the time recorded Mifflin
speaking to the Continental Congress on June 16, 1777.[3] It was to be the first of
Mifflin's lengthy, unexcused absences from his post.

A PHILADELPHIA ADVOCATE

Sometime in early summer 1777, still close to Continental Congress delegates,
Mifflin urged that Congress adjourn, leave Philadelphia, and reconvene in Baltimore. Knowing Philadelphia well, Mifflin thought loyalists, whose numbers were
substantial, might attempt to take the city.[4] Washington, however, chose to increase
resources in the Northern Department rather than in defense of Philadelphia. The
rift between the two men widened, as Mifflin thought that he knew better. Washington had decided defense against a British southward thrust was paramount; Mifflin
thought the highest priority should be Philadelphia's security. "By Spring 1777, Mifflin began openly to disagree with Washington's war strategy."[5] To a certain extent,

Mifflin was prescient, as, following the Battle of Brandywine Creek in September 1777, the British did occupy the American capital. The Continental Congress fled west to Lancaster and then onward to York, Pennsylvania.

Yet victory over Burgoyne and the British at Saratoga saved the union from being split in two and disintegrating, also persuading the French to intervene on the American side. The temporary British occupation of Philadelphia turned out to have inconvenienced the Continental Congress only for a time.

NOT ONLY DISAGREEMENTS BUT ALSO FAILURES

Approximately nine months later, in late 1777 and early in 1778, after the British occupation of Philadelphia, accusations began to fly about Mifflin's Valley Forge failings and his alleged participation in the Conway cabal to depose George Washington and replace him with Horatio Gates as commander in chief (chapters 20 and 26). Around that time (fall 1777), Mifflin appears to have again commenced abandonment of his post. When British occupation of Philadelphia had still seemed imminent, Mifflin moved his family from Philadelphia seventy-seven miles west to Reading. To be sure, concern about his family's safety motivated him, but Mifflin also stayed in Reading—with his family in a comfortable home surrounded by loved ones. Meanwhile, other American officers led troops in the field, absent from homes and families, marching to and fro, imbibing bad water, and consuming marginal food, engaged in skirmishes and battles with British redcoats and American loyalists.

Attempting to explain his failures, Mifflin began to experience ill health, never specified, maintaining that condition as the reason for his absence. He wrote to John Hancock, president of the Continental Congress, "[M]y Health is much impaired and the Possibility of a Recovery of it is so distant that I consider myself a very useless officer."[6] The suspicion arises, however, that Mifflin's continued presence in Reading was proximate to York, where the Continental Congress had settled. York lay fifty miles to the southwest of Reading.[7] Mifflin's ill health never prevented journeys to York, lobbying the Congress and hobnobbing with former colleagues. Then too, eminent politicians such as Timothy Pickering of Massachusetts went to Reading to meet with Thomas Mifflin.[8]

Into the midst of all this—this being Mifflin's failings at Valley Forge and his participation in the Conway cabal—came the Continental Congress. Working at cross purposes, on February 19, Congress promoted Mifflin to major general, along with Lord Stirling (New York), Arthur St. Clair (Pennsylvania), Adam Stephen (Virginia), and Benjamin Lincoln (Massachusetts).[9] The inference that arises, given General Washington's animadversions on Mifflin, was that Mifflin's lobbying and friendship with his fellow politicians paid dividends.

On the contrary side of the ledger, while other colonies had two major generals, Pennsylvania had none. To correct the imbalance, Congress, which did include Mifflin's cronies, selected two Pennsylvania brigadier generals—Thomas Mifflin and Arthur St. Clair—for promotion to major general.[10] Along with Mifflin's stature as a politician, Pennsylvania's deficit may have had more to do with Mifflin's promotion than his merits did.

THE VALLEY FORGE DEBACLE

After the American defeat at Germantown in October and the decision not to attack the British occupying Philadelphia, Washington took his twelve-thousand-man army into winter encampment. He moved his army westward from Whitemarsh, north of Philadelphia, to a defensible position named Valley Forge, eighteen miles northwest of the city. The army stayed there from December 17, 1777, to late May or early June 1778. Soon after the army's arrival, a "disastrous supply crisis" began taking its toll.[11] Estimates are that during the crisis, eighteen hundred to two thousand died from sickness, starvation, and exposure, exacerbated by a rudderless army quartermaster department.

In November 1777, Mifflin had tendered to Congress his resignation as quartermaster general. Congress did not accept it. Instead, Congress resolved that Mifflin should remain in the position, doing a further great disservice to the army, which "paid dearly in the suffering at Valley Forge."[12] In Mifflin's mind, contrary to beliefs in Congress, rather than merely tendering a resignation, he had unilaterally abdicated. "The [quartermaster] department quickly disintegrated" for want of "the presence of its head active in the field."[13] Mifflin instead played politics in Philadelphia while also being a member of the new Board of War that Congress had created.

Among other things, the quartermaster provided the army's transportation. "Because [the absent] Mifflin was unable to procure and supply enough horses, Washington's army at Valley Forge soon ran short of the provisions and equipment it needed to function," Professor Stephen Taaffe explained. Without horses and wagons, supply personnel could neither fetch supplies from urban centers and depots nor forage far afield. Responding to complaints of shortages, "a congressional committee that visited camp . . . recognized that the army required a strong and capable new quartermaster to bring order to the chaos that Mifflin had left. Without one, the army would most likely dissolve before winter ended."[14]

Enter Commander in Chief George Washington and Brigadier "Mad" Anthony Wayne. Because soldiers at Valley Forge were naked and starving, and because Thomas Mifflin "had [effectively] left that office [quartermaster general] . . . and badly managed it," Washington determined to remedy the situation himself.[15] He selected a combat general familiar with the surrounding territory (Anthony Wayne was from west of Philadelphia) to collect foodstuffs and forage from the countryside. Wayne's biographer Thomas Boyd described Wayne's efforts:

> *Wayne rode out and was gone a month, most of the time behind the enemy's lines. Then, long preceded [into camp] by several hundred cattle, many horses, and wagons loaded with forage, he came back to camp over the melting snow. And now, except for clothing, the condition of the army was becoming better.*[16]

While Wayne and his men scoured the countryside, Mifflin was "idle in [his self-imposed] retirement at Reading," despite being quartermaster general and "the deplorable state" of supply to the army. Continental Congress President Henry Laurens wrote to members of Congress that he believed "most of the Evils that had attended our Camp flow from gross neglect and abuse" in Thomas Mifflin's department.[17] A further allegation, not proven but with widespread support, was that Mifflin "warehoused supplies intended for Valley Forge, [and] sold them on the open market."[18]

After Mad Anthony Wayne's successful excursion, grateful soldiers referred to Wayne as "the Great Forager." The troops never coined a nickname for Thomas Mifflin, who had failed them badly.

CARPING UNWORTHY OF A MAJOR GENERAL

Washington not only sent Wayne out into the field but also decided that the army needed a new quartermaster general. The commander in chief decided that Nathanael Greene, "his most trusted lieutenant" and a commander "who had a business background" running a forge and a metal work enterprise in Warwick, Rhode Island, and "who understood the army's logistical difficulties," was his choice. Seconded by a congressional committee, Washington offered the position to Greene. "Greene saw himself first and foremost as a combat commander. In the end, though, Washington's persuasive abilities and Greene's sense of duty prevailed."[19] On March 23, 1778, Congress appointed Nathanael Greene quartermaster general.

Unable to restrain himself, Mifflin openly criticized Nathanael Greene and General Washington's appointment of Greene as a successor. Mifflin was jealous of and disliked Greene, complaining that "the ear of the Commander-in-Chief was exclusively possessed by Greene . . . who is neither the most wise, the most brave, nor the most patriotic of Counselors."[20] Mifflin's dislike of Greene traced its origins to 1775, when Congress had promoted Greene to brigadier general (June 22, 1775) but promoted Mifflin only a year later, on May 16, 1776.[21] The disparity set off a feud with Greene, Mifflin complaining that Congress had unfairly promoted Greene over him. As described by an otherwise sympathetic Mifflin biographer, Professor Kenneth Rossman, the feud "was to divide the army into opposing factions and caused dissention at critical times."[22]

Schooled in politics and its license to advance ideas and contrary opinions, Mifflin appears never to have realized that military organizations differ. Loyalty up the chain of command has a higher value than does open and vociferous criticism of military superiors and their strategic choices. Earlier, in 1777, Mifflin had openly criticized Washington's decisions to keep troops in the north, as aforementioned, publicly stating that Washington should redeploy forces to protect Philadelphia.[23] Earlier, in fall of 1776, Mifflin had openly blamed Washington and Nathanael Greene for the abandonment of Fort Washington in upper Manhattan. Surrender had resulted in the British capture of 2,837 American soldiers.[24] Earlier still, the outspoken Mifflin had begun a campaign of criticizing Washington "behind his back" for "conduct of the Battle of Long Island [August 1776] and subsequent retreat up Manhattan Island."[25] Later, in January 1777, Washington had issued a proclamation urging colonial citizens to make a difficult decision: abandon British protection and swear an oath of allegiance to the new American nation of former colonies. Mifflin publicly advocated for more lenient treatment of Tories.[26]

With mounting criticism by Mifflin, "Washington's regard for Mifflin cooled perceptively," especially following Mifflin's loud expression of resentment of Nathanael Greene and Washington's appointment of Greene as quartermaster general.[27] Mifflin's expostulations fell on deaf ears: "Mifflin had slipped from Washington's favor. . . . [H]is opinion carried little weight."[28]

Chapter Twenty-Six

Thomas Mifflin's Greatest Sin

Mifflin's first transgression was, of course, his bust as quartermaster general, degenerating into the failure at Valley Forge.[1] His second transgression was the role Mifflin played in the Conway cabal, proposing that Horatio Gates replace George Washington as commander in chief.[2] In his defense, "Mifflin steadfastly denied that he ever had any part in any effort to replace Washington as commanding officer."[3]

Agreeing, Professor Stephen Taaffe concluded, "There was no conspiracy. . . . [P]eople griped about Washington's recent lack of success. . . . [T]here was no secret, coordinated plan . . . to remove [Washington] from office."[4] Or, as Chalmers Davidson, Brigadier William Davidson's biographer, saw it, it was only "a whispering campaign."[5] Professor Mark Lender summarizes "prevailing scholarly wisdom generally hold[ing] that the Cabal never existed as a serious threat to Washington's command." But in his book *Cabal*, Lender makes the case that the anti-Washington plot was "broader, deeper, and more serious" than previous scholarship allowed.[6] Ultimately, the affair fizzled out, with the only result being that George Washington further cemented himself in place as the American army's leader.[7]

Gates and Mifflin

Realizing that he needed another battlefield command, Gates thirsted for higher posting. After the Conway cabal, Gates lobbied for command of the Continental Army's Southern Department. The Congress appointed Gates to the position, where he quickly and shamelessly disgraced himself (chapter 20). Disgraced as well, and shot through the mouth in a 1778 duel with Pennsylvania's Colonel John Cadwallader, the badly wounded cabal instigator Major General Conway returned to France.

The alleged third principal in the cabal, Thomas Mifflin, had close connections with Gates. In the summer of 1775, during the siege of Boston, Charles Lee, Gates, "and Mifflin were particularly friendly."[8] At the siege of Boston, Mifflin frequently dined with Charles Lee and Horatio Gates, the two ex–British army officers who became American major generals.[9] Mifflin was "a close friend of Gates."[10] Previously, after university, young Mifflin had spent a year abroad, much of the time in England, on occasion meeting with his father's and grandfather's commercial contacts. Moreover, his heritage was proud British, whose line had done well in America. Last of all, Mifflin's occupation as a merchant required him to spend considerable time dealing with British manufacturers and distributors, who at that time were the primary suppliers to the Mifflins and to the American colonies overall.

Although an ardent revolutionary, Thomas Mifflin possessed an Anglophile streak. That streak would have been an ingredient in his awarding to Gates high marks, as well as his acclaim for Charles Lee. From the war's earliest days, Gates and Lee were critical of George Washington, each believing he would make a far better commander in chief. Did Mifflin agree, placing Horatio Gates on a pedestal?

A close examination also reveals that from a very early point, Mifflin, like Gates, was "an outspoken critic" of George Washington. Mifflin's criticism of Washington began early, as far back as fall 1776, after the siege of Boston. Mifflin took vocal issue with what he believed had been Washington's failings in "the conduct of the army at the Battle of Long Island and the subsequent retreat up Manhattan Island."[11] Mifflin also defied Washington's request that he return to Middlebrook (chapter 25). After Princeton in early 1777, Mifflin defied Washington, remaining AWOL from Middlebrook to accommodate a lengthy Philadelphia stay, busily engaged in politics with Pennsylvania colleagues.[12]

THOMAS MIFFLIN'S VIEWS IN 1777

After the Brandywine and Germantown losses, General Washington knew his credibility was on the line. His battlefield opponents, Generals William Howe and Henry Clinton, had out-generaled him. On the patriot side, Washington's detractors multiplied. For instance, Congressman James Lovell, "showing little faith in the commander in chief, thought that the Philadelphia theater could benefit from an infusion of new leadership."[13] Lovell was joined by Congressman Jonathan Dickinson Sergeant of New Jersey, who had become a "kindred spirit," writing to Lovell, "Thing[s] look gloomy. . . . We want a General; thousands of Lives & Millions of Property are yearly sacrificed to the Insufficiency of our Commander in Chief. Two battles [Brandywine and Germantown] he has lost for us by two Blunders as might have disgraced a Soldier of three Months Standing."[14] That letter was forwarded to others; a copy was found among John Adams's papers, Adams also becoming a Washington detractor.[15]

In late fall 1777, after the Germantown defeat, Washington gathered his senior officers in a council of war at Whitemarsh, north of Philadelphia. The question posed—"Should we attack British forces occupying Philadelphia?"—was answered "in the Negative [almost] unanimously."[16] The "setbacks around Philadelphia," as well as the negative vote, "left Mifflin infuriated. His faith in the commander in chief evaporated." As a Philadelphian since birth, Mifflin's highest priority was to oust the British from his city.

Chapter 25 details how Mifflin "nursed a growing resentment of [General Nathanael] Greene. . . . [H]is agenda against the Rhode Islander was lengthy. [H]e took umbrage as Washington turned increasingly to Greene."[17]

In November 1777, Mifflin tendered his resignation as quartermaster general, "pleading ill health." On November 17, Mifflin wrote to his friend General Horatio Gates, "You have saved the Northern Hemisphere." Mifflin continued, "We have had a noble army melted down by ill-judged marches [occasioning] the severest & most just Sarcasm & Contempt from our Enemies." Mifflin ended with a plea to Gates: "[T]his army will be totally lost unless you come down & collect the virtuous Band who wish to fight under your Banner & . . . save the northern Hemisphere."[18]

AGITATION GROWS

The number of Washington's critics increased. Even Major General Arthur St. Clair, a Washington sycophant, who was in serious disrepute over the Fort Ticonderoga debacle, on November 21, 1777, wrote a letter to Horatio Gates. Showing his political side, St. Clair wrote that he was looking forward to Gates arriving in Pennsylvania. "It seems clear that St. Clair saw Gates's star ascending," Lender deduced in *Cabal*. To Lender, St. Clair's actions "reveal[ed] growing and profound alarm over the state of Continental Army leadership."[19]

The much-ballyhooed Benjamin Rush, hailed as a founding father, had a two-faced side, ready to blame the Revolution's failures on the commander in chief. On January 12, 1778, Rush wrote to Virginia Governor Patrick Henry, "A major genl . . . [probably Thomas Conway] called [the Continental Army] . . . a *Mob*. A Gates . . . would in a few weeks render [Continental soldiers] an irresistible body of men." Rush's letter "fulsomely praised Gates," who supposedly "has shewn us what Americans are capable with a *General* at their head."[20] Of course, the Americans had succeeded at Saratoga in spite rather than because of Horatio Gates.[21] Rush's writing was but one of the critical missives sniping at General Washington.

Despite his protestations of having no involvement in the cabal, Gates did show his true feelings, evincing a lack of respect—indeed, disdain—for his commander. In an act of disloyalty, Gates sent news of the Saratoga victory directly to Congress, bypassing the chain of command and Commander in Chief Washington. Gates's actions were "a deliberate slight of the commanding general." Washington "considered the failure to promptly report . . . a dereliction of duty." Following the battles at

Saratoga, Washington desired Gates to dispatch twenty regiments (at actual rather than theoretical strength, roughly seven thousand men) from the Northern Department to the mid-Atlantic theater. When Gates ignored the command, Washington aide Colonel Alexander Hamilton journeyed to upstate New York to reinforce Washington's order. Gates, though, continued to ignore the directive.[22]

Washington's Reactions

Washington was not oblivious. He knew that in late 1777 and early 1778 he was under attack. On January 30, 1778, Washington wrote to South Carolinian Henry Laurens, president of the Continental Congress and a Washington ally, "A malignant faction has for some time [been] forming to my prejudice . . . [which would result] in dangerous consequences, which interstine [internal] dissentions may produce to the common cause."[23] Early in 1777, cabal adherents approached Virginia Governor Patrick Henry (governor 1776–1779 and again 1784–1786), attempting to enlist his support. Not only did he abjure them, but Governor Henry also notified fellow Virginian Washington that a plot against him was afoot. Henry and Washington remained friends and allies all their days.[24]

The Cabal Goes Underground

As stated previously, many scholars downplay the Mifflin-Gates-Conway association as little but an exchange of gripes that by early 1778 had run its course, going no further. Others term the association a cabal to depose Washington as commander in chief, but short lived as well, evaporating by early 1778. In his excellent book, Professor Mark Lender demonstrated that the cabal evolved over a much longer time, taking an indirect, political approach, mainly through the Board of War's activities. When Mifflin, Gates, and Conway, as well as other activists, calculated that deposing Washington was not feasible, they shifted to attempts at neutering the commander. The trio had Conway appointed inspector in chief of the army, who would operate independently of the commanding general, in marked derogation of the historic military concept "unity of command." Another end run the group attempted to engineer would create quartermaster and commissary departments independent of Washington's command, further in derogation of unity of command.

The Reconfigured Inspector General

Earlier, in June 1776, Congress had created the Board of War, staffing it with congressional delegates (John Adams, Roger Sherman, Edward Rutledge, Benjamin Harrison, and James Wilson). The busy delegates proved unable to do the job, to assist the military rather than attempting to direct the war effort. So Congress returned, several times, to the drawing board, reconstituting the board's staffing.

Finally, using his ample political connections, and despite his manifest failure in the quartermaster general role, on November 2, 1777, Thomas Mifflin obtained appointment to a reconstituted board. Now "[o]ut of favor at [Washington's] headquarters, Mifflin . . . thought he had the trump card in loyal and powerful friends in Congress" and in his Board of War appointment.[25] Of course, Mifflin's earlier performance as quartermaster general should have forestalled any thought about a Mifflin appointment to the board, but Congress had its own agenda.

On November 27, the other wily operative, Horatio Gates ("Granny Gates" to his men), the supposed "Hero of Saratoga," obtained an appointment to the board. According to Mifflin biographer Kenneth Rossman, using his friendship with congressional delegates, "Mifflin nominated his friend Horatio Gates" to the board.[26] Congressional "delegates never consulted the commander in chief on the [War Board's] composition . . . a body charged with supporting critical aspects of the patriot war effort."[27] Washington remained silent but privately thought "[i]t was the elevation of one whose neglect of his duties . . . injured the service."[28]

In December 1777, again carrying on the cabal by other means, the new board appointed Washington's detractor, the Mifflin-Gates confederate Thomas Conway, as inspector general. Congress not only appointed Conway to a drastically reconfigured insector general post but also promoted him to major general. "Washington saw the promotion of Conway as an affront," an affront quadrupled by Congress's appointment of Conway as inspector general.[29]

As Mifflin and Gates had framed the new office, the inspector general was *not* to be a staff officer under the commander in chief but rather an agent of Congress. It was an arrangement that struck directly at Washington's authority. The new inspector general would be a parallel commander of the army, whom Mark Lender characterized as "the Board of War's political commissar."[30]

In one of the few overt steps in his counterattack, Washington announced "that he would issue no orders in cooperation with any steps Conway might attempt to initiate."[31] Washington effectively "stiff-armed" the new inspector general. When Conway showed up at Valley Forge early in 1778, Washington gave him the cold shoulder. Showing the depth of his antipathy toward Conway, Washington wrote to Henry Laurens, "My feelings would not permit me to make professions of friendship to a man I deem my Enemy."[32] Washington aide Alexander Hamilton was blunter, saying of Conway, "He is one of the vermin bred in the entrails of this chimera. . . . [T]here does not exist a more villainous calumniator and incendiary."[33]

Not Done Yet—the Board of War's Further Actions

Professor Lender termed the further actions "Disgust Upon Disgust." In a second, thinly disguised power grab, Mifflin and Gates's Board of War then sought control of field operations by reconfiguring what formerly had been administrative functions. The quartermaster department had been responsible for procurement and distribution of supplies, routine reconnaissance, maintenance of roads and bridges, camps' construction, and supply of horses and wagons. Mifflin put forth a proposal to create four new administrative positions: quartermaster general, commissary general, head of forage, and head of horses and wagons. The proposal's most salient feature "*specifically forbade*" General Washington and his staff to meddle with the board's new arrangements. "[I]t was the Cabal in the form of an administrative coup."[34] Historian Wayne Bodle called the effort "a bold-faced attempt by the board to expand its authority from a supportive role into a day-to-day operation of the army itself."[35] Contrary to the cabal having faded into the 1777 night, in 1778 "[t]he political skill of Thomas Mifflin, the popularity of Horatio Gates, and the acquiescence of Congress . . . deepened the challenge to Washington's command." General "Washington was aghast at this. The general had [merely] wanted reformed and effective army commissary and quartermaster departments."[36]

THE COMMITTEE AT CAMP RIGHTS THE SHIP

Among his midstream machinations, Mifflin obtained a congressional mandate for himself, Horatio Gates, and Thomas Pickering (no admirer of George Washington but short of being a naked usurper) to visit Valley Forge as a committee of inquiry. Ten days later, in January 1778, Congress had second thoughts, deciding not to send the Mifflin-Gates-Pickering trio. Meanwhile, reports of Gates's ineptness began to creep into the picture. Early in November 1777, Congressman Charles Carroll of Maryland began raising doubts about Gates's leadership "at a time most patriots were singing the praises of the Saratoga victor."[37]

A new reconstituted Committee at Camp journeyed to Valley Forge to begin examination of the army's problems. The committee quickly formed part of Washington's counterattack against Mifflin and Gates as any worries about the committee, now again comprised of congressional delegates, evaporated. General Washington and his staff worked well with the political appointees. The Committee at Camp "damned Mifflin's [proposed] reforms at length. [D]ividing the quartermaster department into four capital branches was . . . nonsense." The Board of War's coup became of no moment: "In just days, Mifflin's plan unraveled completely." This development was "galling for Thomas Mifflin."[38]

Washington wholeheartedly believed in the supremacy of civilian authority. But now he had two civilian authorities from which to choose, the Committee at Camp and the Board of War. "[W]ashington virtually ignored the board." Washington refused to acknowledge himself as subordinate to the board, which, in his opinion, had no place in the chain of command.

It took several months, but eventually Washington's allies also became convinced that the Board of War was intent on usurping the commander's authority. So Washington's allies commenced a campaign, by letters and other means, to win over congressional delegates and other influencers who had previously remained silent. Although Washington's chief critics, such as James Lovell and William Duer, did not become his advocates, they ceased being detractors, at least overt ones. More affirmatively, "[t]he Morisses (Robert and Gouverneur), [Benjamin] Harrison, [Tench] Tilghman, the Laurens (Henry and John), [Alexander] Hamilton, [Henry] Knox, Major [John] Clark, [John] Cadwallader, and others" wrote letters praising Washington and condemning the Board of War. Thomas "Mifflin became the lightning rod for [these] counterattacks. [W]ashington's allies vilified him." Mifflin, it turned out, "had made important enemies."[39]

The counterfire "began to hit home." Mifflin left York, Pennsylvania, where the Continental Congress was sitting and he had been politicking, retreating to his home in Reading. "[Mifflin] was incensed over increasing talk linking him to efforts to oust the commander in chief," doubly so because the criticism hit the mark.[40]

ATTACK ON WASHINGTON, ITS END, AND SUBSEQUENT EVENTS

By early spring 1778, both the cabal and the de facto cabal had disintegrated, never to surface again. After the cabal, Gates's relationship with General Washington was strictly professional.

By 1782, Thomas Mifflin had "largely mended fences" with ardent patriots. Indeed, he rose higher. From November 1783 to June 1784, Mifflin served as president of the Congress, elected to a one-year term by delegates. His "political trajectory continued to climb"; in 1787, he was elected to the Constitutional Convention. Following that, Pennsylvania citizens elected Mifflin their initial governor.[41] Today, Pennsylvania schools, towns, cities, and counties bear Mifflin's name (Mifflin County, West Mifflin, North Mifflin, South Mifflin, etc.). In certain quarters, Mifflin is called "a U.S. Founding Father" as well as "a great American."[42] His Revolutionary War service, though, remains unreconstructed, never rising above the level to which it had descended. As Professor Kenneth Rossman begins his Mifflin biography, "His complicity in an intrigue against George Washington . . . as well as bitter controversy over his work as quartermaster-general, deterred biographers who thought about the task of writing a Mifflin biography. There are no other biographies."[43]

CONWAY CABAL: A WHISPERING CAMPAIGN, CABAL, OR CONSPIRACY?

What is a conspiracy? A conspiracy exists even though its objective is unattainable, say, either because of impossibility of achieving it or due to lack of needed resources.[44]

What observers term a "mere pipe dream" may involve conspiracy. A plot to corner the world markets for wheat or corn could not achieve its objective under reasonable scenarios;[45] nevertheless, such a plot would involve a conspiracy. If the Conway cabal had little chance of replacing George Washington as commander in chief, that difficulty or impossibility would have been of no moment.

Nor must a conspiracy involve a "coordinated plot." All that is required is an agreement to achieve an illegal means or an agreement to achieve a legal end by illegal means.[46] Removal and replacement of the commanding general was a legal end. But the means to achieve it, if it were a mutiny involving force of arms, would be illegal. By contrast, if the means suggested were intense lobbying of politicians, that process would involve legal means to achieve a legal end. Conspiracy allegations would not lie.

A second Achilles's heel in conspiracy analysis emanates from the requirement that there must be an overt step toward achievement of the objective.[47] So was the alleged cabal an example of a "gang that couldn't shoot straight" (they were generals, after all)—that is, only an exchange of letters or whispering campaign, with no overt action ensuing? Even a gang that could not shoot straight could be involved in a conspiracy if an agreement, express or implied, and then movement toward the objective, occurred. Again, impossibility of achieving the goal is not a defense.

PART X
WILLIAM WOODFORD

CHAPTER TWENTY-SEVEN

Virginia Planter:
A Brigadier as a Bent Tree

LEST THIS BOOK LEAVE THE IMPRESSION THAT ALL TWENTY-THREE AMERICAN Revolutionary War major generals were less than admirable ("bent trees") and all brigadiers upstanding, the William Woodford biography contradicts that notion.[1] "Tall tree" chapters about Brigadiers Davidson, Mercer, and Muhlenberg portray brigadier generals as leaders of competence and bravery. There were, however, a few outliers.[2] Brigadiers George Weedon, Charles Scott, John Stark, and Daniel Morgan, for example, temporarily resigned commissions with the thought of vindicating their jealousies over the ranking or re-ranking of other brigadiers.[3] Brigadier General William Woodford could have been the paradigm for such conduct.

General William Woodford's wounding, capture by the British, and war-related death tell a stirring story. He ticked all the boxes for heroism. Yet his frequent snits, incessant manipulation, shortcomings in his men's eyes, and arrogant dandyism tell another story. He had a dark, uncomfortable side. Jealousy, anger, suspicion, and envy counterbalanced Woodford's contributions to the patriot cause.

William Woodford was wounded in action (Brandywine, 1777), was taken prisoner (when Charleston fell, 1780), and died a combat-related death (in 1780, in New York City, where the British held him prisoner, aboard a prison ship). His exploits should have ensured him a place in the Revolutionary War pantheon.[4]

A VIRGINIA ARISTOCRAT BORN AND BRED

Woodford was a wealthy planter from Virginia's Tidewater Caroline County. He was a man of privilege with a sense of entitlement. Tantrums in the war's early days were harbingers of what was to come.

At Great Bridge, in December 1775, North Carolina's Colonel Robert Howe moved north with his regiment. Great Bridge, over the Elizabeth River, was a short distance from the Virginia–North Carolina boundary. North Carolina fretted that Lord Dunmore, the feisty colonial governor of Virginia, with five hundred British troops and eight hundred emancipated slaves (Dunmore's "Ethiopian Corps"), might proceed toward North Carolina and its seaboard regions, thought to be Tory strongholds. The American general in charge, Andrew Lewis, wished to cut off that escape route.

On arrival, Colonel Robert Howe (chapters 10–13), Woodford's senior, assumed command. Feeling that he had pulled the laboring oar, Woodford grumbled, loudly and repeatedly. As a consolation, to calm Woodford, Howe decreed that Woodford would be in command of the Virginia troops, which included Woodford's 2nd Virginia along with Culpeper Militia.[5]

A second tantrum followed. Appointed commander of the 2nd, Colonel Woodford was "stunned" to learn that in mid-June 1776 Congress had appointed Hugh Mercer of the newly formed 3rd Virginia to the rank of brigadier.[6] "Woodford had assumed that when Congress had taken Virginia's regiments into continental service back in February [1776], the issue of seniority had been settled with him holding seniority over Mercer due to his [Woodford's] earlier appointment."[7] Woodford felt that the leapfrog Mercer promotion "was an aspersion upon his character." Then came a third blow and another tantrum: Woodford learned that Adam Stephen, colonel of the 4th Virginia, was also to be promoted brigadier over Woodford.

In summer 1776, Woodford penned a resignation letter to General Washington, signaling his umbrage at others' elevations. "I feel myself much hurt by the late promotion of my very worthy friend Col. Mercer. . . . I conceive of the appointment and promotion of an officer at the time serving under me . . . reflected dishonor upon myself." He added, "I am informed from good authority, that a similar promotion is now in contemplation in favor of Col. Adam Stephens [*sic*]. [I] request your permission to retire."[8] Woodford, however, remained in the Continental Army until early September, when he learned that Congress had finally decreed Stephen's promotion. Promotions over his head had now become "the final straw for Woodford; he resigned his commission in protest and returned to Caroline County," deduced biographer Michael Cecere.[9]

STORM CLOUDS OVER THE ENTIRE REVOLUTIONARY MOVEMENT

But other factors may have contributed to Woodford's resignation. In the fall of 1776, it appeared that the revolution would fail. The American army was in disarray after losses at Brooklyn, Kip's Bay, and Harlem Heights on Manhattan, and soon to include White Plains (October 28, 1776) and Fort Washington's surrender (November 16, 1776). Woodford learned of the further defeats when, in November

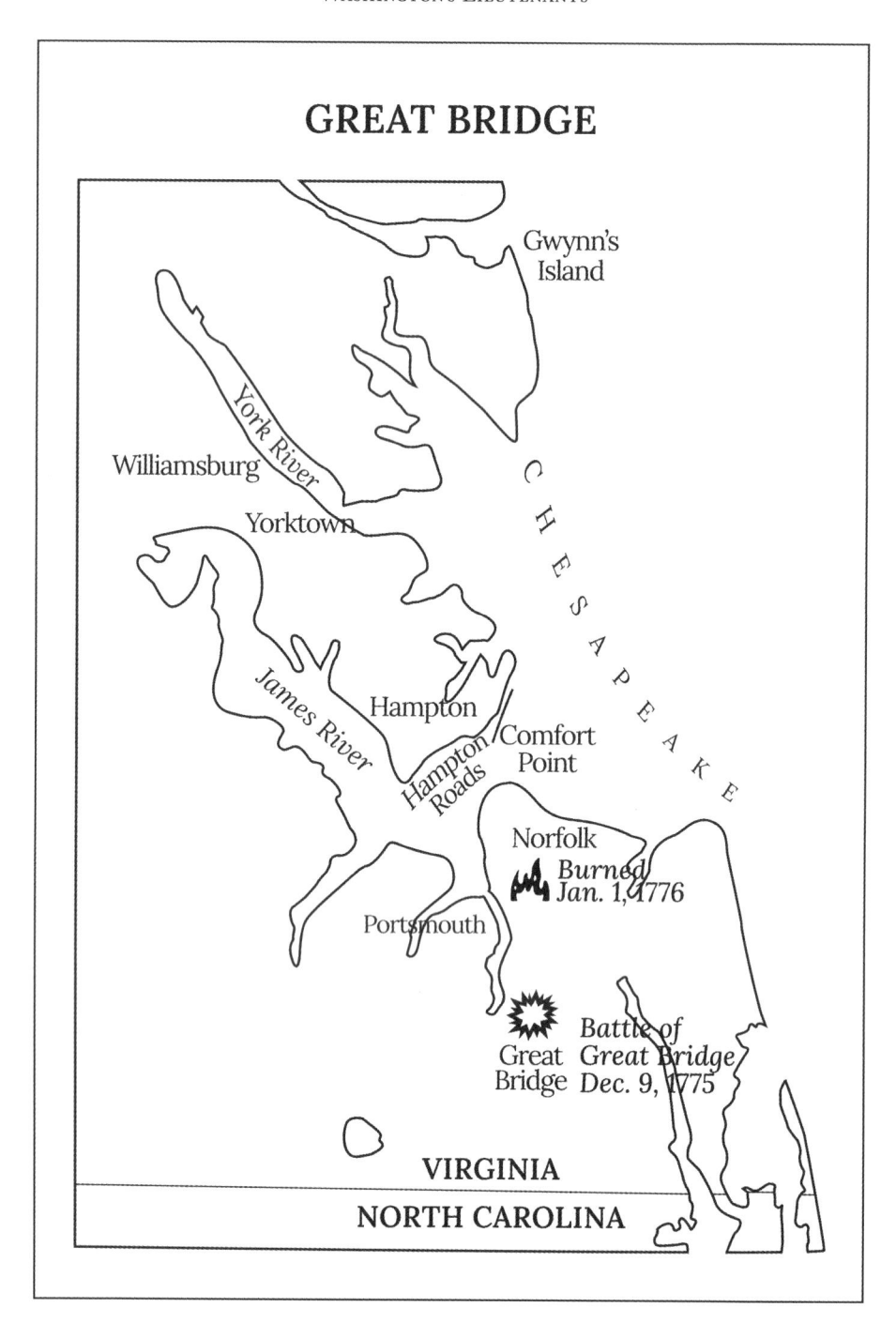

GREAT BRIDGE

Gwynn's
Island

York River

Williamsburg

Yorktown

C H E S A P E A K E

James River

Hampton

Hampton
Roads

Comfort
Point

Norfolk

Burned
Jan. 1, 1776

Portsmouth

Battle of
Great Bridge
Dec. 9, 1775

Great
Bridge

VIRGINIA

NORTH CAROLINA

1776, he rode north to deliver a letter from Washington's brother John Augustine to the general. In person, Woodford witnessed Washington's "Grand Army," having been chased out of New York, vastly diminished and fleeing across New Jersey. "Washington worried that his army might simply melt into nothingness," Ron Chernow wrote in *George Washington: A Life*.[10] General Washington wrote to another brother, Samuel, "I think that the game is pretty near up."[11]

A BETTER-KNOWN WOODFORD SNIT

Yet Woodford is perhaps best known for the additional umbrage he took when Congress listed Woodford as junior to ten other Virginia brigadiers, all (save Peter Muhlenberg) veterans of the French and Indian War.[12] In March 1777, Congress had promoted and then ranked the newly minted generals by seniority, ranking Virginia Generals George Weedon and Peter Muhlenberg over Woodford. Woodford protested. He had been in service longer than the two Virginians whom Congress ranked over him. "[B]ut the majority in Congress, citing Woodford's resignation from the army, placed him at the bottom of the list."[13]

Commander in Chief Washington urged Woodford to accept the seniority list, writing to Woodford, "You may recollect . . . that I strongly advised you against this resignation. I now as strongly recommend your acceptance of the present Appointment. You may feel somewhat hurt, in having two Officers placed before you . . . but remember that this is a consequence of your own Act."[14]

Woodford listened, accepted the promotion, and was back in harness by early May 1777, after an eight- to ten-month absence. General Washington gave Woodford command of a paper brigade consisting of the 3rd, 7th, 11th, and 15th Virginia regiments. The 11th (Col. Daniel Morgan), however, was elsewhere on special assignment, not under Woodford's command. The paper strength of Woodford's force was 3,000, but the brigade had only 999 men fit for duty.

The snits and fits of pique colonial officers such as Woodford (and Weedon and others—Muhlenberg, Sumner, Varnum, and so on—the list was lengthy) over promotions and orders of seniority, what historian Douglas Freeman referred to as "the clash of jealous and ambitious men," are astounding.[15] It is a wonder that these men were able to lead an army that ultimately prevailed. Noteworthy was George Washington's patience, demonstrated time and time again, in dealing with such matters. What an irritant it must have been for the commander to have to deal with such personnel issues when his hands and head were, and had to be, occupied with tactics, strategy, upcoming campaigns, logistics, constantly expiring enlistments, politics, and political interference by Congress's armchair generals.[16]

A VIRGINIA ELITE

Woodford's father was a British army major who, after resigning his commission, immigrated to America. William Senior built up the plantation Windsor, thirty miles northwest of Fredericksburg. Woodford Senior and his spouse had their first son, William, in 1734, followed by four other sons. In 1755, William Senior died suddenly when young William was twenty-one; William Junior became free to pursue his wanderlust. William organized a volunteer company to serve under Washington in the French and Indian War. Woodford spent the war at Fort Loudon (Winchester), where Washington made his rear headquarters.[17]

In the later 1750s, Woodford returned to Caroline County. There he married Mary Thornton, the daughter of George Washington's first cousin. He became a lieutenant colonel in the Caroline County Militia. Citizens elected him to the non-importation committee to enforce the boycott of British goods.[18] He became friends with Edmund Pendleton, first president of the Continental Congress (Woodford served as Pendleton's substitute at the Third Virginia Convention, July 17–August 9, 1775).[19] Woodford was "one of the planter class [who] adhered to the behavior of a southern gentleman."[20] Woodford also owned property in Fredericksburg. In June 1774, Fredericksburg citizens elected him to the Committee on Correspondence, formed as the winds of war blew stronger.[21]

On August 5, 1775, the Third Virginia Convention formally appointed William Woodford colonel, 2nd Virginia Regiment.[22] Patrick Henry's stirring speech at the Second Virginia Convention still rang true: "Is life so dear, or peace so sweet, as to be purchased at the price of chains and slavery? I know not what course others may take, but as for me, give me liberty or give me death!"[23] By that time (spring–summer 1775), through his civic leadership, Woodford had positioned himself for important posts in the coming war for independence.

WOODFORD AND THE 1777 CAMPAIGN

To recap, in May 1777 Woodford, like Lazarus, rose from the ashes after George Washington urged him to rejoin the army. As a brigadier, in command of a brigade, Woodford's actions revealed him to be a martinet. His first orders were to form standing boards of inquiry and a standing court for courts-martial.[24] His troops regarded their new commander's actions as a "shot across the bow." They, too, had heard the scuttlebutt about what had occurred after Great Bridge. "Woodford's efforts to install more discipline in his troops . . . hampered his efforts [at procuring reenlistments]. Many of his men refused to re-enlist under his command."[25] With enlistments expiring, Woodford harangued his men; a senior soldier told him, "They [the other soldiers] say they will only serve under Lt. Col. Scott [Woodford's second-in-command]."[26]

Troops took to calling the general "Beau Woodford" and the "Damndest Partial Rascal on the earth without exception." Historian Harry Ward wrote that Woodford "was not exactly a favorite with the men or the other Virginia generals."[27] In late 1779, Colonel John Neville wrote to General Daniel Morgan, "I am Sorry to inform you [General Woodford] is very Much Disliked in Particular by his Old Brigade." Neville speculated that a cause may have been Woodford's "long held belief in strict discipline."[28]

Renewed Combat: Brandywine

By September 1777, at Brandywine, Virginia Generals Woodford and Scott, now also a brigadier, with their brigades comprised Major General Adam Stephen's division. George Washington placed Stephen's division, Woodford and Scott included, in reserve, on a hill overlooking Brandywine Creek.

When General Washington finally became aware that British commanding general William Howe had split his force, thought unwise in standard military tactics and something that Washington had not anticipated, he acted. He saw that Cornwallis, several miles upstream and having forded two branches of the creek, could turn the Americans' right flank. Washington sent Stephen's division north to meet the challenge, later to be augmented by General John Sullivan with eleven hundred troops. "They [Woodford's troops] doggedly pushed forward . . . towards a hill overlooking the Birmingham Meeting House. [G]eneral Stephen deployed the troops upon a large, cleared field, just west of the Birmingham Road." They thus anchored the far-right flank of the new American line.[29]

Woodford's men performed admirably, but the day's praise went to Generals Weedon and Muhlenberg and their troops, who, at great personal cost, covered the frontline troops' withdrawal from the field as twilight approached. They had prevented Brandywine from being a larger disaster than it actually was.

At Brandywine, British musket fire struck Woodford in the left hand. He spent several weeks at the Moravian settlement in Bethlehem, Pennsylvania, where he recuperated with a wounded Marquis de Lafayette.

Another Rank and Seniority Imbroglio

In early 1778, Woodford was at Valley Forge, where his brigade, now consisting of four regiments, totaled 1,287 men. He spent much time revisiting the Virginia brigadiers' ranking, becoming monomaniacal about it. He was dissatisfied with his ranking as number three of four Virginia brigadiers (Weedon, Muhlenberg, Woodford, and Scott, in that order), as determined by Congress. Because Woodford had left the army for eight months, he garnered little sympathy. Nonetheless, Woodford kept at it. He petitioned Congress, got a board of review appointed, got a second board of review appointed after the first board did little, and finally procured the re-ranking for which he strove. Washington called in the generals' commissions, issuing new ones, with Woodford now senior to Muhlenberg and Scott, and Weedon ranked last.

Woodford had pushed and pushed. He would not be stopped until he obtained what he wanted, at a time when there was a war to fight. In addition, "Beau Woodford" was popular neither with the soldiers he commanded nor with his fellow officers. "Woodford had the reputation of being a dandy [always] dressed to the hilt."[30]

CHAPTER TWENTY-EIGHT

Monmouth Courthouse and Charles Town

In 1777, Lord Germain, secretary of state for America, had replaced Lord William Howe with Henry Clinton as the British forces' North America commander. In spring 1778, Lord Germain ordered Clinton to send five thousand troops to Canada and five thousand to the Caribbean, the latter to defend British sugar interests. With his forces so weakened, Clinton no longer felt he could continue Philadelphia's occupation.[1] In June 1778, the British abandoned the city, beginning the long trek diagonally across New Jersey to Sandy Hook, a spit jutting out into New York's outer harbor. There the army of ten thousand (along with hangers-on) would board transports for New York's inner harbor. Crossing New Jersey, the British army moved two miles per day, impeded by a baggage train several miles in length. The slow-moving caravan made a tempting target. Those events presaged the Battle of Monmouth Courthouse, the war's last major engagement in the mid-Atlantic colonies.

MONMOUTH

In June 1778, Washington led his army out of Valley Forge, journeying straight east, above Philadelphia, eventually to cross the Delaware River. Washington sent General Charles Scott with a brigade of handpicked light infantry ahead to harass the slow-moving British. Lafayette, with one thousand additional men, joined up with Scott. Ultimately, the advance guard swelled to five thousand Americans, nipping at the British's heels.

To recap from chapter 18, in a fit of petulance, brandishing his high rank, Charles Lee expressed to Washington dissatisfaction at not being in command of the army's forward contingent. In reply, "General Washington appeased [Lee] by sending him forward with yet another [advance] contingent of two brigades with instructions to take overall command of the advance guard" when Lee and his force caught up with Scott and Lafayette.[2]

Just short of Tennant's Meeting House, the British turned to face the Americans and engage. On a blistering hot June 28, 1778, the battle commenced; a local woman, Mary Ludwig ("Molly Pitcher"), standing among the American troops, passed them buckets of drinking water.

General Lee, though, ordered his troops to retreat. Washington, unaware of Lee's pullback, ordered a push forward on the American right flank by Nathanael Greene and William Woodford. With Lee's troops in retreat in the center, on the right, Greene's and Woodford's force constituted an exposed salient, its flanks unprotected.[3] With Greene and Woodford off to the right, "General Washington rode ahead of the main body." On reaching a forward position in the American center, "he discovered that his advance guard, which he believed was pushing the enemy, were actually withdrawing in disarray." Generally calm and collected, Washington flashed with anger. He "encountered General Lee on a small knoll . . . and demanded to know why Lee's troops were retreating. Lee, taken aback by Washington's angry tone, stammered, which Washington impatiently dismissed," ordering Lee to the rear.[4]

Unsupported on the side, Woodford's brigade nonetheless moved forward, to be met by swampy terrain. The swampy terrain and fading light made further advance difficult. The force retreated a short way to Comb's Hill, there unlimbering artillery pieces. "With the use of artillery, he [Woodford with his men] crushed the British army's left flank."[5] During the night, Clinton and his troops turned, resuming their march northeast.[6] The results of the fight, with six hundred American and seven hundred British casualties, indicated a draw, which amounted to a *de facto* American victory.[7]

FOR WOODFORD: NORTH, THEN SOUTH

In May 1779, Washington decided to send a force south to Charles Town, reinforcing the Southern Army there. General Benjamin Lincoln, who commanded the Charles Town defense, had requested reinforcement.[8] Early in 1780, British General Henry Clinton, with an eight-thousand-man force, had left New York, their ships landing infantry near the Savannah River mouth. An advance British force that previously had occupied Savannah marched overland eighty miles north to Charles Town, first crossing the Savannah River, the Georgia–South Carolina boundary. Coming north, the Clinton-led British force wheeled to the right, advancing in a southeasterly direction, down the peninsula on which Charles Town sits at the tip, nestled between the Cooper and Ashley Rivers. Two-thirds of the way down the peninsula, the British force halted to prepare "parallels" to overcome the American fortifications strung along the peninsula's width, including a wide and deep ditch. Meanwhile, south of the city, British men-of-war blockaded the entrance to the Charles Town harbor, preparing to bombard the city.

Woodford's Role

In December 1779, George Washington ordered Woodford and his brigade south.[9] In March, "We arrived . . . to the great joy of the garrison."[10] "We" meant Woodford, two thousand troops, and six brass cannons. A short time later, Washington sent General Charles Scott south to Charleston with additional soldiers. On April 6, 1780, "[t]he bells pealed joyously, with people celebrating as a relief column of 750 soldiers from North Carolina and Virginia arrived."[11] Washington had intended to send General Peter Muhlenberg, but Muhlenberg, reluctant to serve under Woodford, resisted. Muhlenberg still disputed Woodford's advance in seniority over himself and the way Woodford had achieved it.[12]

In Charles Town, General Lincoln's councils of war urged him to quit the city. Some rank-and-file citizens condemned the Southern Army's continued presence, saying that "[Lincoln's] strategy will send us all to our graves" because of continuing British bombardment if patriot forces remained. "General Washington is in favor of withdrawing," others said.[13] By contrast, pressured by the city fathers to stay, Lincoln dallied. Then the dreaded Banastre Tarleton and his green-coated cavalry smashed the American cavalry, cutting off the sole escape route the Americans had left. General Clinton reinforced the position Tarleton had cleared north of the city, along the Cooper River, with two thousand men.[14] Escape from the besieged city was no longer an option.

Serving the British, Hessian Captain Hinrichs wrote of the dire American position: "All their cavalry was annihilated. Our works come up to their ditch [the defensive moat the Americans had flooded]. Fort Moultrie [on Sullivan's Island] and the entire harbor were in our hands. They could not entertain the least hope of succor."[15]

On May 11, 1780, General Benjamin Lincoln accepted British General Henry Clinton's terms of capitulation, no terms offered, with formalities to be concluded the following day, May 12. Fifty-six hundred American troops, twenty-six hundred Continental regulars, and three thousand militia surrendered, fenced in by British forces that now numbered twelve thousand.[16] The British put American prisoners in densely packed barracks and on prison ships in Charles Town harbor. They imprisoned American officers across the Cooper River, at Haddrell's Point. The officers would remain there until the British offered them parole or the prisoner and his representative could engineer an exchange for a British officer of equal rank.[17]

The British did not act with alacrity. With the capture of both Savannah and Charles Town ("Pearl of the South"), the two major coastal cities, the British felt they had the keys to the American South on their belt, so they could act at leisure. Later, the British impression was reinforced by Lord Cornwallis's overwhelming victory over Horatio Gates and the American Southern Army at Camden, South Carolina, on August 16, 1780.

Woodford's Slow, Lengthy Demise

Imprisoned at Charles Town, Woodford could arrange neither exchange nor parole. In stark confinement, he languished. The British refused to provide adequate food supplies to Haddrell's Point on the grounds that the officers were inflating the prisoner count. Among the officers, Generals James Hogun from North Carolina and Woodford of Virginia suffered diseases that eventually proved fatal.[18]

> *Yellow fever broke out. . . . [T]here was a lack of medicine. Without hard money [the officers] found it almost impossible to make purchases. Haddrell's Point . . . seemed a land of desolation—a "flat country" where the water was not fit to drink and "the soil is nothing but sand which burns the flat of the foot and blinds one when the wind blows." The pine trees give no shade.*[19]

In autumn 1780, the British shipped William Woodford to New York. History does not reveal from what illness Woodford suffered. Probably the British continued his imprisonment aboard a British prison ship in the East River's Wallabout Bay. There, while still in captivity, William Woodford died, the date of death given as November 13, 1780. The British buried him in Trinity Churchyard, on Broadway at the foot of Wall Street. A partial epitaph read, "The fatigues of the siege, in which he bore a very active part, together with the mortification of becoming a prisoner, and the rigorous confinement he suffered, proved too much for his delicate condition. [He] fell a cheerful sacrifice to his country's glorious cause."[20]

Postscript: Barbaric Imprisonment of American Soldiers

The British jailers were cruel, regarding the Americans as traitors, rebels against the Crown. Captured Americans were criminals rather than prisoners of war and were treated accordingly. Further, American troops were "clodhoppers" to whom the British owed not even common courtesy. No greater inhumanity toward prisoners may be found than the British prison ships in the East River, where General Woodford endured barbarous captivity. The East River extends north and south, with one exception. After the Brooklyn Bridge and Manhattan Bridges and Vinegar Hill, the river turns east for a mile, bordered by the now defunct Brooklyn Navy Yard.[21] The notch created by the irregular Brooklyn shoreline is Wallabout Bay.

In Wallabout Bay, the British anchored demasted, rotting hulks of men-of-war. There they imprisoned more than one thousand men per ship. The prisoners were crammed "into lower decks reeking of urine, excrement, and vomit with little ventilation owing to sealed gunports." Mortality rates approached 100 percent "from scurvy, dysentery, and typhus." Food and water were nonexistent. "Malnourishment, as a consequence of fetid water and scarce provisions, was rampant, as were rats and mosquitos."[22]

One estimate is that 11,500 Americans perished at Wallabout Bay, another 18,000. British warders threw corpses overboard.[23] In contrast, on the American side, in the entire war 6,800 men perished in combat.[24] For decades, bones of deceased prisoners washed up on Brooklyn's shores or worked to the surface of sand landfill extending the navy yard.

Barbarous conditions such as these hastened William Woodford's death. The prison ships and British treatment of prisoners are the most shocking legacies of the Revolutionary War.[25]

Part XI

Thomas Conway

Chapter Twenty-Nine

Sedition Afloat

Thomas Conway was Irish born and advanced to the rank of colonel in the French army's Irish Brigade. He then procured from the Continental Congress commissions as a brigadier and later as a major general. He was a "black Irishman," a descendent of Spanish sailors shipwrecked on Irish shores after the British had vanquished the Armada in 1588.[1] However, Conway was not an Irish resident for long. In the mid-eighteenth century, when he was a young boy, his family moved to France. There Conway grew to maturity. Retaining his English fluency, Conway became multilingual.

Searching for Fame

When the Revolutionary War broke out in America, like many others, the English-speaking Conway sought adventure and glory.[2] He journeyed across the Atlantic. From the Continental Congress, Conway wrangled a brigadier's commission. For the next two years he served in the Pennsylvania Continental Line, leading a brigade at Germantown in October 1777.

History remembers Conway primarily, perhaps solely, as a principal in the plot to replace George Washington with General Horatio Gates, now enshrined as the Conway cabal. One view, perhaps a revisionist one, looks on Conway as "a vain, whiny weasel . . . generally disliked." The view of Conway that survives is as "one of the Revolution's most notorious goats."[3]

Earliest Negatives

George Washington "took a violent dislike to [Conway] . . . for reasons not altogether clear."[4] Or was it easily understandable? Washington took a dislike to many foreign appointments, at least over the heads of his battle-tested colonels and other senior officers who had endured countless hardships in service to the cause.[5] Perhaps, to top off his dislike for Conway, Washington also knew that from his earliest days in America, an ungrateful Brigadier Conway had wheedled and lobbied for a second promotion, to major general, without battlefield exploits to justify such a promotion and without consulting the commander in chief. Congress granted Conway the promotion in October 1777. Congress had leapfrogged Conway over twenty-three battle-hardened brigadier generals, many (perhaps all) of whom Washington knew personally.[6] Congressman Richard Henry Lee reported that Washington "regarded Conway as a braggart and a mediocre general."[7]

Among his other negative attributes, Conway "was an indiscrete letter writer."[8] That characteristic began both the cabal and the makings of its downfall. James Lender finds that before a Conway letter, the earliest "origins of the cabal were murky at best."[9]

PERHAPS NOT SO MURKY

In late October 1777, Colonel James Wilkinson, a Gates aide, carried a report of victory at Saratoga in upstate New York to York, Pennsylvania, where the Continental Congress was sitting, seventy miles west of British-occupied Philadelphia. Wilkinson was playing a key role in carrying out a Gates political gesture designed to bypass the chain of command, thereby currying favor with the Congress and simultaneously embarrassing Gates's superior, George Washington. Wilkinson stopped for the night in Reading, Pennsylvania, where he spent the evening eating and drinking in a tavern with General William Alexander's (Lord Stirling's) aides. "In the course of a brimmingly pleasant evening, Wilkinson informed Major [William] McWillaims, aide to Lord Stirling, of a gossipy letter General Conway had written to Gates. McWilliams confided it to Lord Stirling, who forwarded the Conway letter to Washington."[10] The gossipy letter (neither the original nor a copy of which has ever been found) was one "extolling [Gates's] generalship in effusive terms."

Then, as General Alexander reported to Washington, the Conway letter "took a swipe at General Washington." Lord Stirling quoted the derogatory lines as having said, "Heaven has been determined to save your [Gates's] Country; or a weak General and bad Councellors [sic] would have ruined it."[11] This was the last straw. Seeking a promotion to major general over the heads of senior brigadiers confirmed a widespread view of Conway as a self-promoting pest. "Conway had become a major thorn in Washington's side. It was *enough*. [T]he chief's vaunted patience ended. At last he would counterattack."

THE RESPONSE

On November 4, Washington wrote a brief missive directly to General Conway, repeating the offending sentence, with nothing more, and signing the letter, "I am

Sir Yr Hble Svrt."[12] On November 16, in a response to General Washington, Conway mounted a lengthy, obsequious defense, with Conway informing Washington that he had asked Congress to accept his resignation. With France entering the war, Conway stated that he wished to return to his home country to reassume a position in the French army.[13]

WASHINGTON LEAVES CONWAY TWISTING IN THE WIND

Taking note of Conway's resignation but not, however, accepting it, Washington informed the disgraced Conway that the Continental Congress would need to act to accept the resignation. Almost simultaneously, Mifflin and Gates, acting as the Board of War and working at cross purposes, appointed Conway inspector general of the army, rehabilitating him, or so it seemed. Moreover, in the newly created position, Conway would have reporting responsibilities to the board rather than to the commander in chief.[14]

With his new commission as inspector general in hand, Conway showed up at Valley Forge early in 1778. "Washington's reception was colder still."[15] A reason was that in addition to Conway's self-promotion, Conway had written Washington an obsequious explanation for his actions in promoting Gates and criticizing the commander in chief. In the letter explaining his seeming disloyalty, Conway turned snarky, penning "a sarcastic comparison of Washington to Frederick the Great," which Washington took "as a calculated affront."[16] A fair appraisal was that, as a sophisticated European, Conway thought the over-the-top, tongue-in-cheek comparison to Frederick the Great was one that he could put over on someone (Washington) he regarded as a colonial rube.

With multiple reasons for his growing dislike of Conway, Washington announced "that he would issue no orders in cooperation with any steps Conway might attempt to initiate. [W]ashington had effectively stiff-armed the [new] inspector general."[17] After several days at Valley Forge, Conway returned to York, where he conferred with Thomas Mifflin.

CONWAY'S FURTHER DOWNFALL

Congress did not act on Conway's offer to resign until April or May 1778. Then, in summer 1778, in Philadelphia, Pennsylvania, Militia General John Cadwallader accused Conway of cowardice at the Battle of Germantown. Conway "dropped a glove," challenging Cadwallader to a duel. The two men and seconds met outside Philadelphia on July 4, 1778. They chose pistols as weapons for the face-off. "Cadwallader fired first. [H]is shot smashed into Conway's cheek. The wound to [Conway's] mouth was terrible but not fatal."[18]

Unrepentant, Cadwallader broadcast, "I've stopped the damned rascal's tongue anyhow."[19] A staunch acolyte of Washington, Cadwallader had led troops at Trenton, Princeton, and elsewhere.[20] A disfigured Conway underwent a long, slow recuperation and healing, leaving him markedly scarred. Afterward he returned to France, fading into obscurity. His rise and fall were compressed into a short time span, but the legacy he left behind ranks him as an intentionally egotistical, seditious, and disloyal officer, on the list only slightly below Benedict Arnold. Of General Washington's major generals, Thomas Conway certainly ranks last.

Chapter Thirty

Final Thoughts and Conclusions

OVER TIME, MANY OF THE MAJOR GENERALS' REPUTATIONS HAVE BECOME SACRO-sanct, as untouchable as if they were preserved in amber. Those reputations, however, do not always accord with historical reality, as this book attempts to demonstrate. Arthur St. Clair and Thomas Mifflin certainly are in this group, political accolades obscuring their abject failures as military leaders. During the years when the new nation governed itself as a collection of former colonies under the Articles of Confederation, first Mifflin and later St. Clair became president. They did not serve as presidents of the country, for there was no such office, but rather as presidents of the Congress, Mifflin from November 1783 to early June 1784 and St. Clair from February to early November 1787. The fact that in the 1780s members of Congress elected Mifflin and then St. Clair whitewashed all that had occurred previously. Then as now, members of Congress had short memories. Mifflin's and St. Clair's elections followed from false narratives that the two men had been able leaders and courageous fighters.

A few biographies are closer to the mark, reflective of reality (or at least probable truth). Those accounts have remained constant over the centuries. Four of the other generals—Stephen, Lee, Gates, and Conway—are in that group, regarded over time and coming down to us as disloyal or subverted by vice. No subsequent events have blurred those fundamental shortcomings, including long-lasting and egregious conflicts of interest (Stephen), cowardice (Gates), drunkenness (Stephen), arrogance (Stephen, Lee, Gates, and Conway), and disloyalty (Conway and Lee). Certainly there were no "butterfly minds" in the group: all had backgrounds, intelligence, and capacity for leadership. Yet the misuse of those talents, along with their innate faults, have remained sufficient to continue condemning them.

Major General Robert Howe stands alone. His womanizing and fondness for drink became scandalous, causing his loss of the Southern Army command. His attempted defense of Savannah demonstrated a lack of military acumen. After

General Washington ordered him north, however, Howe redeemed himself. His accomplishment of several difficult missions that Washington assigned him reflect belated professional growth and accomplishment.

The paradox is that the men to whom Congress gave the senior leadership positions, the major generals, on whom it was incumbent to pursue victory in the Revolution, faded rather quickly. Several—especially the seven discussed in this book—engaged in active wrongdoing. They were "bent trees in the forest." Only two of the twenty-three American generals on whom the politicians bestowed the senior rank steadfastly led men through the course of the war. The service of Generals Nathanael Greene and Benjamin Lincoln alone fits that description.

For the most part, along with Commander in Chief George Washington, the brigadier generals won the war. Thirteen died in combat or from combat-related causes. As a group and as individuals, they were "tall trees in the forest." This book includes the stories of Hugh Mercer, Peter Muhlenberg, and William Davidson to support the "tall trees" hypothesis. Lest the assertion be given universality, though, the book recounts the story of one other, William Woodford, who represents a mixed bag—but Woodford was one of the brigadiers who died in service to his country. Otherwise, the brigadiers' pantheon is crowded, including Lachlan McIntosh (Georgia), William Moultrie (South Carolina), Francis Nash (a North Carolina brigadier who died in combat), Charles Scott (Virginia), Joseph Warren (a Massachusetts physician killed at Bunker Hill), Enoch Poor (killed by a junior French officer in a duel growing out of Poor's charge of insubordination at Monmouth), and John Stark (New Hampshire) (we are victorious, "or Molly Stark sleeps a widow tonight").

Among Revolutionary War leaders, an interesting factoid—a geographic one—concerns the leaders' heritages. Not even a majority were of English stock, contrary to popular belief. Instead, most were Scottish, Irish, or Welsh (twenty-two of the thirty-eight about whom information exists), with several others having French, Swiss, or Dutch roots.[1] Irishmen, Scots, and Welshmen or their ancestors had been under English thumbs for generations. Many shared the sentiments of rank-and-file colonists, resenting English heavy-handedness. In the British Isles, the English severely restricted land acquisition, lodging title to vast tracts in English hereditary peers. In the 1640s, Cromwell, the Lord Protector, commissioned English as lords throughout Ireland, masters of the Irish people and Irish lands. Irish towns lost their traditional names and were rechristened with English names. Birr in County Offaly became Parsons Town, named for the ruling English lord. Cobb, the port town for Cork, became Queenstown (although upon Irish independence it reverted to its Irish name).

Another misleading impression that persists, and indeed grows stronger, is the notion that political leaders were our nation's sole founders, or the politicians helped by a few outliers. For instance, in *The Virginia Dynasty*, historian and former Second Lady Lynne Cheney chronicles "four presidents"—Washington, Jefferson, Madison, and Monroe—"who led a revolution and created a nation."[2] Cheney makes no mention of the military leaders who fought, historical figures who also can lay claim to having "led a revolution and created a nation."[3] The late Winston Groom's historical work *The Patriots* is the same, naming Alexander Hamilton, Thomas Jefferson, and John Adams as the "founding brothers."[4] Pulitzer finalist Professor H. W. Brands, in *Our First Civil War*, mainly writes about Ben Franklin, reprising his book *The First American: The Life and Times of Benjamin Franklin*, sprinkled with quotations from George Washington and John Adams.[5] Brands omits any mention of the men who fought the war. Current historical books call for recognition of pamphleteer Thomas Paine, physician Benjamin Rush, and Boston revolutionary Samuel Adams, to name several of the outliers, as additional founding fathers.[6]

A recent volume that argues for adding a seventh, eighth, or ninth founding father is Brooke Barbier's *King Hancock: The Radical Influence of a Moderate Founding Father* (2023).[7] In her introduction of a historical figure known primarily for his florid signature (a "John Hancock"), Barbier wrote, "[T]here is always a danger that an overfamiliar narrative will rehearse the heroics of a few great men at the expense of others now overlooked or undervalued despite the crucial role they played."[8] Biographies of "the heroics of a few great men" confine themselves to the politicians who spent the war in comfortable lodgings, eating three meals and imbibing a good bit of drink every day. Little mention is given to the "overlooked and undervalued" men who carried the war to the enemy.

On that side of the ledger, the seven major generals criticized in this book at times endured hardships and served well. They were bent, not broken.

Notes

Chapter 1—Overview

1. Quoted in Rick Atkinson, *The British Are Coming: The War for America, Lexington to Princeton, 1775–1777*, at 550 (New York: Henry Holt, 2019).

2. See, for example, Joseph M. Waterman, *With Sword and Lancet: The Life of General Hugh Mercer*, at 156–58 (Richmond, VA: Garrett & Massie, 1941). See also chapters 8 and 9.

3. See, for example, chapter 14 (Brigadier William Lee Davidson) and chapters 22–23 (Brigadier Peter Gabriel Muhlenberg). See generally Douglas Branson, *Southern Brigadier Generals in the Revolutionary War* (Jefferson, NC: McFarland, 2024) (of eighteen generals chronicled, seven died, eleven were wounded, and ten were captured and held by the British as prisoners of war).

4. See Henry Augustus Muhlenberg, *The Life of Major-General Peter Muhlenberg, of the Revolutionary Army*, appendix, at 454–55 (Philadelphia: Carey & Hart, 1849). Author Muhlenberg counted fifty-eight brigadiers, but three on his list (John De Haas of Pennsylvania and John Cadwallader, also of Pennsylvania, twice) refused to accept their commissions as brigadiers.

5. They were Richard Montgomery of New York, Daniel Wooster of Connecticut, Hugh Mercer of Virginia, Enoch Poor of New Hampshire, Francis Nash of North Carolina, William Woodford of Virginia, Casmir Pulaski of Poland, and James Hogan of North Carolina. Muhlenberg, *Life of Major-General Peter Muhlenberg*, at 454–55.

6. John Thomas expired from smallpox as he led the retreat from the disastrous American attempt to take Quebec in 1775. A foreign general, Major General Johann von Robais, Baron De Kalb, died leading the American right wing at the Battle of Camden, South Carolina, on August 16, 1780. He died three days after the battle, a devastating American defeat. He had at least eleven saber, bayonet, and bullet wounds. David Lee Russell, *The American Revolution in the Southern Colonies*, at 172 (Jefferson, NC: McFarland, 2000); John Buchanan, *The Road to Guilford Courthouse*, at 167 and 172 (New York: Wiley & Sons, 1997).

7. One foreign major general, Baron Johann De Kalb, was killed in action at Camden South Carolina. See, for example, chapter 17.

8. Hilary Mantel, quoted in Mark G. Spencer, "A Shock to the System," review of Stacy Schiff, *The Revolutionary: Samuel Adams*, *Wall Street Journal*, October 8, 2022, at B-1, B-2.

9. Artemas Ward of Massachusetts, Philip Schuyler of New York, Israel Putnam of Connecticut, William Heath of Massachusetts, Joseph Spencer of Connecticut, John Sullivan of New Hampshire, Alexander McDougal of New York, and Thomas Conway of Ireland.

William Smallwood of Maryland resigned in January 1781, and Samuel Holden Parsons of Connecticut in July 1782. Compilation by the author.

10. Mark Edward Lender, *Cabal: The Plot Against General Washington*, at 55 (Yardley, PA: Westholme, 2019).

11. Two foreign volunteers (ultimately awarded major general commissions), Marquis de Lafayette of France and Friedrich Wilhelm von Steuben of Prussia, also remained in service until the war's end. Both European major generals were present for Lord Cornwallis's surrender at Yorktown in October 1781. Washington never permitted a third foreign volunteer, Philippe Charles Tronson du Coudray, whom the Continental Congress commissioned a major general, to command in the field. The Congress also handed out major general commissions to Baron Johann De Kalb (killed in action at Camden, South Carolina) and Louis Lebeque Duportail (France).

12. See Ken Alder, *Engineering the Revolution: Arms and Enlightenment in France* (Chicago: University of Chicago Press, 2010).

13. See https://fr.wikipedi.org/wiki/Philippee_Hubert_Prudhomme_de_Borre (accessed February 16, 2022).

14. Robert P. Broadwater, "General Roche de Fermoy," in *American Generals of the Revolutionary War: A Biographical Dictionary* (Jefferson, NC: McFarland, 2007).

15. His name also is forever linked to a plot (some say just a few letters and some idle thoughts but not a plot) to replace George Washington with Horatio Gates or Conway himself. The Conway cabal is described in Lender's *Cabal: The Plot Against General Washington*.

16. Douglas S. Freeman, *George Washington*, vol. 4, at 594 (Washington, DC: Library of Congress, 1949). See also Worthington Chauncey Ford, *Journals of the Continental Congress*, vol. 10, at 63 (1937; London: Forgotten Books, 2014).

17. George Washington was "incensed to learn about [Irishman Thomas] Conway's impending promotion" to major general, Ron Chernow wrote. The Continental Congress was set to and did award a promotion whereby Conway "would be jumped over twenty more senior [and American] brigadiers." Ron Chernow, *George Washington: A Life*, at 317 (New York: Penguin, 2010).

18. H. W. Brands, *The First American: The Life and Times of Benjamin Franklin*, at 535 (New York: Doubleday, 2000) (description of supplicants to Benjamin Franklin, who collected "[a] small army of young men—some not so young—[who] besieged [him] seeking commissions in the American army").

19. Chernow, *George Washington: A Life*, at 205.

CHAPTER 2—BANNED FROM COMBAT DUTY

1. See R. W. Dick Phillips, *Arthur St. Clair: The Invisible Patriot*, at 29, 60, 66, 135, 187, and 291 (Bloomington, IN: iUniverse, 2014).

2. Phillips, *Arthur St. Clair*, at ix (quoting Joseph Dooley, professor of history, Ohio University).

3. Phillips, *Arthur St. Clair*, at 127 (Congress further directed that the army court-martial St. Clair, but it was never convened).

4. Formed by the Northwest Ordinance of 1787, today the territory has become the states of Ohio, Michigan, Indiana, Illinois, Wisconsin, and a smallish part of Minnesota. "Northwest Territory," http://www.britannica.com/northwest/territory (accessed May 22, 2023). See also

David McCullough, *The Pioneers: The Heroic Story of the Settlers Who Bought the American Ideal West* (New York: Simon & Schuster, 2000).

5. See generally Patrick Feng, "The Battle of the Wabash: The Forgotten Disaster of the Indian Wars" (2021), https://www.Armyhistory.org (accessed June 10, 2022). See also Alan D. Graff, *Field of Corpses and the Death of the American Army* (Brentwood, TN: Knox Press, 2023). Custer's last stand, officially the Battle of Little Bighorn, in 1876, involved the loss of 268 officers and soldiers, with 55 wounded, 6 of whom later died, falling far short of the losses at the Battle of a Thousand Slain. See generally Gregory J. W. Urwin, "The Battle of the Little Bighorn," https://www.britannica.com/event/Battle-of-the-little-bighorn (accessed October 17, 2023).

6. See, for example, Dean Snow, *1777: Tipping Point at Saratoga*, at 45 (New York: Oxford University Press, 2016).

7. Phillips, *Arthur St. Clair*, at 5.

8. Phillips, *Arthur St. Clair*, at 29.

9. See, for example, "Average Height in England in the Early Eighteenth Century," https://www.epub.ub.uni.menchen.de/572/1/european_heights_in_the_early_eighteenth_century (accessed June 10, 2022).

10. Ron Chernow, *George Washington: A Life*, at 21 (New York: Penguin, 2010).

11. Portrait by Revolutionary War artist John Trumbull, New York Metropolitan Museum of Art, https://www.metmuseum.org/art/collection/search/12820 (accessed June 16, 2022).

12. Stephen R. Taaffe, *Washington's Revolutionary War Generals*, at 43, 84 (Norman: University of Oklahoma Press, 2019) (promotion to brigadier, personal characteristics).

13. Purchase rather than merit was the means of obtaining a commission in a British regiment. Horatio Gates (chapter 19), who also came to North America to fight in the French and Indian War, similarly purchased his commission (Phillips, *Arthur St. Clair*, at 5–6). Ensign was then the lowest officer rank in British forces. Today, of course, at least in the United States, only the navy has retained the ensign rank.

14. Phillips, *Arthur St. Clair*, at 29, 35.

15. See, for example, Emory G. Evans, *Thomas Nelson and the Revolution in Virginia*, at 28 (Williamsburg, VA: Virginia Bicentennial Commission, 1978): "[M]ost [Virginians] had little or no military experience." Professor Evans was chair, Department of History, University of Maryland.

16. Phillips, *Arthur St. Clair*, at xiii.

17. See, for example, chapters 16 and 18 (Lee) and 19 and 20 (Gates).

18. See Douglas Branson, *Southern Brigadier Generals in the Revolutionary War*, at 67–68 (Jefferson, NC: McFarland, 2024). Generals Andrew Pickens, William Davidson, Henry Laurens, Francis Marion, and Isaac Huger had fought in the Cherokee Wars.

19. See, for example, Richard V. Polhemus and John F. Polhemus, *Stark: The Life and Wars of John Stark*, at 43–79 (Delmar, NY: Black Dome Press, 2014).

20. After a short interval, Washington no longer chose his senior officers or controlled promotions. Indeed, the Continental Congress arrogated this task to itself, in the process expressly ignoring or overriding Washington's recommendations. See Taaffe, *Washington's Revolutionary War Generals*, at 17 ("Congress chose subordinate generals") and 43 (congressional promotion of Joseph Spencer to major general "despite Washington's dislike").

21. See "Fredericksburg Masonic Lodge No. 4," https://masoniclodge4.org/history (accessed June 14, 2022).

22. See generally M. Baigent, R. Leigh, and H. Lincoln, *Holy Blood, Holy Grail* (New York, Dell, 2005); Robert Brydon, *The Guild, the Masons, and the Rosy Cross* (Jacksonville, FL: Grand Lodge of Florida, 2012).

23. See generally James Webb, *Born Fighting: How the Scots-Irish Shaped America* (New York: Random House, 2011).

24. Vermont was the fourteenth state admitted to the union, in 1791.

25. The distance from Albany, New York, to Montreal is 198 miles.

26. Phillips, *Arthur St. Clair*, at 82.

27. Cf. John Boyd, *Mad Anthony Wayne*, at 33–34 (New York: Scribner & Sons, 1929): "St. Clair, who had service for the king in common with [Horatio] Gates, was being favored for his experience with military routine . . . though he had done nothing at Three Rivers other than running a snag through his foot."

CHAPTER 3—CREDIT WAS NOT DUE

1. Recounted in Isaac Makos, "The Surrender of Fort Ticonderoga," https://www.battle fields.org/fort_ticonderoga (accessed June 9, 2022).

2. Stephen R. Taaffe, *Washington's Revolutionary War Generals*, at 104 (Norman: University of Oklahoma Press, 2019).

3. See Mark Puls, *Henry Knox: Visionary General of the American Revolution*, at 140, 145–47, 195, 210, and 234–37 (New York: Palgrave Macmillan, 2008).

4. Dean Snow, *1777: Tipping Point at Saratoga*, at 9 (New York: Oxford University Press, 2016). Other works refer to the hill as Mount Defiance. See, for example, John Boyd, *Mad Anthony Wayne*, at 38 (New York: Scribner & Sons, 1929).

5. Boyd, *Mad Anthony Wayne*, at 34.

6. Compare Makos, "Surrender of Fort Ticonderoga" (British force of eight thousand) with Snow, *1777*, at 380 (nine thousand). When the British later surrendered, in October 1777, Burgoyne's "shrunken army" numbered fifty-eight hundred. Snow, *1777*, at 207. Burgoyne's force also included approximately three hundred women.

7. Snow, *1777*, at 18.

8. Makos, "Surrender of Fort Ticonderoga," at 2.

9. R. W. Dick Phillips, *Arthur St. Clair: The Invisible Patriot*, at 118 (Bloomington, IN: iUniverse, 2014).

10. Phillips, *Arthur St. Clair*, at 125–27.

11. Taaffe, *Washington's Revolutionary War Generals*, at 232, 238.

12. Taaffe, *Washington's Revolutionary War Generals*, at 227.

13. Taaffe, *Washington's Revolutionary War Generals*, at 235.

14. Phillips, *Arthur St. Clair*, at 119, 65.

15. Some 250 years later Fort Ticonderoga stands intact, in good condition. Indeed, it is a New York State Park. See https://www.fortticonderoga.org (accessed June 16, 2022).

16. Taaffe, *Washington's Revolutionary War Generals*, at 84.

17. See, for example, Admiral Sandy Woodward, *Memoirs of the Falkland Island British Group Commander* (Annapolis, MD: Naval Institute Press, 1992).

18. See Rick Atkinson, *The British Are Coming: The War for America, Lexington to Princeton, 1775–1777*, at 514–17 (New York: Henry Holt, 2019). Cf. Phillips, *Arthur St. Clair*, at 87 (two thousand troops).

19. Phillips, *Arthur St. Clair*, at 104.

20. See Phillips, *Arthur St. Clair*, at 101.

21. Atkinson, *British Are Coming*, at 525.

22. Taaffe, *Washington's Revolutionary War Generals*, at 69 (council of war following Trenton "to discuss the army's response to the all-out British assault" of Cornwallis's troops).

23. "[H]istorians have admitted that strategic military planning did not happen to be one of Washington's strong suits. . . . It was, however, a primary strength of St. Clair, a talent that he repeatedly demonstrated . . . during 1775, 1776 and 1777." Phillips, *Arthur St. Clair*, at 102.

24. After Trenton, Washington had taken his army back across the Delaware to spend a few days recharging. The army then recrossed the Delaware once more, camping below Trenton.

25. Phillips, *Arthur St. Clair*, at 103.

26. See Douglas Branson, *Southern Brigadier Generals in the Revolutionary War* (Jefferson, NC: McFarland, 2024), chapter 17, at 124 and 127–28.

27. Robert Beale, quoted in Dennis P. Ryan, "Robert B. Memoirs," in *A Salute to Courage: The American Revolution as Seen Through the Wartime Writings of Officers of the Continental Army and Navy*, at 56 (New York: Columbia University Press, 1979).

28. See "Continental Army Generals: Charles Scott," *RevWarTalk*, http://www.revwartalk .com/charles-scott, at 4 (accessed May 9, 2020).

29. Michael Cecere, *Second to No Man but the Commander in Chief: Hugh Mercer, American Patriot*, at 143–46 (Second Battle of Trenton generally) (Berwyn Heights, MD: Heritage, 2015).

30. Phillips, *Arthur St. Clair*, at 109–10.

31. Gerald M. Carbone, *Nathaniel Greene: A Biography of the American Revolution* (New York: St. Martin's Press, 2010). See also Taaffe, *Washington's Revolutionary War Generals*, at 70: "[Arthur St. Clair] knew that there was a road around the British left flank. He suggested the Americans use it to slip away." After discussion, the council of war, with one dissenter, "endorsed it."

32. "When Brig. Gen. Arthur St. Clair learned that rain had rendered officers' weapons useless, he responded, 'You have nothing for it but to push on and charge.'" Quoted in James Wilkinson, *Memories of My Own Times*, vol. 1 (Philadelphia, PA: Abraham Small, 1816), cited in Taaffe, *Washington's Revolutionary War Generals*, at 68.

33. Recounted in Atkinson, *British Are Coming*, at 525.

34. After the battle, General Washington detailed Colonel George Weedon and his men to conduct the 919 Hessian prisoners captured at Trenton to Philadelphia, thirty-five miles away. See generally Harry W. Ward, *Duty, Honor or Country: General George Weedon and the American Revolution*, at 75 (Philadelphia: American Philosophical Society, 1979).

Chapter 4—St. Clair's Generalship: Battle of a Thousand Slain

1. See generally David McCullough, *The Pioneers: The Heroic Story of the Settlers Who Bought the American Ideal West*, at 14ff. (New York: Simon & Schuster, 2019).

2. McCullough, *Pioneers*, at 11 (Putnam and Tupper).

3. See https://www.google maps.com/Marietta/Ohio (accessed June 9, 2022). Generals Butler, Scammel, Warren, and Wooster died in the war because of wounds suffered in combat.

4. McCullough, *Pioneers*, at 57.

5. R. W. Dick Phillips, *Arthur St. Clair: The Invisible Patriot*, at 164 (Bloomington, IN: iUniverse, 2014).

6. Phillips, *Arthur St. Clair*, at 178.

7. See generally Charles River and Colin Fluxman, *Little Turtle's War: The History and Legacy of the 18th Century Conflict between the United States and Native Americans in the Northwest* (Audible Books, 2020); Calvin M. Young, *Little Turtle (Me-she-kin-no-quah): The Great Chief of the Miami Indian Nation* (CreateSpace, 2014); Alan D. Graff, *Field of Corpses and the Death of the American Army* (Brentwood, TN: Knox Press, 2023).

8. McCullough, *Pioneers*, at 87.

9. Phillips, *Arthur St. Clair*, at 183.

10. Recounted in Mark Puls, *Henry Knox: Visionary General of the American Revolution*, at 303 (New York: Palgrave Macmillan, 2008).

11. See Patrick Feng, "The Battle of the Wabash: The Forgotten Disaster of the Indian Wars," https://www.amhistroy.org/the/battle_of_the_Wabash (accessed June 8, 2022).

12. Many Americans believe that the 1876 Battle of the Little Bighorn, also known as Custer's Last Stand, represents the most lopsided Native American conquest of US troops. See chapter 2, note 5. In that engagement, the Seventh Cavalry suffered 268 killed and 55 wounded, 6 of whom later died, compared with 919 US troops slain on the Wabash River. See also https://en.wikipedia.org/wiki/Battle_of_the_Little_Bighorn (accessed June 18, 2022).

13. See generally Feng, "Battle of the Wabash."

14. Phillips, *Arthur St. Clair*, at 190.

15. Phillips, *Arthur St. Clair*, at 185, 190, and 203.

16. See Mayo Clinic, *Family Health Guide*, 2nd ed., at 916 (New York: William Morrow, 1996): the discomfort of a gout attack "will subside generally over the next 1 or 2 weeks, leaving the [affected] joint normal and pain free."

17. Phillips, *Arthur St. Clair*, at 184 and 193.

18. Phillips, *Arthur St. Clair*, at 189.

19. Phillips, *Arthur St. Clair*, at 256.

20. Phillips, *Arthur St. Clair*, at 199.

21. Phillips, *Arthur St. Clair*, at 187 and 204.

22. Phillips, *Arthur St. Clair*, at 189.

23. Phillips, *Arthur St. Clair*, at 200.

24. Phillips, *Arthur St. Clair*, at 172 and 199.

25. Phillips, *Arthur St. Clair*, at 194.

26. An example gives flesh to the idea of total responsibility. While officer of the deck (OOD), a junior officer has command when a US man-of-war runs aground. The ensuing court of inquiry may hold him or her (probably) responsible or not responsible (the author served in the US Navy from 1965 to 1972). At the inquiry, the young OOD may point a finger at the ship's navigator, alleging that the chart the navigator provided lacked accurate water depth information (or any information at all). But whether the court finds the OOD or the navigator at fault or not (or both), the court always will hold the ship's captain responsible, even though he may have been sound asleep in his cabin.

Chapter 5—A Second Scottish Physician

1. See generally Serena Zabin, *The Boston Massacre: A Family History* (New York: Houghton Mifflin Harcourt, 2019).

2. Harry M. Ward, *Major General Adam Stephen and the Cause of American Liberty*, at x (Charlottesville: University of Virginia Press, 1989).

3. Ward, *Major General Adam Stephen*, at 161.

4. Quotation from Lauren Wilkinson, *American Spy*, at 68 (New York: Random House, 2019).

5. George Washington, quoted in Ron Chernow, *George Washington: A Life*, at 128 (New York: Penguin, 2010).

6. Ernest Randolph Trice, "Adam Stephen: Virginia Physician, Soldier of Misfortune," *Virginia Medical Journal* (July 1980): 470, 471.

7. Ward, *Major General Adam Stephen*, at 4, quoting Adam Stephen.

8. At least one source gives Stephen's birthdate as 1718 rather than 1721. See Dallas B. Sharpe, "Adam Stephen," in *The West Virginia Encyclopedia*, December 8, 2015, https://www.wvencylopedia,org/articles/587 (accessed March 11, 2020).

9. See generally Michael Cecere, *Second to No Man but the Commander in Chief: Hugh Mercer, American Patriot* (Berwyn Heights, MD: Heritage Books, 2015); Joseph M. Waterman, *With Sword and Lancet: The Life of General Hugh Mercer* (Richmond, VA: Garrett & Massie, 1941).

10. Ward, *Major General Adam Stephen*, at 4–5.

11. See generally Fred Anderson, *Crucible of War: The Seven Years' War and the Fate of Empire in British North America, 1754–1763*, at 42–54 (New York: Vintage, 2001). The French and Indian War is also known as the Seven Years' War.

12. Described in Robert Lisle, "The Court Martial of Adam Stephen, Major General, Continental Army," *Madison College Bulletin* 30, no. 3 (1972): 33–34.

13. Charles H. Ambler, *Washington and the West*, at 89–90 (Whitefish, MT: Kessinger, 2010).

14. See, for example, H. W. Brands, *The First American: The Life and Times of Benjamin Franklin*, at 247 (New York: Doubleday, 2000).

15. Walter Isaacson, *Benjamin Franklin: An American Life*, at 166 (New York: Simon & Schuster, 2004).

16. Edward Braddock, quoted in Isaacson, *Benjamin Franklin*, at 167.

17. See Anderson, *Crucible of War*, at 86–107 (chapter 8, "Braddock Takes Command," and chapter 9, "Disaster on the Monongahela").

18. See generally David L. Preston, *Braddock's Defeat: The Battle of Monongahela and the Road to Revolution* (New York: Oxford University Press, 2015).

19. Interview with Andrew Masich, president & CEO, Senator John Heinz History Center, History Center of Western Pennsylvania, Pittsburgh, PA, February 13, 2010.

20. Ward, *Major General Adam Stephen*, at 43.

21. Ward, *Major General Adam Stephen*, at 42–43.

22. Letter of September 6, 1758, quoted in Ward, *Major General Adam Stephen*, 43 (spelling and capitalization converted).

CHAPTER 6—BUSINESS OVER GENERALSHIP

1. These included the Cherokee Wars referenced in the text and the expedition against tribes in the Ohio Territory, known also as Pontiac's War (1763). See generally Robert Lisle, "The Court Martial of Adam Stephen, Major General, Continental Army," *Madison College Bulletin* 30, no. 3 (1972): 34.

2. Letter from Lewis Ourry to British Colonel Henry Bouquet, August 27, 1763, quoted in Harry Ward, *Major General Adam Stephen and the Cause of American Liberty*, at 84 (Charlottesville: University of Virginia Press, 1989).

3. Ward, *Major General Adam Stephen*, at 90.

4. See generally H. R. McIlwaine, *Legislative Journals of the Convention of Virginia*, vol. 3, at 1334 (Richmond, VA, 1918–1919; republished, New York: Wentworth Press, 2016).

5. He and other veterans could not receive title to those lands until they had had them surveyed, a task difficult to achieve in territory still populated by hostile Native Americans.

6. Max W. Grove, *Reconstructed Census of Berkeley County, Virginia*, at 13 (Colesville, MD: Eastern West Virginia Press, 1970).

7. Stan Cohen, *Historic Springs of Virginia*, at 132–33 (Charleston, WV: Pictorial History Publishing, 1981).

8. Ward, *Major General Adam Stephen*, at 96. Stephen had one additional military episode in the interval between wars. In 1774, Stephen and Andrew Lewis led a twenty-seven-hundred-man force, including one thousand Virginia volunteers, and split into two divisions to quell the Native American villages and tribes in Ohio. Lewis and his division proceeded down the Ohio River, where they fought the Indians at the Battle of Point Pleasant, the point at which West Virginia's principal river, the Kanawha, flows into the Ohio. After the battle, great Shawnee chief Cornstalk sued for peace. Stephen had led his division overland toward south central Ohio and did not see appreciable action. See generally chapter 17.

9. Samuel K. Fore, "Adam Stephen," https://www.mountvernon.org/library/digital-en cyclopedia/artivle/adam-stephen/ (accessed March 11, 2020). Washington won the election "but was piqued and had a long memory." Gene Procknow, "Drunken or Deserter—The Case of Major General Adam Stephen," July 26, 2017, https://www.geneprock.com/2017/07/26 /drunken-or-deserter-the-case-of-major-general-adam-stephen/ (accessed March 12, 2020).

10. Willis F. Evans, *History of Berkeley County* (Martinsburg, WV: n.p., 1928).

11. See Charles R. Lingley, *The Transition in Virginia from Colony to Commonwealth*, at 97 (1910; New York: Legare Street Press, 2021).

12. Ward, *Major General Adam Stephen*, at 117.

13. Ward, *Major General Adam Stephen*, at 131.

14. Ward, *Major General Adam Stephen*, at 123.

15. Cf. Rick Atkinson, *The British Are Coming: The War for America, Lexington to Princeton, 1775–1777*, at 193 (New York: Henry Holt, 2019) (seven new regiments).

16. Ward, *Major General Adam Stephen*, at 133.

17. Historical accounts overstate Stephen's role in Dunmore's War. "Together [General Charles Lee and Adam Stephen] forced British Governor to flee to his Royal Navy ships and prevented a loyalist insurgency," Gene Procknow wrote in "Drunken or Deserter," at 1.

18. Atkinson, *British Are Coming*, at 190–93 and 345–46. Fleeing from Williamsburg, Dunmore had recruited Blacks to his little army, promising them their freedom. "A grisly sight [on Gwynn's Island] were the dead and dying blacks strewn along a path for two miles. Small-pox had taken a heavy toll among Dunmore's 'Ethiopian Brigade.' . . . [H]undreds of blacks had died." Inoculation vastly reduced the whites' exposure to the dread disease, but Dunmore had denied inoculation to the African Americans.

19. Atkinson, *British Are Coming*, at 193.

20. Benjamin Rush to Congressman Richard Henry Lee, December 21, 1776, quoted in Stephen R. Taaffe, *Washington's Revolutionary War Generals* (Norman: University of Oklahoma Press, 2019).

21. See generally Charles H. Lessler, *The Sinews of Independence: Monthly Strength Reports of the Continental Army*, at 43 (Chicago: University of Chicago Press, 1976).

22. Trice, "Adam Stephen," at 472. See also Fore, "Adam Stephen," at 3 (recording the incident as having occurred on the previous day).

23. See Samuel S. Smith, *The Battle of Princeton*, at 8–15 (Monmouth Beach, NJ: Philip Freneau Press, 1967).

24. See generally "Largely Forgotten: Brigadier Andrew Lewis of Virginia," in Douglas Branson, *Southern Brigadier Generals in the Revolutionary War: Eighteen Commandeers Instrumental in the America's Victory* (Jefferson, NC: McFarland, 2024).

25. Ward, *Major General Adam Stephen*, at 160–61.

26. Ward, *Major General Adam Stephen*, at 161.

CHAPTER 7—EGREGIOUS SINS

1. The British forces' bases were at Perth Amboy, twenty miles to the southeast, and across Arthur Kill, on Staten Island, straight east of Perth Amboy.

2. Leonard Lundin, *Cockpit of the Revolution: The War for Independence in New Jersey*, at 222–25 (1972; New York: Legare Street Press, 2023).

3. Samuel K. Fore, "Adam Stephen," https://www.mountvernon.org/library/digital-encyclopedia/artivle/adam-stephen/ (accessed March 11, 2020), at 3.

4. Adam Stephen to John Sullivan, June 4, 1777, quoted in Harry M. Ward, *Major General Adam Stephen and the Cause of American Liberty*, at 175 (Charlottesville: University of Virginia Press, 1989).

5. Samuel Adams to Richard Henry Lee, July 22, 1777, quoted in Ward, *Major General Adam Stephen*, at 177.

6. "Adams often pictured himself as a soldier." In early 1776, Adams had written to Abigail, "Oh, that I was a soldier." With war on the horizon, "[h]e was reading military books." David McCullough, *John Adams*, at 28 (New York: Simon & Schuster, 2001).

7. Gene Procknow, "Drunken or Deserter—The Case of Major General Adam Stephen," July 26, 2017, https://www.geneprock.com/2017/07/26/drunken-or-deserter-the-case-of-major-general-adam-stephen/, at 1 (accessed March 12, 2020). Of course, at Brandywine both General George Weedon and General Peter Muhlenberg demonstrated gallantry and bravery, as did the Virginian troops they commanded; after the battle, their actions were lauded as the brightest points in an otherwise "overwhelming defeat."

8. Ward, *Major General Adam Stephen*, at 185.

9. Harry M. Ward, *Duty, Honor or Country: George Weedon and the American Revolution*, at 106 (Philadelphia: American Philosophical Society, 1979) ("the most Horrid fog I ever saw").

10. See, for example, Procknow, "Drunken or Deserter," at 1–3.

11. While leading a newly created corps of light infantry, General William Maxwell of New Jersey similarly had been drunk, allegedly evidencing cowardly behavior on Maxwell's part. See, for example, Don Higginbotham, *Daniel Morgan: Revolutionary Rifleman*, at 78–79 (Williamsburg, VA: Omohundro Institute of Early American History and Culture, 1979). A subsequent court-martial acquitted Maxwell.

12. Henry Augustus Muhlenberg, *The Life of Major-General Peter Muhlenberg, of the Revolutionary Army*, at 112 (Philadelphia: Carey & Hart, 1849).

13. Ward, *Major General Adam Stephen*, at 188.

14. Ward, *Major General Adam Stephen*, at 189.

15. See, for example, chapter 3.

16. Letter from Adam Stephen to Benjamin Rush, Lyman H. Butterfield, *Letters of Benjamin Rush*, vol. 2, at 1120 (Princeton, NJ: University of Princeton Press, 1951); Procknow, "Drunken or Deserter," at 1.

17. James Madison, quoted in James Thomas Flexner, *George Washington: The Forge of Experience*, at 300 (Boston: Little, Brown, 1965). See also H. W. Brands, *The First American: The Life and Times of Benjamin Franklin*, at 499 (New York: Doubleday, 2000).

18. Quoted in Robert Lisle, "The Court Martial of Adam Stephen, Major General, Continental Army," *Madison College Bulletin* 30, no. 3 (1972): 37.

19. For instance, in a letter to several of his squabbling generals, Washington wrote, "Let us all be a band of brothers and rise superior to every injury whether real or imaginary and persevere in the arduous but glorious struggle in which we are engaged until peace and independence are secured to our country." George Washington to Anthony Wayne, September 6, 1780, quoted in Stephen R. Taaffe, *Washington's Revolutionary War Generals*, at 210 (Norman: University of Oklahoma Press, 2019).

20. Ward, *Major General Adam Stephen*, at 201.

21. Benjamin Rush, quoted in Edward G. Lengel, *General George Washington: A Military Life*, at 300 (New York: Random House, 2005).

22. Paul David Nelson, "Lee, Gates, and Stephen: Revolutionary War Generals in the Lower Shenandoah Valley," *West Virginia History* 37, no. 3 (1976): 185.

23. Albert Louis Zambone, *Daniel Morgan: A Revolutionary Life*, at 12 (Yardley, PA: Westholme, 2018) ("Morgan sought, from the very beginning, to get ahead in colonial Virginia").

24. Ward, *Major General Adam Stephen*, at 100.

CHAPTER 8—YET ANOTHER SCOTTISH PHSICIAN

1. See generally Rand McNally, Inc., *2022 Road Atlas*, at 129–36 (Chicago: Rand McNally, 2022) (compilation by the author). Counties are in Illinois, Kentucky, New Jersey, Ohio, Pennsylvania, Virginia, and West Virginia.

2. Dating from the nineteenth century and named for Hugh Mercer's probable descendents, Thomas and Asa Mercer, early Seattle pioneers. See Mercer Island Historical Society, "Mercer Island History," available at http://www.mercerislandhistory.org (visited March 12, 2025).

3. See Historical Monuments Data Base, "Mercer Monuments," available at http://www.hmdb.org/results/hugh-mercer (visited March 11, 2025). Monuments are in Fredericksburg, Virginia; Mercer County, New Jersey; Princeton, New Jersey; National Park, New Jersey; and Philadelphia, Pennsylvania's Laurel Hill Cemetary.

4. See, for example, Geoffrey Plank, *Rebellion and Savagery: The Jacobite Rising and the British Empire* (Philadelphia: University of Pennsylvania Press, 2005).

5. See John T. Goolrick, *The Life of General Hugh Mercer*, at appendix A (1906; Hungerford, UK: Legare Street Press, 2022). Mercer's mother was Ann Munro. "Revolutionary War Biography: Hugh Mercer," http://www.battlefields.org/learn/biographies/hugh-mercer, at 1 (accessed July 6, 2020).

6. "Revolutionary War Biography: Hugh Mercer," at 2.

7. See Stuart Reid, *Culloden Moor 1746: The Death of the Jacobite Cause* (Oxford: Osprey, 2002); Reid, *Like Hungry Wolves: Culloden Moor 16 April 1746* (London: Windrow & Greene, 2000).

8. Cf. Michael Cecere, *Second to No Man but the Commander in Chief: Hugh Mercer, American Patriot*, at 3 (Berwyn Heights, MD: Heritage Books, 2015), listing Mercer as an assistant surgeon's mate.

9. Additionally, in return for loyalty oaths to the Crown, the king not only granted pardons but also bestowed grants of American land on a group of Highland Scots. They settled, forming a colony, on the Cape Fear River in southeastern North Carolina. Throughout the Revolution, the Scottish enclave remained loyalist, thoroughly Tories. See Joe E. Mobley, *North Carolina Governor Richard Caswell: Founding Father and Revolutionary Hero*, at 51–53 (Charleston, SC: The History Press, 2016).

10. The area was the site of Fort Chambers (now Chambersburg, Pennsylvania), which founder Benjamin Chambers built for protection against Indian raids. See Waterman, *With Sword and Lancet*, at 8–9.

11. Author Cecere records Mercer as practicing in the same general vicinity, along Conocoheague Creek, but in Cumberland County, abutting Franklin County to the east (seat: Carlisle).

12. See, for example, H. W. Brands, *The First American: The Life and Times of Benjamin Franklin*, at 161 (New York: Doubleday, 2000) (in the Quaker-dominated Pennsylvania Assembly, "[t]here remained an uneasiness with war and war preparations, especially when they entailed expense and risk"); Walter Isaacson, *Benjamin Franklin: An American Life*, at 123 (New York: Simon & Schuster, 2004) (when in 1747 Benjamin Franklin tried to organize a militia "in response to ongoing threats by the French and their Indian allies . . . [the] Assembly, dominated by pacifist Quakers, dithered and failed to authorize any defenses").

13. See also chapter 14.

14. Quoted in Francis Packman, *Montcalm and Wolfe*, at 195 (1884; New York: Wentworth Press, 2019).

15. Waterman, *With Sword and Lancet*, at 20.

16. Kittanning, which still exists, today is the seat of Armstrong County, Pennsylvania.

17. Cecere, *Second to No Man*, at 15.

18. Henry Wadsworth Longfellow, *The Song of Hiawatha* (1855).

19. Cecere, *Second to No Man*, at 14.

20. Waterman, *With Sword and Lancet*, at 30.

21. New York *Mercury*, October 4, 1756.

22. See generally Cecere, *Second to No Man*, at 8–16.

23. Roughly, US 30 ("the Lincoln Highway") today.

24. Waterman, *With Sword and Lancet*, at 38.

25. See Israel D. Rupp, *Early History of Western Pennsylvania*, at 97 (Los Angeles: Hard-Press, 2019).

26. See "Revolutionary War Biography: Hugh Mercer," at 2–3 (George Washington, Hugh Mercer, George Weedon, William Woodford, Fielding Lewis, Thomas Posey, Gutavus Wallace, and Marquis de Lafayette).

27. "Revolutionary War Biography: Hugh Mercer," at 3.

28. Waterman, *With Sword and Lancet*, at 71. And, as many other immigrants did, Mercer bought land, several thousand acres of agricultural land, lots in the town of Fredericksburg, purchased jointly with George Weedon, and Ferry Farm, where George Washington had been born and his mother had lived before moving to Fredericksburg proper. Mercer, who had emigrated from Scotland, where arable land and buildable sites were precious, found Virginia expansive, the land inexpensive. Coming from a background of privation, Mercer gobbled up raw land, as did others of newly found means in America.

29. George Weedon, as quoted in part in Waterman, *With Sword and Lancet*, at 91.

30. John T. Goolrick, *Historic Fredericksburg*, at 33 (Richmond, VA: Whittel & Shepperson, 1922). See also chapter 10 (distinctions between county and district militias).

31. See *William & Mary Quarterly* 5 (1948): 249.

CHAPTER 9—"GIVE ME LIBERTY OR GIVE ME DEATH"

1. Ron Chernow, *George Washington: A Life*, at 281 (New York: Penguin, 2010).

2. Militia Colonel Robert Byrd to Colonel Henry Bouquet, on Mercer's tenure in the Virginia Militia, quoted in Joseph Waterman, *With Sword and Lancet: The Life of General High Mercer*, at 38 (Richmond, VA: Garrett & Massie, 1941). See also Bouquet Papers, 211, Pennsylvania Archives, Philadelphia, Pennsylvania.

3. Waterman, *With Sword and Lancet*, at 56.

4. Michael Cecere, *Second to No Man but the Commander in Chief: Hugh Mercer, American Patriot*, at 53 (Berwyn Heights, MD: Heritage Books, 2015).

5. Cecere, *Second to No Man*, at 63.

6. See "Revolutionary War Biography: Hugh Mercer," at 3, http://www.battlefields.org/learn/bioraphies/hugh-mercer (accessed July 6, 2020).

7. Alfred Thayer Mahan, *The Influence of Sea Power upon History: 1660–1783* (Boston: Little, Brown, 1890).

8. General Hugh Mercer to General George Washington, July 29, 1776, quoted in Waterman, *With Sword and Lancet*, at 111.

9. For example, in August 1776, Mercer sent Smallwood's Marylanders, a battalion of Pennsylvania riflemen, and a battalion of Pennsylvania militia north to General Washington, then superintending defense of Brooklyn and Long Island. See, for example, Waterman, *With Sword and Lancet*, at 83.

10. "Revolutionary War Biography: Hugh Mercer," at 4.

11. Cf. Waterman, *With Sword and Lancet*, at 134 (2,634 officers and men surrendered). Following defeats at Long Island, White Plains, and elsewhere, General Washington had given Nathanael Greene a discretionary order regarding Fort Washington, a fateful decision that resulted in Greene's attempt to retain the fort, leading to the complete surrender. This was an event that Greene lamented for the remainder of his career.

12. General Hugh Mercer to General George Washington, September 17, 1776, quoted in Waterman, *With Sword and Lancet*, at 128.

13. See, for example, Cecere, *Second to No Man*, at 104–5.

14. Reproduced in Stephen Fried, *Rush: Revolution, Madness, and the Visionary Doctor Who Became a Founding Father*, at 233 (New York: Crown Books, 2018). See also Harlow Giles Unger, *Benjamin Rush: The Founding Father Who Healed a Wounded Nation* (New York: Da Capo Press, 2018).

15. General Hugh Mercer to Colonel Durkee et al., reproduced in William S. Stryker, *The Battles of Trenton and Princeton*, at 379 (1898; Trenton, NJ: Old Barracks Association, 2001).

16. Quoted in Isaac Greenwood, *The Revolutionary Service of John Greenwood*, at 39 (1922; New York: Legare Street Press, 2022).

17. John Greenwood, of General John Sullivan's division, quoted in *Revolutionary Service of John Greenwood*, at 41.

18. Stryker, *Battles of Trenton and Princeton*, at 318. Over the course of the Revolutionary War, the petty princes of German states, particularly Hesse and Brunswick, and also Hanover, hired out to the British thirty thousand soldiers.

19. Quoted in William M. Dwyer, *The Day Is Ours: An Inside View of the Battles of Trenton and Princeton, November 1776–January 1777*, at 219 (New Brunswick, NJ: Rutgers University Press, 1998).

20. Waterman, *With Sword and Lancet*, at 149, 151.

21. Stryker, *Battles of Trenton and Princeton*, at 394, quoting General Lord Stirling to New Jersey Governor Robert Livingston.

22. See generally David Hackett Fischer, *Washington's Crossing* (New York: Columbia University Press, 2004).

23. Quoted in Colonel James Wilkinson, *Memoirs of My Own Times*, vol. 1, at 146 (Philadelphia: Abraham Small, 1816).

24. Waterman, *With Sword and Lancet*, at 154.

25. Cecere, *Second to No Man*, at 154–55.

26. Waterman, *With Sword and Lancet*, at 153–54.

27. Benson J. Lossing, *Pictorial Field Book of the Revolution*, at 29 (Philadelphia, 1860).

28. Ron Chernow, *George Washington: A Life*, at 281 (New York: Penguin, 2010). Historical accounts differ, although the differences amount to no more than a distinction without a difference. In another account, General Washington sent Mercer and his men as an advance party to secure the bridge at Stony Brook, which spans the Princeton Turnpike nearer Princeton than Trenton. The Mercer contingent left camp at one o'clock, in advance of the main American army.

29. "Revolutionary War Biography: Hugh Mercer," at 4–5. A reproduction of the tree is the seal of Mercer County, New Jersey.

30. Benjamin Rush, *A Memorial Containing Travels through Life of Sundry Incidents in the Life of Dr. Benjamin Rush*, at 98 (Philadelphia: Louis Biddle, 1905).

31. General Hugh Mercer, quoted in George Washington Parke Custis, *Recollections and Memoirs of Washington*, at 13 (Richmond, VA, 1860).

32. Waterman, *With Sword and Lancet*, at 159.

33. Inscription on the General Hugh Mercer Monument, Fredericksburg, Virginia.

34. Barbara Tuchman, *A Distant Mirror: The Calamitous 14th Century*, at 571 (New York: Ballantine Books, 1978), eulogizing the French Baron de Coucy.

CHAPTER 10—A PHILANDERER?

1. Ebenezer Hazard, "A View of Coastal South Carolina in 1778," *South Carolina Historical Magazine* 73 (1972): 189; Marquis de Chastellux, *Travels in North America in 1780 & 1781*, vol. 1, at 111 (Chapel Hill: University of North Carolina Press, 1963).

2. David K. Wilson, *The Southern Strategy: Britain's Conquest of South Carolina and Georgia*, at 67 (Columbia: University of South Carolina Press, 2005).

3. Charles E. Bennett and Donald R. Lennon, *A Quest for Glory: Major General Robert Howe and the American Revolution*, at 154 (Chapel Hill: University of North Carolina Press, 1991).

4. John Buchanan, *The Road to Guilford Courthouse: The American Revolution in the Carolinas*, at 128 (New York: John Wiley and Sons, 1997).

5. Stephen R. Taaffe, *Washington's Revolutionary War Generals*, at 82 (Norman: University of Oklahoma Press, 2019).

6. Taaffe, *Washington's Revolutionary War Generals*, at 182.

7. Taaffe, *Washington's Revolutionary War Generals*, at 184.

8. Wilson, *Southern Strategy*, at 67.

9. Quoted in Wilson, *Southern Strategy*, at 67.

10. Bennett and Lennon, *Quest for Glory*, at 7.

11. See Bennett and Lennon, *Quest for Glory*, at 7, 147 (quotation), 153.

12. Hugh Rankin, *The North Carolina Continentals*, at 18 (Chapel Hill: University of North Carolina Press, 1991).

13. See generally Bennett and Lennon, *Quest for Glory*, at 1–7.

14. Janet Schaw, *Journal of a Lady of Quality; Being the Narrative of a Journey to the West Indies and North Carolina in the Years 1774–1776*, at 142 (New Haven, CT: Yale University Press, 1939).

15. South Carolina had a markedly smaller Regulator-like movement. As David Russell explains, though, "[t]he basis of the conflict" in South Carolina was "much like it was for its northern neighbor . . . and was centered in the difference between the Lowcountry and Upcountry regions." Russell expands: "In the Lowcountry were the aristocracy with their plantations, their capital their Charles Town, slaves, rice and indigo crops, Anglican religion, wealth, and a heritage of English peoples." By contrast, "[t]he Upcountry was populated with small farmers, of moderate means and [with] few slaves, from Scotch-Irish and German families with some English. . . . These people were poorly educated and lacked the social standing of the Tidewater Lowcountry populace." David Lee Russell, *The American Revolution in the Southern Colonies*, at 22 (Jefferson, NC: McFarland, 2000).

16. Wilson, *Southern Strategy*, at 21 (Columbia: University of South Carolina Press, 2005), describes colonial North Carolina as comprised of three sections: the tidewater, the piedmont, and the frontier. "[T]he piedmont or backcountry [was] a vast, relatively flat inland region between the tidewater and the mountains." The mountain region was "almost entirely patriot." Other regions were mixed.

17. Wilson, in *Southern Strategy*, defines the Regulator movement through a description of its causes: "[C]itizens felt neglected by the tidewater-dominated legislatures. Lawlessness was rampant in the backcountry, and yet the problem was ignored by those in power on the coast." In addition, "[t]he backcountry settlements bore the brunt of keeping the Indian nations in check—something the backcountry settlers felt the tidewater elites failed to appreciate." *Southern Strategy*, at 21.

18. Russell, *American Revolution in the Southern Colonies*, at 19. See also Hugh Owen Nash Jr., *Patriot Sons, Patriot Brothers*, at 16 (Nashville, TN: Westview, 2006): in 1764, "[a] group of North Carolina insurgents began to protest abuses of power by public officials and what was considered to be 'the ruling class' in North Carolina."

19. Marjoleine Kars, *Breaking Loose Together: The Regulator Rebellion in North Carolina*, at 159 (Chapel Hill: University of North Carolina Press, 2002).

20. William Stevens Powell, *The War of Regulation and the Battle of Alamance, May 16, 1771*, at 17 (Raleigh: North Carolina Department of Archives and History, 1957).

21. Nash, *Patriot Sons*, 27.

22. Kars, *Breaking Loose Together*, at 199–203.

23. Powell, *War of Regulation*, at 34; Mobley, *North Carolina Governor*, at 34.

24. One historian, David Russell, peered more deeply, coming to regard Tryon as a tyrant:

North Carolina's political landscape had been damaged by the tyrannical administration of Governor Tryon. His oppressive regime had created an atmosphere that . . . fostered the Reg-

ulator Movement throughout the western counties of the Carolinas. . . . [But] hatred of the English tyrant had the effect of nurturing the seeds of discontent in the colony and served the idea of independence well.

Russell, *American Revolution in the Southern Colonies*, at 43.

25. William L. Saunders, *Colonial Records of North Carolina*, vol. 10, at 96 (Raleigh, NC: 1886–1890).

26. Bennett and Lennon, *Quest for Glory*, at 27–28.

27. See Michael Cecere, *General William Woodford of Virginia, Revolutionary War Patriot*, at 59 (Berwyn Heights, MD: Heritage Books, 2019).

28. The title of chapter 4 in Cecere, *General William Woodford of Virginia*, at 57. The Battle of Bunker Hill took place on June 17, 1775.

29. Future chief justice John Marshall was present as a member of the Culpepper Militia, in which his father, Thomas Marshall, was a senior officer. Justice Marshall described the conflict in John Marshall, *The Life of George Washington*, vol. 2, at 132ff. (Fredericksburg, VA: Citizens Guild, 1926).

30. William S. Powell, *North Carolina Through Four Centuries*, at 192 (Chapel Hill: University of North Carolina Press, 1989).

31. Russell, *American Revolution in the Southern Colonies*, at 64.

32. Russell, *American Revolution in the Southern Colonies*, at 64.

33. See Harry M. Ward, *Major General Adam Stephen and the Cause of American Liberty*, at 133 (Charlottesville: University of Virginia Press, 1989).

34. Six were promoted: John Armstrong (Pennsylvania), William Thomas (Pennsylvania), Andrew Lewis (Virginia), James Moore (North Carolina), William Alexander aka Lord Stirling (New Jersey), and Robert Howe. See Taaffe, *Washington's Revolutionary War Generals*, at 29.

35. See generally Rick Atkinson, *The British Are Coming: The War for America, Lexington to Princeton, 1775–1777*, at 324ff. (New York: Henry Holt, 2019).

36. Alexander Garden, *Anecdotes of the American Revolution, Illustrative of the Talents and Virtues of Heroes and Patriots*, at 7 (Charleston, SC: Miller, 1828).

37. C. L. Bragg, *Crescent Moon over Carolina: William Moultrie & American Liberty*, at 87 (Columbia: University of South Carolina Press, 2013) ("the other two being Saratoga and King's Mountain").

38. As a result of the 1776 victory, "the state now had [a] new symbol—the palmetto tree—an emblem that would endure as a central element of the state seal and the state flag." E. Stanley Godbold Jr. and Robert H. Woody, *Christopher Gadsden and the American Revolution*, at 160–61 (Knoxville: University of Tennessee Press, 1982).

Chapter 11—Howe's Downward Spiral

1. Quoted in Harvey H. Jackson, *Lachlan McIntosh and the Politics of Revolutionary Georgia*, at 118 (Athens: University of Georgia Press, 1979).

2. Jackson, *Lachlan McIntosh*, at 111.

3. Stephen R. Taaffe, *Washington's Revolutionary War Generals*, at 184 (Norman: University of Oklahoma Press, 2019).

4. Charles E. Bennett and Donald R. Lennon, *A Quest for Glory: Major General Robert Howe and the American Revolution*, at 56 (Chapel Hill: University of North Carolina Press, 1991).

5. "Muhlenberg himself suffered all his life from the consequences of disease contracted on the futile Georgia-Florida campaign." Edward W. Hocker, *The Fighting Parson of the American Revolution: A Biography of General Peter Muhlenberg*, at 52–53 (Mechanicsburg, PA: Sunbury Press, 1936).

6. See generally Bennett and Lennon, *Quest for Glory*, at 72–75.

7. Bennett and Lennon, *Quest for Glory*, at 79.

8. Bennett and Lennon, *Quest for Glory*, at 81.

9. Bennett and Lennon, *Quest for Glory*, at 83.

10. Bennett and Lennon, *Quest for Glory*, at 51.

11. Taaffe, *Washington's Revolutionary War Generals*, at 132 (New York's Alexander McDougall and Howe promoted to major general on October 20, 1777).

12. "[A] basic tenet of the revolutionary movement [was] that each state should provide logistical support for it own Continental forces." Bennett and Lennon, *Quest for Glory*, at 67.

13. See Taaffe, *Washington's Revolutionary War Generals*, at 184.

14. Robert Howe to South Carolina's Henry Laurens, October 9, 1778, Laurens Papers, Letterbook No. 16, at 104 (College of Charleston, South Carolina Historical Society, Charleston, SC).

15. David Lee Russell, *The American Revolution in the Southern Colonies*, at 101 (Jefferson, NC: McFarland, 2000).

16. See, for example, Taaffe, *Washington's Revolutionary War Generals*, at 210.

17. David K. Wilson, *The Southern Strategy: Britain's Conquest of South Carolina and Georgia*, at 69 (Columbia: University of South Carolina Press, 2005).

18. Quoted in Richard Rankin, "Mosquitoe Bites: Caricatures of Lower Cape Fear Whigs and Tories on the Eve of the American Revolution," *North Carolina Historical Review* 65 (1988): 188.

19. Cornelius Harnett to Richard Caswell, September 26, 1778, Clark, *State Records* 22, at 982 (Raleigh: North Carolina History and Archives).

20. Taaffe, *Washington's Revolutionary War Generals*, at 184.

21. See David Palmer, *The River and the Rock* (New York: Greenwood Press, 1969).

22. See Hugh Rankin, *The North Carolina Continentals*, at 18 (Chapel Hill: University of North Carolina Press, 1991).

23. Bennett and Lennon, *Quest for Glory*, at 112.

24. Taaffe, *Washington's Revolutionary War Generals*, at 210.

25. See, for example, E. Stanley Godbold Jr. and Robert H. Woody, *Christopher Gadsden and the American Revolution*, at 178–81 (Knoxville: University of Tennessee Press, 1982).

26. Wilson, *Southern Strategy*, at 72 ("anemic"), 79 (854). Cf. Russell, *American Revolution in the Southern Colonies*, at 101 (700).

27. Wilson, *Southern Strategy*, at 72.

28. Wilson, *Southern Strategy*, at 78, 80 (casualty totals).

29. Wilson, *Southern Strategy*, at 77. Earlier in the war, a similar scenario played out in the Battle of Long Island when the retreating Maryland Continentals came to Gowanas Creek, which they had to cross to reach Brooklyn Heights and the American line. Several of the men drowned in the wide creek. See generally Jon J. Gallagher, *The Battle of Brooklyn, 1776*, at 129 (Edison, NJ: Castle Books, 2002).

30. Quoted in Wilson, *Southern Strategy*, at 77.

31. Wilson, *Southern Strategy*, at 78.
32. Bennett and Lennon, *Quest for Glory*, at 100.

CHAPTER 12—PARTIAL REDEMPTION

1. Charles E. Bennett and Donald R. Lennon, *A Quest for Glory: Major General Robert Howe and the American Revolution*, at 124 (Chapel Hill: University of North Carolina Press, 1991).

2. Much as in the Civil War, Vicksburg, Mississippi, was the Gibraltar of the Confederacy, from its height above the Mississippi able to command river traffic below.

3. Quoted in Bennett and Lennon, *Quest for Glory*, at 104.

4. See, for example, Stephen Brumwell, *Turncoat: Benedict Arnold and the Crisis of American Liberty* (New Haven, CT: Yale University Press, 2018); Nathaniel Philbrick, *Valiant Ambition: Benedict Arnold and the Fate of the American Revolution* (New York: Penguin, 2017). There have been attempts to resuscitate Benedict Arnold. See, for example, James K. Martin, *Benedict Arnold, Revolutionary Hero: An American Warrior Reconsidered* (New York: New York University Press, 2000); Charles B. Biddle, *The Case of Major André*, at 317 (Philadelphia: Historical Society of Pennsylvania, 1884).

5. Philbrick, *Valiant Ambition*, at 127.

6. See Stephen R. Taaffe, *Washington's Revolutionary War Generals*, at 204 (Norman: University of Oklahoma Press, 2019).

7. Taaffe, *Washington's Revolutionary War Generals*, at 204.

8. See, for example, Bennett and Lennon, *Quest for Glory*, at 118.

9. See Biddle, *The Case of Major André*, at 317. More recent works include D. A. B. Ronald, *The Life of John André: The Redcoat Who Turned Benedict Arnold* (Haverton, PA: Casemate, 2019), and Winthrop Sargent, *The Life and Career of Major John André, Adjutant-General of the British Army in America* (New York: Legare Street Press, 2022).

10. See "John André: British Military Officer," https://www.britannica.com/biography /John-Andre (accessed August 1, 2022).

11. See Bennett and Lennon, *Quest for Glory*, at 133.

12. Bennett and Lennon, *Quest for Glory*, at 133.

13. Quoted in Michael Schellhammer, "Mutiny of the New Jersey Line," *Journal of the American Revolution*, March 19, 2014, https://www.allthingsliberty.com/2014/3/mutiny-of -the-New-Jersey-line (accessed August 1, 2022).

14. Schellhammer, "Mutiny of the New Jersey Line," at 3.

15. See generally John A. Nagy, *Rebellion in the Ranks: Mutinies of the American Revolution* (Yardley, PA: Westholme, 2007).

16. See, for example, R. W. Dick Phillips, *Arthur St. Clair: The Invisible Patriot*, at 113 (Bloomington, IN: iUniverse, 2014) (Arthur St. Clair); Bennett and Lennon, *Quest for Glory*, at 138 (Robert Howe).

17. Bennett and Lennon, *Quest for Glory*, at 139–40.

18. Bennett and Lennon, *Quest for Glory*, at 141.

19. See generally "The Philadelphia Mutiny of 1783," https://www.military-history.fan dom.com/Philadelphia-Mutiny-of-1783 (accessed August 1, 2022).

20. Bennett and Lennon, *Quest for Glory*, at 146.

21. Bennett and Lennon, *Quest for Glory*, at 147.

22. See, for example, Francis Apthorp Foster, *The Institution of the Society of Cincinnati, 1783–1920*, at 15 (Boston: General Society of the Cincinnati, 1923); Charles Luken Davis, *North Carolina Society of the Cincinnati*, at 7–26 (1907; New York: Legare Street Press, 2022).

23. See generally Gary Forsythe, *A Critical History of Rome: From Prehistory to the First Punic War* (Berkeley: University of California Press, 2006). Many have asserted that George Washington's example, as the planter from Mount Vernon in Virginia who left his farm to command the revolutionary forces, inspired the founders' choice of Cincinnatus in naming their society.

CHAPTER 13—ADDENDUM: INTOXICATING BEVERAGES

1. Michael Schellhammer, "Mutiny of the New Jersey Line," *Journal of the American Revolution*, March 19, 2014, at 3, https://www.allthingsliberty.com/2014/3/mutiny-of-the-New -Jersey-line (accessed August 1, 2022).

2. See, for example, chapter 7.

3. See Robert Howe to Edward Heath, September 26, 1779, in Edward Heath Papers, vol. 14, at 89 (Boston: Massachusetts Historical Society): Howe wrote to recommend "a very smart application of port wine. . . . I have known this wine course, pursued by others who [have lost] their Argue. . . . I never had the Argue in my life."

4. Jeff Dacus, "The Neglected Andrew Lewis," *Journal of American History*, September 28, 2015, text following note 8, https://www.allthingsliberty.com/2015/09/the-neglected-an drew-lewis (accessed September 8, 2020).

5. Congressman Charles Carroll to General George Washington, September 27, 1777, quoted in Philander Chase, ed., *Papers of George Washington*, at 564 (Charlottesville: University of Virginia Press, 2001).

6. Cf. Daniel McDonald Johnson, *This Cursed War; Lachlan McIntosh and the American Revolution*, at 15 (Allendale, SC: Self-published, 2018): Continental troops at Darien, Georgia, were given "a half pint of rum three times a week." The British measure of a gill, followed at that time and dating from the fourteenth century, was five fluid ounces, amounting to five "shots" if a one-ounce shot glass were used. See, for example, Amy Tikkman, "Gill," in *Encyclopedia Britannica*, http://britannica.com/gill (accessed April 5, 2020). The gill liquid measurement is no longer widely used, although the European Union's regulations provide that the amount of alcoholic beverage in a mixed drink must be one-sixth of a gill.

7. Dean Snow, *1777: Tipping Point at Saratoga*, at 174 (New York: Oxford University Press, 2016). General Gates later rescinded the order.

8. Johnson, *This Cursed War*, at 95.

9. Ben Franklin, quoted in Walter Isaacson, *Benjamin Franklin: An American Life*, at 170 (New York: Simon & Schuster, 2003).

10. At the 1780 Battle of Camden, General Gates led the Southern Army out of Hillsborough, North Carolina, before quartermasters could resupply the army. On the eve of the battle, in lieu of the gill of rum customary before a major fight, Gates and commissary men substituted a gill of molasses for rum, with catastrophic intestinal results for the men (especially diarrhea—with soldiers constantly disappearing into the woods as they marched toward the engagement). "[I]t was unluckily conceived that molasses would be an acceptable substitute [for rum]. . . . [M]olasses . . . operated so carthartically as to disorder the men, who were breaking ranks all night . . . certainly much debilitated before the action commenced." Colonel

Ortho Holland Williams, quoted in Jim Piecuch, *The Battle of Camden*, at 29 (Charleston, SC: The History Press, 2006).

11. See, for example, Edward W. Hocker, *The Fighting Parson of the American Revolution: A Biography of General Peter Muhlenberg*, at 56 (Mechanicsburg, PA: Sunbury Press, 1936) ("Sutlers selling liquor caused trouble" in army encampments).

12. Gordon S. Wood, "The Age That Made the Man," *Wall Street Journal*, September 26, 2020, at C-7.

13. Of Revolutionary War encampments, Chalmers Davidson recorded much the same thing: "[R]oaring fires served to roast the belly while the buttocks froze." Chalmers Gaston Davidson, *Piedmont Partisan: The Life and Times of Major General William Lee Davidson*, at 48 (Davidson, NC: Davidson College, 1951).

14. George Washington, quoted in Jared Sparks, *The Writings of George Washington*, vol. 4, at 199–200 (Boston, 1840).

15. Barbara Tuchman, *A Distant Mirror: The Calamitous 14th Century*, at 54, 141 (New York: Ballantine Books, 1978).

16. See Harry M. Ward, *Major General Adam Stephen and the Cause of American Liberty*, at 71–72 (Cherokee expedition) and 82–84 (Pontiac's War) (Charlottesville: University of Virginia Press, 1989).

17. See, for example, Ron Chernow, *George Washington: A Life*, at 18–20 (New York: Penguin, 2010) ("Surveying suited Washington's talents perfectly" and "toughened" him through experiences on the frontier).

18. See chapter 6.

19. Richard V. Polhemus and John F. Polhemus, *Stark: The Life and Wars of John Stark*, at 254–68 (Delmar, NY: Black Dome Press, 2014); Ben Z. Rose, *John Stark: Maverick General*, at 114–24 (Waverly, MA: TreeLine Press, 2007).

20. Account of George Washington of the Capitulation, July 19, 1754, in W. W. Abbot et al., eds., *The Papers of George Washington*, vol. 1, at 159–65 (Charlottesville: University of Virginia Press, 1985). See also Ward, *Major General Adam Stephen*, at 11.

21. Harry W. Ward, *Duty, Honor or Country: General George Weedon and the American Revolution*, at 119 (Philadelphia: American Philosophical Society, 1979).

22. John Jakes, *Charleston*, at 51 (New York: Dutton, 2002).

23. Quoted in Harry M. Ward, *Charles Scott and the Spirit of '76*, at 19 (Charlottesville: University of Virginia Press, 1988) (internal quotation marks omitted).

24. Noel Moore Lee, *Patriot Above Profit*, at 348 (Nashville, TN: Rutledge Hill Press, 1988).

25. Albert Louis Zambone, *Daniel Morgan: A Revolutionary Life*, at 38 (Yardley, PA: Westholme, 2018).

26. David McCullough, *The Pioneers: The Heroic Story of the Settlers Who Bought the American Ideal West*, at 4–5 (New York: Simon & Schuster, 2019).

27. See, for example, Walter Isaacson, *John Adams: An American Life*, at 8 (New York: Simon & Schuster, 2003) ("they wanted to go even further and 'purify' the church of all Roman Catholic traces . . . lingering pollutants from the Church of Rome").

28. See, for example, Tuchman, *Distant Mirror*, at 383: in defense of Ghent, in Flanders, "[t]he militia of [neighboring] Bruges . . . caroused through the night and staggered forth on the morrow, May 5 [1382] shouting and singing in drunken disorder."

29. Quoted in Rick Atkinson, *The British Are Coming: The War for America, Lexington to Princeton, 1775–1777*, at 49 (New York: Henry Holt, 2019).

30. Benjamin Franklin, as a commissioner in negotiations with the Indians leading to the Carlisle Treaty of 1753, described the effect of alcohol on that occasion:

We found that they [the approximately 100 Indians in attendance] had made a great bonfire in the middle of the square. They were all drunk, men and women, quarreling and fighting . . . by the gloomy light of the bonfire, running after and beating one another with firebrands, accompanied by horrid yelling.

Ben Franklin, quoted in H. W. Brands, *The First American: The Life and Times of Benjamin Franklin*, at 227 (New York: Doubleday, 2000).

31. Marquis de Lafayette, quoted in Ward, *Duty, Honor or Country*, at 201.

32. Atkinson, *British Are Coming*, at 552. A hogshead is a large cask—in terms of more precise measurement, a larger barrel containing sixty-three gallons.

33. General Charles Scott, quoted in Ward, *Charles Scott and the Spirit of '76*, at 56–57.

34. Ron Chernow, *Grant*, at 246 (New York: Penguin, 2017).

35. Jonathan W. Jordon, paraphrasing author Patrick O'Donnell, in "Maryland's Finest," *Wall Street Journal*, March 5, 2016, at C-6.

36. See Ward, *Major General Adam Stephen*, at 182; Stephen R. Taaffe, *Washington's Revolutionary War Generals*, at 108 (Norman: University of Oklahoma Press, 2019) ("[h]is doctor ascribed [a] breakdown in Sullivan's health to alcohol").

37. The court acquitted General Maxwell. Robert Lisle, "The Court Martial of Adam Stephen, Major General, Continental Army," *Madison College Bulletin* 30, no. 3 (1972): 37, n18.

38. George Washington, quoted in Ward, *Charles Scott and the Spirit of '76*, at 120.

39. Ward, *Major General Adam Stephen*, at 191 (emphasis added).

40. Marquis de Chastellux, *Travels in North America in the Years, 1780-1782*, at 64 (New York, 1828).

41. See Jakes, *Charleston*, at 91. Marion was fond of pointing out that in assembling a far-reaching empire, Roman soldiers drank only a water-vinegar mix. "The Roman Legions marched and conquered the world drinking nothing else," Marion exhorted his men.

42. Francis Marion, the Swamp Fox, quoted in Jakes, *Charleston*, at 54.

43. The story told to young US Navy officers is that early in the eighteenth century the navy ceased flogging as a means of punishment, although until recently confinement with limitation of nourishment to bread and water ("piss and punk") remained as a potential form of punishment. When regulations eliminated flogging, the navy extracted a quid pro quo: American sailors had to give up their entitlement to a daily grog ration, marking the beginning of the broader prohibition of alcohol in the armed services.

CHAPTER 14—PIEDMONT PARTISON: TALL TREE DAVIDSON

1. Nikole Hannah-Jones, "The 1619 Project," *New York Times* (*Sunday Magazine*), August 14, 2019.

2. There is a sequel to the original volume: Nikole Hannah-Jones, Caitlin Roper, Ilene Silverman, and Jack Silverstein, eds., *The 1619 Project: A New Origin Story* (New York: Random House, 2021). In the preface, Ms. Hannah-Jones summarizes her earlier writing. See, for example, on page xxv ("I wrote about the motivations of the colonists who declared independence from Britain [who] wanted to protect the institution of slavery") and page xxxi ("How do you romanticize a revolution . . . that built white freedom on Black slavery").

3. See "Populations of Great Britain and United States (1775)," http://www.encyclo pedia.com (visited January 10, 2022). Massachusetts had 280,166 persons (4,595 enslaved), Pennsylvania 282,186 (6,769 enslaved), and New Hampshire 81,300 (656 enslaved). The only colonies with significant slaveholdings were three of the thirteen—namely, Virginia, North Carolina, and South Carolina. Georgia was a relatively new colony with a sparse population of 8,000–10,000 persons. Even in these three primary slaveholding jurisdictions, a dichotomy existed, with wealthy, Church of England, slaveholding planters in the eastern lowlands and hardscrabble, Presbyterian, slaveholding-opponent farmers on the Piedmont and in the western hill country.

4. See, for example, Graham Harrington, "10 Key Stops of the Underground Rail-road in Pennsylvania," *The Keystone*, January 31, 2025, available at www.keystonenewsroom .com/2025/01/31/10-key-stops-on-the-underground-railroad (visited March 11, 2025): "Pennsylvania played a key role. . . . As the first free state north of [Maryland and Virginia], Pennsylvania provided many the entry point to freedom."

5. Herrmann Schuricht, *History of the German Element in Virginia*, at 85 (Baltimore: Theo. Kroh & Sons, 1898).

6. Schuricht, *History of the German Element in Virginia*, at 84.

7. "They [migrants from Pennsyvania and the north] did not possess the conventional forms and social polish of the English aristocracy" (Schuricht, *History of the German Element in Virginia*, at 76).

8. Other heroes of the Revolution—Andrew Pickens, Hugh Mercer, Andrew Lewis, and Peter Muhlenberg, and their families, among others—exasperated by the Pennsylvania colo-ny's failure to protect them, left Pennsylvania. Many refugees from Pennsylvania, Muhlenberg included, settled in the northern Shenandoah Valley.

9. Chalmers Gaston Davidson, *Piedmont Partisan: The Life and Times of Brigadier General William Lee Davidson*, at 87 (Davidson, NC: Davidson College, 1951).

10. Ryan Cole, *Light-Horse Harry Lee: The Rise and Fall of a Revolutionary Hero*, at 52 (Washington, DC: Regnery History, 2019).

11. Henry Lee, *Memoirs of the War in the Southern Department*, vol. 2, at 399 (Philadelphia, 1812) (internal quotation marks omitted).

12. James K. Swisher, *The Revolutionary War in the Southern Backcountry*, at 277 (Gretna, LA: Pelican, 2008).

13. See, for example, "Fast Facts," https://www.davidson.edu/fast-facts (accessed August 3, 2021).

14. Tennessee has named what is now its most populous county after William Lee David-son. Davidson County is the site of Nashville, Tennessee's capital. See Rand McNally, Inc., *2022 Road Atlas*, at 94–95 (Chicago: Rand McNally, 2022); http://www.tennesseeencyclope dia.net/entries/davidson-county (visited March 11, 2025).

15. Swisher, *Revolutionary War in the Southern Backcountry*, at 175–76: "[P]artisan activities [became] a critical part of that effort in the lower south."

16. Davidson, *Piedmont Partisan*, at 3.

17. See, for example, Walter Isaacson, *Benjamin Franklin: An American Life*, at 156–57, 154 (New York: Simon & Schuster, 2004) ("The Quakers opposed military spending on principle, and the Penns [acting through a series of appointed lackey governors] opposed anything that would cost them money or subject their land to taxes"); H. W. Brands, *The First American: The Life and Times of Benjamin Franklin*, at 160 (New York: Doubleday, 2000) ("[H]orror stories

of women and children being slaughtered by fiendish red men, provoked and provisioned by the French. . . . [In the] theology of the Quakers there remained an uneasiness with war and war preparation") and 209 ("Failure of the politicians to provide defense . . . demonstrated that politicians could not be trusted to accomplish what needed to be done").

18. See chapter 8.

19. Davidson, *Piedmont Partisan*, at 15.

20. Davidson, *Piedmont Partisan*, at 7. Important to note is that many Native Americans had no sense of the concept "private property." What people in modern eras think of as instances of thievery would not always have been considered stealing by the first Americans.

21. Governor William Tryon to Earl of Shelburne, July 8, 1767, quoted in Douglas Branson, *Southern Brigadier Generals in the Revolutionary War*, at 190 (Jefferson, NC: McFarland, 2024).

22. See Steven Beauregard Weeks, *Church and State in North Carolina*, at 43 (1893; New York: Wentworth Press, 2019). A description of Davidson at the time noted, "[D]avidson was a son of the frontier. . . . He was open-hearted, sympathetic, and a trifle credulous. He was physically brave to the point of fool-heartedness. To his thinking, arms and a man were inseparable. He respected authority, political or religious. . . . Throughout his life he remained a personable, gregarious extrovert." Davidson in Davidson, *Piedmont Partisan*, at 27.

23. Christine R. Swager, *Heroes of Kettle Creek, 1779–1782*, at 13 (West Conshohocken, PA: Infinity Publishing, 2008); Weeks, *Church and State in North Carolina*, at 43.

24. William R. Reynolds Jr., *Andrew Pickens: South Carolina Patriot in the Revolutionary War*, at 104 (Jefferson, NC: McFarland, 2012).

25. What the literature universally refers to as the backcountry conjures up visions of mountain cabins and rough-hewn frontiersman. The backcountry then was around Salisbury and Charlotte, the respective seats of Rowan and Mecklenburg Counties, which lie in central North Carolina's southern tier. Beyond Charlotte, a traveler must transit at least three additional counties before reaching the Appalachians and what today's observer might term "backcountry." Rand McNally, Inc., *2022 Road Atlas*, at 74 (Chicago: Rand McNally, 2021).

26. For a detailed description of the Regulator movement, see Robert O. DeMond, *The Loyalists of North Carolina during the Revolution*, at 23–33 (Durham, NC: Duke University Press, 1940; Greenville, SC: Southern Historical Press, 2019).

27. Davidson, *Piedmont Partisan*, at 29.

28. Charles E. Bennett and Donald R. Lennon, *A Quest for Glory: Major General Robert Howe and the American Revolution*, at 28 (Chapel Hill: University of North Carolina Press, 1991).

29. See Hugh F. Rankin, *North Carolina in the American Revolution*, at 12 (Raleigh: North Carolina Division of Archives and History, 1959):

In 1746 [this group of Highlanders] had revolted against the King of England and led by "Bonnie Prince Charlie," they had been defeated in the Battle of Culloden. After that, and before they migrated to the New World, they had taken an oath of allegiance to the King. Highlanders were people who believed in keeping their word. They settled in eastern North Carolina around Cross Creek.

30. Joe A. Mobley, *North Carolina Governor Richard Caswell: Founding Father and Revolutionary Hero*, at 52 (Charleston, SC: History Press, 2016) (land grants).

31. Mobley, *North Carolina Governor*, at 52.

32. See generally J. D. Lewis, "The Battle of Moore's Creek Bridge," https://www.carolina.com/revolution_battle_of_moores_creek_bridge (accessed August 16, 2021). See also Rankin, *North Carolina in the American Revolution*, at 10–19.

33. Davidson, *Piedmont Partisan*, at 37.

34. Rankin, *North Carolina in the American Revolution*, at 11; Mobley, *North Carolina Governor*, at 51.

35. Although none of the states ever filled the troop quota Congress assigned them, North Carolina had a particularly difficult time because "[a] large part of the population were loyalists unwilling to fight against the Crown." Mobley, *North Carolina Governor*, at 60. At its peak, "North Carolina supplied ten regiments—6,086 to 7,663 soldiers—to the Continental Line in the Revolution. [The militia] was not as competent a fighting force as the regular army, although 10,000 North Carolinians served in its ranks during the war." Mobley, *North Carolina Governor*, at 60. Cf. Rankin, *North Carolina in the American Revolution*, at 73: "It has been estimated that nearly 22,000 North Carolinians (continental and militia) saw service during the War of the Revolution."

36. Described by historian James Swisher as "crusty old Gen. Griffith Rutherford . . . a warrior, the veteran of many a backwoods fight." *Revolutionary War in the Southern Backcountry*, at 71. He "was not a great military mind but he was a leader of focus and will." He was badly wounded at the Battle of Camden, captured by the British, and exchanged by the Americans in 1781. *Revolutionary War in the Southern Backcountry*, at 151.

37. See Mobley, *North Carolina Governor*, at 66.

38. Rankin, *North Carolina in the American Revolution*, at 28.

39. Davidson, *Piedmont Partisan*, at 39.

40. William S. Powell, *North Carolina Through Four Centuries*, at 192 (Chapel Hill: University of North Carolina Press, 1989).

41. Cole, *Light-Horse Harry Lee*, at 52.

42. Otherwise, William Davidson's movements are difficult to track—until, that is, he returned to North Carolina. See Davidson, *Piedmont Partisan*, at 51.

43. Davidson, *Piedmont Partisan*, at 60.

44. See, for example, William A. Graham, *General Joseph Graham and His Papers on North Carolina Revolutionary History*, at 238 (Raleigh: North Carolina Department of Archives and History, 1904).

45. Russell, *American Revolution in the Southern Colonies*, at 178.

46. Davidson, *Piedmont Partisan*, at 65.

47. Davidson, *Piedmont Partisan*, at 69.

Chapter 15—Cowan's Ford

1. Lawrence E. Babbits, *A Devil of a Whipping: The Battle of Cowpens* (Chapel Hill: University of North Carolina Press, 2011).

2. Albert Louis Zambone, *Daniel Morgan: A Revolutionary Life* (Yardley, PA: Westholme, 2018).

3. See, for example, Hugh F. Rankin, *North Carolina in the American Revolution*, at 31 (Raleigh: North Carolina Division of Archives and History, 1959): "In 1779 the British government made a major change in its military strategy. From now on . . . they would concentrate their primary efforts in the southern states."

4. Chalmers Gaston Davidson, *Piedmont Partisan: The Life and Times of Brigadier General William Lee Davidson*, at 71–72 (Davidson, NC: Davidson College, 1951).

5. See generally Rankin, *North Carolina in the American Revolution*, at 41–44.

6. William Davidson to General Horatio Gates, October 10, 1780, in Horatio Gates Papers, Archives Division, New York Public Library.

7. See generally "Battle of King's Mountain," This Day in History—October 7 (2010), https://www.history.com/this-day-in-history/october-7/battle-of-kings-mountain (accessed August 19, 2021); L. C. Draper, *King's Mountain and Its Heroes* (Cincinnati, OH, 1881) ("The victory ranks with Saratoga and Yorktown as one of decisive engagements of the Revolution").

8. Rankin, *North Carolina in the American Revolution*, at 40.

9. Davidson, *Piedmont Partisan*, at 82.

10. See, for example, John Buchanan, *The Road to Guilford Courthouse: The American Revolution in the Carolinas*, at 242 (New York: Wiley & Sons, 1997) (quoting Charles Stedman, an officer under Cornwallis). The British had a reputation for moving very slowly when in force. The pace was attributed to British soldiers' and their mercenary colleagues' (Hessians and Brunswickers) proclivity to range six and eight miles on either side of the main force, looting, marauding, raping, and burning crops, farm buildings, and houses. See, for example, Hilary Mantel, *Wolf Hall*, at 108 (New York: Picador, 2009):

> *The English will never be forgiven for the talent for destruction they have always displayed when they get off their own island. English armies laid waste to the land they moved through. [S]ystematically, they perform every act proscribed by the code of chivalry, and broke every one of the laws of war. The battles were nothing; it was what they did between the battles that left its mark. They robbed and raped for forty miles around the line of their march. They burned the crops in the fields, and the houses with people in them.*

Ministers premised the southern strategy on the plurality or even majority of loyalists and closet sympathizers who lived there. A fruitful exercise might be research into how the British army's lack of discipline contributed to reversal of loyalist sympathizer attitudes, not only in the south but also throughout the colonies.

11. Rankin, *North Carolina in the American Revolution*, at 44.

12. Babbits, *Devil of a Whipping*, at 84.

13. See, for example, Babbits, *Devil of a Whipping*, at 137–38.

14. General William Davidson to General Daniel Morgan, January 21, 1781, in Theodorus Bailey Myers Collection, New York Public Library.

15. Davidson, *Piedmont Partisan*, at 102.

16. Davidson, *Piedmont Partisan*, at 113.

17. Compare William A. Graham, *General Joseph Graham and His Papers on North Carolina Revolutionary History*, at 257 (Raleigh: North Carolina Department of Archives and History, 1904) (250 men) with Henry Lee, *Memoirs of the War in the Southern Department*, vol. 2, at 398 (Philadelphia, 1812) (300 men).

18. James K. Swisher, *The Revolutionary War in the Southern Backcountry*, at 275 (Gretna, LA: Pelican, 2008). See also David L. Russell, *The American Revolution in the Southern Colonies*, at 218 (Jefferson, NC: McFarland, 2000): "Greene put General Davidson in charge of slowing Cornwallis at the fords."

19. Swisher, *Revolutionary War Southern Backcountry*, at 10, 275–77, recounts events at Cowan's ford.

20. Swisher, *Revolutionary War in the Southern Backcountry*, at 277.

21. Hugh Rankin, *North Carolina in the American Revolution*, at 50 (Raleigh: North Carolina Division of Archives and History, 1959).

22. John S. Pancake, *This Destructive War: The British Campaign in the Carolinas, 1780–1782*, at 163 (Tuscaloosa: University of Alabama Press, 1985).

23. Russell, *American Revolution in the Southern Colonies*, at 219.

24. See generally Robert Henry, *Narrative of the Battle at Cowan's Ford* (Greensboro, NC, 1891).

25. Swisher, *Revolutionary War in the Southern Backcountry*, at 10.

26. Swisher, *Revolutionary War in the Southern Backcountry*, at 278.

27. Editor, "Davidson College, Watchman of the South," *Richmond Times Dispatch*, March 23, 1843: "[He was] a man of influence, and, as tradition says, more beloved than any other man in the country."

28. Davidson, *Piedmont Partisan*, at 129. Today the Catawba has been dammed. The site of Cowan's Ford lies beneath the water of a large man-made lake, Lake Norman.

Chapter 16—Professional Soldier Lee

1. For example, Hugh Mercer and Adam Stephen had both emigrated from Scotland a generation before the war commenced. Peter Muhlenberg was not himself an immigrant, but his parents were, with German spoken in the home. Andrew Lewis's parents had emigrated from Ireland.

2. Indeed, Lee may never have achieved citizenship before the Revolution began. Charles Lee purchased his estate in Berkeley County, Virginia, only in 1775, buying 3,284 acres of Jacob Hite's Honeywell Plantation for £5,504. Harry M. Ward, *Major General Adam Stephen and the Cause of American Liberty*, at 107 (Charlottesville: University of Virginia Press, 1989).

3. Stephen R. Taaffe, *Washington's Revolutionary War Generals*, at 15 (Norman: University of Oklahoma Press, 2019).

4. Artemas Ward was the first major general, not because of merit but because, prior to General Washington's arrival, Ward commanded the troops besieging Boston. Congress commissioned Philip Schuyler of New York as the third major general and Israel Putnam of Connecticut as the fourth. Taaffe, *Washington's Revolutionary War Generals*, at 15–16.

5. Taaffe, *Washington's Revolutionary War Generals*, at 31.

6. See Ward, *Major General Adam Stephen*, at 108: "[Lee] did not settle on his estate until 1779 after his suspension from the army."

7. Ward, *Major General Adam Stephen*, at 218.

8. See, for example, Richard John Alden, *General Charles Lee: Traitor or Patriot?* (Baton Rouge: Louisiana State University Press, 1951); Dominick Mazzagetti, *Charles Lee: Self Before Country?* (New Brunswick, NJ: Rutgers University Press, 2013); Christian McBurney, *George Washington's Nemesis: The Outrageous Treason and Unfair Court-Martial of Charles Lee during the Revolutionary War* (El Dorado Hills, CA: Savas Beatie, 2020); Phillip Pappas, *Renegade Revolutionary: The Life of General Charles Lee* (New York: New York University Press, 2014); Theodore Thayer, *The Making of a Scapegoat: Washington and Lee at Monmouth* (Port Washington, NY: Kennikat Press, 1976); Samuel White Patterson, *Knight Errant of Liberty: The*

Triumph and Tragedy of General Charles Lee (New York: Lantern Press, 1958); Hilary Mantel, *Wolf Hall* (New York: Picador, 2009).

9. Paul J. Burrow, "The Treachery of Charles Lee," https://www.twu.edu/history (accessed August 7, 2020).

10. George Washington, quoted in Rick Atkinson, *The British Are Coming: The War for America, Lexington to Princeton, 1775–1777*, at 330 (New York: Henry Holt, 2019).

11. Atkinson, *British Are Coming*, at 330, 488. Lee had been educated at a private academy in Switzerland. "There he not only learned the classics and Shakespeare but also acquired a working knowledge of French, Greek, Latin, and Italian." Taaffe, *Washington's Revolutionary War Generals*, at 14.

12. David K. Wilson, *The Southern Strategy: Britain's Conquest of South Carolina and Georgia*, at 41–42 (Columbia: University of South Carolina Press, 2005).

13. As long ago as the sixteenth century, English royalty and nobility treated small dogs as children. See, for example, Mantel, *Wolf Hall*, at 572–73, in which a fictional Henry VIII speaks of his then wife, Anne Boleyn: "[Y]ou have seen him [the dog] on her arm. She takes him everywhere. . . . I think she loves him better than me. Yes, I am second to the dog." The practice seems to have continued to the present day, at least in part, exemplified perhaps by the late Elizabeth II's treatment of her beloved corgis.

14. Alden, *General Charles Lee: Traitor or Patriot?*, at 302.

15. Burrow, "Treachery of Charles Lee," at 4.

16. See, for example, "Revolutionary War Biography: Charles Lee," https://www.battle fields.org/learn/biographies/charles-lee, at 2 (accessed August 7, 2020).

17. Taaffe, *Washington's Revolutionary War Generals*, at 60.

18. See, for example, Atkinson, *British Are Coming*, at 501 ("He planned to harass Howe [and Cornwallis] from behind").

19. See "General Charles Lee Captured at Widow White's Tavern," This Day in History—December 13 (2009), https://www.history.com/this-day-in-history/december-13/general-charles-lee-leaves-his-troops-for-widow-whites-tavern (accessed August 7, 2020).

20. "General Charles Lee Captured at Widow White's Tavern," at 1.

21. Atkinson, *British Are Coming*, at 503.

22. See, for example, "General Charles Lee Captured at Widow White's Tavern," at 1–3.

23. Benjamin Rush to Richard Henry Lee, December 21, 1776, quoted in Harry M. Ward, *Charles Scott and the Spirit of '76*, at 23 (Charlottesville: University of Virginia Press, 1988).

24. Mark Edward Lender and Garry Wheeler Stone, *Fatal Sunday: George Washington, the Monmouth Campaign, and the Politics of Battle*, at 116–17 (Norman: University of Oklahoma Press, 2016).

25. Quoted in Mark Edward Lender, *Cabal: The Plot Against General Washington*, at 211 (Yardley, PA: Westholme, 2019).

CHAPTER 17—LEE'S PRIVILEGED BACKGROUND

1. A grammar school is the elite among British state-sponsored schools, all of which stand in contradistinction to public schools, which are not public at all (Eton, Harrow, Rugby, and the like).

2. See, for example, Carol Karels, *A Disobedient Servant: The Revolutionary War and the Times That Tried Men's Souls*, at 105–11 (Cheltenham, UK: The History Press, 2007).

3. David K. Wilson, *The Southern Strategy: Britain's Conquest of South Carolina and Georgia*, at 40 (Columbia: University of South Carolina Press, 2005).

4. See, for example, Harry M. Ward, *Major General Adam Stephen and the Cause of American Liberty*, at 107 (Charlottesville: University of Virginia Press, 1989).

5. Rick Atkinson, *The British Are Coming: The War for America, Lexington to Princeton, 1775–1777*, at 330 (New York: Henry Holt, 2019).

6. Atkinson, *British Are Coming*, at 330.

7. See, for example, Hal T. Shelton, *General Richard Montgomery and the American Revolution*, at 202 (New York: New York University Press, 1994).

8. Ron Chernow, *George Washington: A Life*, at 175 (New York: Penguin, 2010).

9. There were dissents to Washington's appointment. James Madison castigated Washington as "one of a class of tidewater gentry" who demonstrated "a pusillanimity little comporting with their professions and the name of Virginians." James Madison, quoted in James Thomas Flexner, *George Washington: The Forge of Experience, 1772–1775*, at 330 (Boston: Little, Brown, 1965).

10. Chernow, *George Washington: A Life*, at 185.

11. Christian M. McBurney, "Ten Quotes of Major General Charles Lee," *Journal of American History* (January 2020), https://www.allthingsliberty.com/2020/01/top-ten-quotes-of-major-general-charles-lee/ (accessed August 10, 2020). See also Chernow, *George Washington: A Life*, at 184.

12. David McCullough, *John Adams*, at 91 (New York: Simon & Schuster, 2001).

13. "Revolutionary War Biography: Charles Lee," at 2.

14. Atkinson, *British Are Coming*, at 501.

15. Albert Louis Zambone, *Daniel Morgan: A Revolutionary Life*, at 167 (Yardley, PA: Westholme, 2018).

16. See generally Mark Edward Lender, *Cabal: The Plot Against General Washington* (Yardley, PA: Westholme, 2019).

17. See generally Ron Chernow, *Alexander Hamilton*, at 101–4 (London: Penguin, 2008).

18. Chernow, *George Washington: A Life*, at 175, 213.

19. David McCullough, *1776*, at 65 (New York: Simon & Schuster, 2005).

20. Quoted in Harry M. Ward, *Duty, Honor or Country: General George Weedon and the American Revolution*, at 166 (Philadelphia: American Philosophical Society, 1979).

21. Atkinson, *British Are Coming*, at 332.

22. Atkinson, *British Are Coming*, at 333.

23. Attributed to Captain Clement Lampriere, a well-regarded American privateer, in Wilson, *Southern Strategy*, at 45.

24. William Moultrie, *Memoirs of the American Revolution*, vol. 1, at 141 (1802; New York: Arno Press, 1968).

25. Wilson, *Southern Strategy*, at 49.

26. In addition, the British landed ground troops on the next barrier island to the north, Long Island, present-day Isle of Palms. Intelligence, lacking reconnaissance by British General Clinton, informed the British that the troops could splash through the several inches of water that separated Long and Sullivan's islands at low tide. Instead, the channel between islands was not eighteen inches deep at low tide, but rather a swampy morass up to seven or more feet deep in places. Across the channel, a force of 780 Americans under Colonel

William Thompson stood to impede any British advance down Sullivan's Island toward Fort Moultrie. The British ground troops were marooned, unable to leave Long Island to attack Sullivan's Island.

27. After wet cement has been in place for a time, it becomes hardened and resistant to change. See, for example, Paul J. Burrow, "The Treachery of Charles Lee," https://www.twu.edu/history, at 1 (accessed August 7, 2020): "[H]e repelled a British assault at Fort Moultrie." In fact, Lee recommended just the opposite: rather than stand and fight, the defenders should abandon the fort.

28. Adam Gopnik, "Original Gangsters: The New York Mob," *New Yorker*, December 7, 2020, at 65, 67. The myth was "that gangsters were melancholic men of honor . . . legendary and, in a black way, lovable."

29. Privately Rutledge advised Moultrie, "General Lee wishes you to evacuate [Fort Sullivan]. You will not without an order from me. I would sooner cut off my hand than write one." Quoted in Atkinson, *British Are Coming*, at 333–34.

CHAPTER 18—LEE'S FALL FROM GRACE

1. Charles Lee, quoted in Albert Zambone, *Daniel Morgan: A Revolutionary Life*, at 176 (Yardley, PA: Westholme, 2018).

2. Only General Anthony Wayne supported an attack—and an all-out one at that. See, for example, Thomas Boyd, *Mad Anthony Wayne*, at 112 (New York: Scribner & Sons, 1929).

3. Stephen R. Taaffe, *Washington's Revolutionary War Generals*, at 163 (Norman: University of Oklahoma Press, 2019).

4. See Taaffe, *Washington's Revolutionary War Generals*, at 163 (letters to Washington by Generals Greene, Lafayette, and Wayne).

5. See, for example, Michael Cecere, *General William Woodford of Virginia, Revolutionary War Patriot*, at 171 (Berwyn Heights, MD: Heritage Books, 2019). See also "Continental Army Generals: Charles Scott," *RevWarTalk*, http://www.revwartalk.com/charles-scott, at 5–6 (accessed May 9, 2020). See, for example, Harry M. Ward, *Major General Adam Stephen and the Cause of American Liberty*, at 157–62 (Charlottesville: University of Virginia Press, 1989).

6. Cf. Taaffe, *Washington's Revolutionary War Generals*, at 164 ("somewhat less than 5,000 men").

7. Harry M. Ward, *Charles Scott and the Spirit of '76*, at 49. Lee stated to Washington that "it would look bad for everyone if Lee did not get the job" (164). In another demonstration of arrogance, in 1778 Lee expressed to Congress "contempt for Washington, his army, and his strategy," and lobbied Congress to elevate him to lieutenant general, arguing that it was only fair, despite a lack of noteworthy achievements. "[H]is captivity," he maintained, "had prevented him from distinguishing himself on the battlefield." Taaffe, *Washington's Revolutionary War Generals*, at 162.

8. Ward, *Charles Scott and the Spirit of '76*, at 50.

9. Quoted in Theodore B. Lewis, "Was Washington Profane at Monmouth?" *New Jersey History* 89 (1971): 162. See also "Continental Army Generals: Charles Scott," *RevWarTalk*, at 45 ("Tradition holds that . . . Scott witnessed Washington excoriating Lee in a profanity-laden tirade").

10. Quoted in Edward Lengel, *General George Washington: A Military Life*, at 300 (New York: Random House, 2005).

11. See Taaffe, *Washington's Revolutionary War Generals*, at 166.

12. Taaffe, *Washington's Revolutionary War Generals*, at 166.

13. Mark Edward Lender, *Cabal: The Plot Against General Washington*, at 212 (Yardley, PA: Westholme, 2019).

14. Zambone, *Daniel Morgan*, at 177.

15. See Salina Baker, "Twenty Quotes from George Washington and His Generals," http://www.salinabakerauthor.com/Twenty/Quotes/from/George/Washington/and/his/gen erals (accessed September 2, 2022).

16. Taaffe, *Washington's Revolutionary War Generals*, at 168.

17. See chapter 7.

18. Taaffe, *Washington's Revolutionary War Generals*, at 169.

19. Charles Lee to Horatio Gates, December 18, 1779, in Lee Papers, vol. 3, Archives and Manuscripts, Duke University Libraries, at 278.

20. Lender, *Cabal*, at 212.

21. Charles Lee to Horatio Gates, December 19, 1779, in Lee Papers, vol. 4, Archives and Manuscripts, Duke University Libraries, at 401 (commas absent in original).

22. A 1779 letter by Lee to General Anthony Wayne, congratulating Wayne on leading the capture of Stony Point below West Point, presented a contradictory view of Lee, showing that Lee had mellowed in retirement in Virginia. Lee wrote, "I do most sincerely declare that your action in the assault of Stony Point is not only the most brilliant, in my opinion, through the whole course of this war, on either side, but that it is the most brilliant I am acquainted with in history." Charles Lee to General Anthony Wayne, August 11, 1779, in Lee Letters, vol. 3. at 357, on file at New York, New York State Historical Society (1873).

23. Paul J. Burrow, "The Treachery of Charles Lee," https://www.twu.edu/history, at 2 (accessed August 7, 2020).

24. George Henry Moore, *Mr. Lee's Plan—March 29, 1777: The Treason of Charles Lee, Major General, Second in Command in the American Army of the Revolution* (Port Washington, NY: Kennikat Press, 1860).

25. Richard John Alden, *General Charles Lee: Traitor or Patriot?*, at 302 (Baton Rouge: Louisiana State University Press, 1951).

26. See Theodore Thayer, *The Making of a Scapegoat: Washington and Lee at Monmouth*, at 12 (Port Washington, NY: Kennikat Press, 1976).

27. See Dominick Mazzagetti, *Charles Lee: Self Before Country?*, at 142 (New Brunswick, NJ: Rutgers University Press, 2013).

28. Phillip Pappas, *Renegade Revolutionary: The Life of General Charles Lee* (New York: New York University Press, 2014).

CHAPTER 19—GENUINE BATTLE EXPERIENCE?

1. See, for example, H. W. Brands, *The First American: The Life and Times of Benjamin Franklin*, at 161 (New York: Doubleday, 2000) (in the Quaker-dominated Pennsylvania Assembly, "[t]here remained an uneasiness with war and war preparations, especially when they entailed expense and risk"); Walter Isaacson, *Benjamin Franklin: An American* Life, at 123 (New York: Simon & Schuster, 2003) (when in 1747 Benjamin Franklin tried to organize a militia "in response to ongoing threats by the French and their Indian allies . . . [the] Assembly, dominated by pacifist Quakers, dithered and failed to authorize any defenses").

2. Dean Snow, *1777: Tipping Point at Saratoga*, at 31 (New York: Oxford University Press, 2016).

3. See John R. Luzader, *Decision on the Hudson: A Military History of the Decisive Campaign of the American Revolution*, at 204 (New York: Savas Beatie, 2010).

4. Snow, *1777*, at 58, 84.

5. Snow, *1777*, at 25.

6. Johann Friedrich Specht, *A Military Journal of the Burgoyne Campaign*, at 81 (Westport, CT: Greenwood Press, 1995).

7. Reported in Snow, *1777*, at 105.

8. In theory, a regiment contained 600 plus men, but in actuality convalescence from wounds, sickness, desertion, and the like lowered that number to 350 or 400 "effectives." A brigade consisted of two or more regiments, so perhaps 1,200 plus on the roster, but only 700–800 effectives.

9. Charles Neilson, *An Original, Compiled, and Corrected Account of Burgoyne's Campaign*, at 144 (Port Washington, NY: Kennikat Press, 1970).

10. Snow, *1777*, at 121.

11. Snow, *1777*, at 154.

12. John Buchanan, *The Road to Guilford Courthouse: The American Revolution in the Carolinas*, at 149 (New York: Wiley & Sons, 1997).

13. In the Thirty Years' War, Swedish King Gustavus Adolphus (1594–1632) artfully combined disparate elements (infantry, cavalry, artillery, etc.) of his army. He and his forces prevailed in battle after battle, conquering Danes, Poles, and Germans, until Gustavus fell at the Battle of Lutzen on November 16, 1632. Historians term him the father of modern warfare. See, for example, Theodore Ayrault, *Gustavus Adolphus: A History of the Art of War after the Middle Ages to the End of the Spanish Succession War, with a Detailed Account of the Campaigns of the Great Swede* (Salisbury, NC: Pervasive Books, 2019) ("one of the greatest military commanders of all time"). See also Nils Ahnlund, *Gustavus Adolphus, the Great Warrior King* (Des Moines, IA: History Book Club, 1999); Lars Erickson Wolke, *Gustavus Adolphus, Sweden, and the Thirty Years War* (Barnsley, South Yorkshire, UK: Pen & Sword Military, 2022).

Undoubtedly Daniel Morgan never heard of Gustavus Adolphus or the Thirty Years' War. Nonetheless, as a great battlefield tactician, Morgan emulated many of the warrior king's innovations.

14. Snow, *1777*, at 169, 178–79, 82.

15. Snow, *1777*, at 181.

16. Snow, *1777*, at 243.

17. As remembered by Lieutenant Colonel James Wilkinson, Gates's adjutant at Saratoga. See James Wilkinson, *Memories of My Own Times*, vol. 1, at 267 (Philadelphia: Abraham Small, 1816).

18. See, for example, Henry Dearborn, "A Narrative of the Saratoga Campaign," *Bulletin of Fort Ticonderoga Museum* 1, no. 5 (1929): 2–12.

19. Jim Piecuch, *The Battle of Camden*, at 13 (Charleston, SC: The History Press, 2006).

20. See, for example, Kenneth R. Rossman, *Thomas Mifflin and the Politics of the American Revolution*, at 4 (Chapel Hill: University of North Carolina Press, 1952). See also at 100: after Saratoga, "[t]he eyes of the nation turned gratefully and expectantly to the mighty Caesar of North [Horatio Gates]."

21. Stepehn R. Taaffe, *Washington's Revolutionary War Generals*, at 142 (Norman: University of Oklahoma Press, 2019).

Chapter 20—Gates's Cowardice at Camden

1. Washington's officers, including the generals, "questioned . . . the extent Gates contributed to the victory at Saratoga." Stephen R. Taaffe, *Washington's Revolutionary War Generals*, at 143 (Norman: University of Oklahoma Press, 2019).

2. See Taaffe, *Washington's Revolutionary War Generals*, at 207–8. Gates was currently on an extended leave, in residence at his Virginia plantation.

3. See generally Mark Edward Lender, *Cabal: The Plot Against General Washington* (Yardley, PA: Westholme, 2019).

4. David McCullough, *John Adams*, at 171 (New York: Simon & Schuster, 2001).

5. Jonathan Dickinson Sergeant, November 20, 1777, quoted Taaffe, *Washington's Revolutionary War Generals*, at 138.

6. George Washington, quoted in John C. Fitzpatrick, *The Writings of George Washington: Revolutionary War Series*, vol. 14, at 385 (Washington, DC: United States Government Printing Office, 1931–1944).

7. Taaffe, *Washington's Revolutionary War Generals*, at 142.

8. Chalmers Gaston Davidson, *Piedmont Partisan: The Life and Times of Major General William Lee Davidson*, at 47 (Davidson, NC: Davidson College, 1951).

9. See generally Lender, *Cabal*.

10. Kenneth R. Rossman, *Thomas Mifflin and the Politics of the American Revolution*, at 134 (Chapel Hill: University of North Carolina Press, 1952).

11. Taaffe, *Washington's Revolutionary War Generals*, at 144.

12. See Taaffe, *Washington's Revolutionary War Generals*, at 207.

13. Ortho Holland Williams, "A Narrative of the 1780 Campaign by Ortho Holland Williams, Adjutant General," in *The Papers of General Nathanael Greene*, vol. 1, at 486 (Charleston, SC: 1822).

14. Ortho Holland Williams, quoted in Jim Piecuch, *The Battle of Camden*, at 29 (Charleston, SC: The History Press, 2006).

15. The actual number of "effectives" in Gates's "Grand Army," as he called it, was 3,052 according to one source. See John Buchanan, *The Road to Guilford Courthouse: The American Revolution in the Carolinas*, at 161 (New York: Wiley & Sons, 1997).

16. Buchanan, *Road to Guilford Courthouse*, at 153, 157–58.

17. See postscript in chapter 28.

18. See, for example, Hilary Mantel, *Wolf Hall*, at 108 (New York: Picador, 2009):

The English will never be forgiven for the talent for destruction they had always displayed when they get off their own island. English armies laid waste to the land they moved through. [T]hey performed every action proscribed by the codes of chivalry, and broke every one of the laws of war. The battles were nothing; it was what they did between battles that left its mark. They robbed and raped for forty miles around their line of march. They burned the crops in the fields, and the houses with people in them.

19. See, for example, Barbara Tuchman, *A Distant Mirror: The Calamitous 14th Century*, at 267 (New York: Ballantine Books, 1978): "Covering eight or nine miles a day [was the usual line] of march" for an English army moving through France. That slowed considerably for the English army "better to live off the country, gather loot," and otherwise rape and pillage.

20. Buchanan, *Road to Guilford Courthouse*, at 161.

21. Williams, "Narrative of the 1780 Campaign," at 494–95.

22. Buchanan, *Road to Guilford Courthouse*, at 163.

23. Buchanan, *Road to Guilford Courthouse*, at 160.

24. Buchanan, *Road to Guilford Courthouse*, at 168.

25. General Horatio Gates to the Continental Congress, August 20, 1780, in Horatio Gates Papers, Archives Division, New York Public Library.

26. Garrett Watts, quoted in John C. Dann, *The Revolution Remembered: Eyewitness Accounts of the War for Independence*, at 194 (Chicago: University of Chicago Press, 1980).

27. See "The Hero Rides Hard," in Buchanan, *Road to Guilford Courthouse*, at 170.

28. Buchanan, *Road to Guilford Courthouse*, at 172.

29. See Salina Baker, "Twenty Quotes from George Washington and His Generals," http://www.salinabakerauthor.com/Twenty/Quotes/from/George/Washington/and/his/generals (accessed September 2, 2022).

30. Buchanan, *Road to Guilford Courthouse*, at 393.

31. Albert Zambone, *Daniel Morgan: A Revolutionary Life*, at 271 (Yardley, PA: Westholme, 2018).

32. Taaffe, *Washington's Revolutionary War Generals*, at 221.

33. Taaffe, *Washington's Revolutionary War Generals*, at 218.

34. Taaffe, *Washington's Revolutionary War Generals*, at 218.

35. See also Buchanan, *Road to Guilford Courthouse*, at 394.

36. Buchanan, *Road to Guilford Courthouse*, at 172.

CHAPTER 21—A GATES ROADMAP OF WHAT NOT TO DO

1. Walter Isaacson, *Benjamin Franklin: An American Life*, at 399 (New York: Simon & Schuster, 2003).

2. For instance, Colonel John Laurens of South Carolina, who had served as aide-de-camp to George Washington and was a son of Continental Congress President Henry Laurens, died on August 27, 1782, shot in a skirmish at Combahee River, South Carolina. He thus died in combat nearly a year after Yorktown. See, for example, "John Laurens: American Army Officer," https://www.britannica.com/biography/john-laurens (accessed November 5, 2020).

3. Lord North, quoted in David McCullough, *John Adams*, at 267 (New York: Simon & Schuster, 2001).

4. A behind-the-scenes agitator was Major General Horatio Gates, whom Washington had summoned from semiretirement in Virginia (see chapter 18). Gates warned the Society of the Cincinnati founders and other plotters that without protections, come peace, they would "grow old in poverty, wretchedness, and contempt." See, for example, Ron Chernow, *George Washington: A Life*, at 433 (New York: Penguin, 2010) (attributing authorship to Gates's aide-de-camp, John Armstrong Jr.). In reference to the Newburgh letters, Gates advised the officers to "assume a bolder tone—and suspect the man who would advise to more moderation and longer forbearance," the latter probably a poke at George Washington. Quotations from John Rhodehamel, *George Washington: Writings*, at 239 (New York: Library of America, 1997).

5. Chernow, *George Washington: A Life*, at 434.

6. See generally H. W. Brands, *The First American*, at 687–88 (New York: Doubleday, 2000). Another detailed account can be found in Chernow, *George Washington: A Life*, at 433–36.

7. John C. Fitzpatrick, *The Writings of George Washington: Revolutionary War Series*, vol. 26, at 239 (Washington, DC: United States Government Printing Office, 1931–1944).

8. George Washington, quoted in Brands, *First American*, at 668.

9. George Washington, quoted in Brands, *First American*, at 668.

10. Chernow, *George Washington: A Life*, at 436.

11. Stephen Howard Browne, *The First Inauguration: George Washington and the Invention of the Republic* (College Park: Pennsylvania State University Press, 2020).

12. But see Stephen Howard Browne, *The Ides of War: George Washington and the Newburgh Crisis* (Columbia: University of South Carolina Press, 2016).

13. Stephen R. Taaffe, *Washington's Revolutionary War Generals*, at 217 (Norman: University of Oklahoma Press, 2019).

14. "Memoirs of C. P. Bennett, Delaware Continentals," *Pennsylvania Magazine of History and Biography* 9 (1885): 454–56.

15. Quoted in William P. Robinson, *The Revolutionary Sketches of William R. Davie*, at 18 (Chapel Hill: University of North Carolina Press, 1976).

16. Colonel Thomas Rodney to Delaware Governor Caesar Rodney, on file, folder 18, box 6, Delaware Historical Society, Wilmington, Delaware.

17. Taaffe, *Washington's Revolutionary War Generals*, at 217.

18. Jim Piecuch, *The Battle of Camden*, at 27 (Charleston, SC: The History Press, 2006). See also Taaffe, *Washington's Revolutionary War Generals*, at 217 ("[M]any of the soldiers succumbed to diarrhea from eating a diet of green corn, unripened peaches, and molasses").

19. "Journal of Sergeant William Seymour, Delaware Regiment," in *Journal of Southern Expedition, 1780–1783*, at 5–7 (Wilmington, DE: Historical Society of Delaware, 1783).

20. General Gates did proceed, accompanied by a small cavalry contingent under Colonel Charles Armand, a French volunteer. See John Buchanan, *The Road to Guilford Courthouse: The American Revolution in the Carolinas*, at 155 (New York: Wiley & Sons, 1997).

21. See, for example, Piecuch, *Battle of Camden*, at 27.

22. Henry Lee, *The Revolutionary War of General Henry Lee*, at 178 (New York: Da Capo Press, 1998).

23. Piecuch, *Battle of Camden*, at 30.

24. Horatio Gates to Samuel Huntington, President of the Continental Congress, August 20, 1780, in Horatio Gates Papers, Archives Division, New York Public Library.

25. Quoted in John C. Dann, *The Revolution Remembered: Eyewitness Accounts of the War of Independence*, at 194–95 (Chicago: University of Chicago Press, 1980).

26. Alexander Hamilton to James Duane, September 6, 1781, reproduced in Harold G. Syrett, *The Papers of Alexander Hamilton*, at 420 (New York: Columbia University Press, 1961).

27. Blackwell Robinson, ed., *Sketches of William Davie*, at 17 (reprint, Raleigh: North Carolina Department of Archives and History, 1976).

28. Quoted in Piecuch, *Battle of Camden*, at 32.

29. Piecuch, *Battle of Camden*, at 31.

30. Robert Scott Davis Jr., "Thomas Pinckney and the Last Campaign of Horatio Gates," *South Carolina Historical Magazine* 86, no. 2 (1985): 93.

31. See, for example, James M. Gavin, *On the Road to Berlin: Battles of an Airborne Commander, 1943–1946* (New York: Viking, 1978).

32. Quoted in Piecuch, *Battle of Camden*, at 20.

33. John Iredell to Hannah Iredell, September 28, 1781, reproduced in Donald Higginbotham, ed., *The Papers of John Iredell*, at 172 (Raleigh: North Carolina Division of Archives, 1976).

34. Syrett, *Papers of Alexander Hamilton*, at 421.

35. Ortho Holland Williams to Alexander Hamilton, August 30, 1780, reproduced in Piecuch, *Battle of Camden*, at 25.

36. Quoted in Davis, "Thomas Pinckney and the Last Campaign of Horatio Gates," 84.

37. Lieutenant Christopher Richmond to Thomas Sim Lee, August 30, 1780, reproduced in Piecuch, *Battle of Camden*, at 33.

38. Quoted in James Thacher, *A Military Journal during the American Revolutionary War*, at 116 (Plymouth, MA, 1823).

39. Benjamin Rush to John Adams, August 25, 1780, reproduced in Gregg Lint, ed., *The Papers of John Adams*, at 92 (Cambridge, MA: Belknap Press, 1996).

CHAPTER 22—ANOTHER TALL TREE: FIGHTING PASTOR MUHLENBERG

1. On Statuary Hall, see generally the historical account of the US Capitol Architect, available at http://www.aoc.gov/explore-capitol-campus/building-grounds/statuary-hall (visited March 13, 2025).

2. Virginia ordered the removal of Robert E. Lee's likeness, bringing the total to twenty-five rather than twenty-six. See aoc.gov/explore-capitol-campus.

3. Henry Augustus Muhlenberg, *The Life of Major-General Peter Muhlenberg*, at 33 (Philadelphia: Carey & Hart, 1849).

4. See, for example, chapter 12.

5. See generally Arthur J. Mekeel, *The Relation of the Quakers to the American Revolution* (Washington, DC: University Press of America, 1979).

6. Albert Louis Zambone, *Daniel Morgan: A Revolutionary Life*, at 8 (Yardley, PA: Westholme, 2018), citing Pierre Marambaud, *Byrd of Westover*, at 51, 250 (Charlottesville: University of Virginia Press, 1971).

7. The northern end of the Valley near Woodstock, Winchester, and Front Royal, stretching into what today is the panhandle of West Virginia, is lower than the southern portion (Staunton, Lexington, Roanoke, etc.), so under a view prevalent then the upper area was known as the "lower valley"—that is, lower in elevation. The east and west branches of the Shenandoah subsequently flow north—that is, downhill—merging and then turning toward the east, where the Shenandoah flows into the Potomac at Harper's Ferry, West Virginia.

8. Edward W. Hocker, *The Fighting Parson of the American Revolution: A Biography of General Peter Muhlenberg*, at 44 (Mechanicsburg, PA: Sunbury Press, 1936).

9. Bruce Catton, *Stillness at Appomattox*, at 307 (Garden City, NY: Doubleday, 1962).

10. Muhlenberg, *Life of Major-General Peter Muhlenberg*, at 53. See also Hocker, *Fighting Parson of the American Revolution*, at 45 (the sermon was based on Eccles. 3:1).

11. Bill Federer, "Sometimes Even Pastors Must Go to War," World Net Daily, September 30, 2019, https://wnd.com/2019/9/sometimes-even-pastors-must-go-to-war, at 2 (accessed February 2, 2020).

12. Muhlenberg's brother, Frederick Augustus Muhlenberg, who later served in Congress with his sibling, "did not approve of [brother Peter] going into the army until the British burned down his church, Christ Lutheran in New York City in front of him. Then Frederick

joined the military himself." American War History, "Peter Muhlenberg," http://www.revwar talk.com/peter-muhlenberg (accessed February 3, 2020).

13. Cf. Muhlenberg, *Life of Major-General Peter Muhlenberg*, at 50: "[The incident] shows of what sterling metal the patriots of old time were formed."

14. The twenty-two-hundred-student Allentown, Pennsylvania, college is named after Peter Muhlenberg's father, Reverend Henry Melchior Muhlenberg, rather than after the Revolutionary War general. See http://www.muhlenberg.edu (accessed February 6, 2020).

15. Further, Pennsylvania labored under a double disability. While the Crown and Parliament ruled other colonies, the proprietors (William Penn and later Thomas Penn) ruled Pennsylvania, with the Crown and Parliament in the background. The proprietors did not permit any taxation whatsoever on their vast land holdings, even entering into secret nontaxation pacts with the colonial governors apponted by and beholden to the Penns. So, even had the Pennsylvania Assembly voted a tax, the royal governors would have vetoed it. Even if the Quaker-dominated Assembly had conceded the need for defense against Indian raids (which it eventually did), the colony lacked the ability to fund a defense. See generally H. W. Brands, *The First American*, at 37, 211 (New York: Doubleday, 2000).

16. Hocker, *Fighting Parson*, at 7.

17. See Peter Veth, "Henry Melchior Muhlenberg," in Living Lutheran, October, 2018, available http://www.livinglutheran.org/2018/10/henry-melchior-muhlenberg (visited March 7, 2025). Henry Melchior Muhlenberg, who emigrated from Eimbeck, Germany, in 1742, is considered the patriarch of Lutheran churches in America. "[H]e exercised superintendence for many years over virtually all of the Lutheran congregations of Pennsylvania, New Jersey, Maryland, and Virginia." He is frequently termed "the venerated Father Muhlenberg." Muhlenberg, *Life of Major-General Peter Muhlenberg*, at 17, 40.

18. See "Muhlenberg College History," available http://www.muhlenberg.edu/aboutus /college-history (visited March 6, 2025). The college is located in Allentown, Pennsylvania.

19. Quoted in Muhlenberg, *Life of Major-General Peter Muhlenberg*, at 27–28.

20. Muhlenberg, *Life of Major-General Peter Muhlenberg*, at 25.

21. Letter from James Wood, Esq., to Peter Muhlenberg, May 4, 1777, in Muhlenberg Papers, Trexler Library, Muhlenberg College, Allentown, Pennsylvania.

22. American War History, "Peter Muhlenberg," 2 ("Since the Anglican Church was the state church of Virginia, he was required to be ordained in the Anglican Church in order to serve a congregation in Virginia").

23. Hocker, *Fighting Parson*, at 31–32.

24. Muhlenberg, *Life of Major-General Peter Muhlenberg*, at 44 (Committee of Safety and Correspondence).

25. Muhlenberg, *Life of Major-General Peter Muhlenberg*, at 47.

26. Rick Atkinson, *The British Are Coming: The War for America, Lexington to Princeton, 1775–1777*, at 565 (New York: Henry Holt, 2019), reports that the HMS (His or Her Majesty's Ship) designation did not come into regular use "until several years after the American Revolution had ended." I have continued to use the HMS designation on the theory that its descriptive value outweighs the historical inaccuracy.

27. Muhlenberg, *Life of Major-General Peter Muhlenberg*, at 56.

28. See generally Atkinson, *British Are Coming*, at 324ff.

29. Contemporaries, including George Washington, characterized Lee as "rather fickle and violent" but "the first officer in military knowledge and experience." Atkinson, *British Are Coming*, at 330.

30. See, for example, Henry Lumpkin, *From Savannah to Yorktown*, at 11, 17 (New York: Paragon, 1981).

31. David L. Russell, *The American Revolution in the Southern Colonies*, at 94 (Jefferson, NC: McFarland, 2000).

32. Hocker, *Fighting Parson*, at 51.

33. Quoted in Muhlenberg, *Life of Major-General Peter Muhlenberg*, at 62.

34. Savannah (then Georgia's largest town) sat at the northernmost point of the Georgia coast. The colony of Georgia, however, was the southern extremity of the thirteen colonies and, of the thirteen, the least populated. Located as they were on the fringe, Georgia residents worried about a lack of support from the Continental Line and northern politicians.

Chapter 23—Muhlenberg the Brigadier General

1. Henry Augustus Muhlenberg, *The Life of Major-General Peter Muhlenberg, of the Revolutionary Army*, at 71 (Philadelphia: Carey & Hart, 1849).

2. Muhlenberg, *Life of Major-General Peter Muhlenberg*, at 77–78.

3. Edward W. Hocker, *The Fighting Parson of the American Revolution: A Biography of General Peter Muhlenberg*, at 57 (Mechanicsburg, PA: Sunbury Press, 1936).

4. Cf. Harry M. Ward, *Major General Adam Stephen and the Cause of American Liberty*, at 180 (Charlottesville: University of Virginia Press, 1989): "[T]he Virginia troops distinguished themselves. The 3rd Regiment in Weedon's brigade (Greene's division) was the last to leave the field, and most of its officers were killed."

5. Muhlenberg, *Life of Major-General Peter Muhlenberg*, at 96.

6. Quoted in Hocker, *Fighting Parson*, at 60.

7. Ward, *Major General Adam Stephen*, at 185. See also generally 184–89.

8. See chapter 7.

9. Hocker, *Fighting Parson*, at 63.

10. Nathanael Greene, quoted in Ward, *Major General Adam Stephen*, at 188.

11. Muhlenberg, *Life of Major-General Peter Muhlenberg*, at 114.

12. See generally Bob Drury and Tom Clavin, *Valley Forge* (New York: Simon & Schuster, 2018).

13. Hocker, *Fighting Parson*, at 68. To the British, especially strong incentives existed for Muhlenberg's capture. "The British would surely have been delighted to lay their hands on him, for in view of his having been a parson of the established Church of England, his treason was looked upon as especially heinous."

14. Muhlenberg, *Life of Major-General Peter Muhlenberg*, at 24.

15. Ward, *Major General Adam Stephen*, at 197.

16. George Washington to Peter Muhlenberg, April 10, 1778, quoted in Muhlenberg, *Life of Major-General Peter Muhlenberg*, at 131.

17. By contrast, in summer 1777, the disgruntled George Weedon retired, seemingly on a permanent basis, to Fredericksburg. See chapter 2.

18. Muhlenberg, *Life of Major-General Peter Muhlenberg*, at 149, records that General Anthony Wayne dissented from an otherwise unanimous vote not to attack Philadelphia.

19. See Muhlenberg, *Life of Major-General Peter Muhlenberg*, at 156: "Although the Virginians fought with their usual steadiness and gallantry [and] although [General Muhlenberg] displayed the same skill and impetuous ardour . . . the actions of this particular body of troops were lost in those of the main force. They did their duty . . . but more cannot be claimed."

20. At White Plains, General Muhlenberg commanded a body of picket troops that undertook reconnaissance in the direction of the enemy's lines. Later in the year, General Washington, having sent Nathanael Greene to the southern campaign, commanded Muhlenberg and his troops across the Hudson, where they were stationed at West Point. Muhlenberg and his men spent winter encampments in 1778 at West Point, New York; in 1779 at Middlebrook, New Jersey; and in 1780 at Morristown, New Jersey, the latter of which was without General Muhlenberg, whom Washington had sent south to superintend the defense of Virginia. Muhlenberg, *Life of Major-General Peter Muhlenberg*, at 157, 176.

21. Hocker, *Fighting Parson*, at 76.

22. Friedrich Kapp, *The Life of Frederick William von Steuben, Major General of the Revolutionary Army*, at 60 (CreateSpace, 2015).

23. For example, in October 1780 British Commander in Chief "[C]linton sent 3,000 British troops from New York, under [Major] General [Alexander] Leslie to Virginia. They arrived in the James River at Portsmouth on October 15." The British forces raided country along the James River, pointing northwest toward Richmond. Muhlenberg and Brigadier George Weedon, whose resignation Congress had never accepted, recruited troops but stayed well back from engagement until they gathered what the generals calculated was the needed strength. See, for example, Muhlenberg, *Life of Major-General Peter Muhlenberg*, at 205.

24. Muhlenberg, *Life of Major-General Peter Muhlenberg*, at 210.

25. In January 1781, the British attempted the last of their Virginia diversions. Benedict Arnold, now a British general, sailed with two thousand troops up the James River to Westover, twenty-five miles below Richmond. Arnold and his men raided up the river, taking possession of Richmond for a short time, causing damage there, and engaging in skirmishes against the colonials. British General Phillips and Arnold threw their forces into a major skirmish at City Point on April 24, 1781. Muhlenberg, *Life of Major-General Peter Muhlenberg*, at 220–21. Between sixty and seventy colonials, untrained and inexperienced militiamen, were killed, while "the British loss was trifling." See generally Hocker, *Fighting Parson*, at 77–81.

26. An interesting sidelight: The traitor Arnold questioned a captured colonial, "What would be my fate if the Americans captured me?" The colonial soldier replied, "We would cut off the shortened leg wounded at Quebec and Saratoga and bury it with the honors of war, and hang the rest of you." Recounted in Hocker, *Fighting Parson*, at 78.

27. See Hocker, *Fighting Parson*, at 83.

28. See, for example, David Lee Russell, *The American Revolution in the Southern Colonies*, at 289 (Jefferson, NC: McFarland, 2000) (noting only that Muhlenberg, with seven hundred troops, was present at Yorktown) and 296 (Hamilton commanded the force attacking the British redoubt).

29. Stephen R. Taaffe, *Washington's Revolutionary War Generals*, at 236 (Norman: University of Oklahoma Press, 2019).

30. Eighty-five years later, another minister, Leonidas Polk, left behind his miter and crozier to enter the military. Polk left his position as an Episcopal bishop to accept a commission as a general in the Confederate army in the War Between the States, as many southerners term the Civil War. See Ron Chernow, *Grant*, at 153–54 (New York: Penguin, 2017).

CHAPTER 24—A POLITICAL GENERAL

1. William M. Welsch, "The 10 Worst Continental Army Generals," *Journal of the American Revolution*, https://www.allthingsliberty.com/2013/10/10-worst-continental-army -generals (accessed September 15, 2022).

2. See, for example, Robert K. Wright Jr. and Morris MacGregor, *Thomas Mifflin: Soldier-Statesman of the Constitution*, at 109–11 (Fort McNair, DC: US Army Center of Military History, 1987).

3. See, for example, https://history.gov/People/Continental-Congress/Presidents (accessed January 14, 2023). Mifflin was fifth of ten congressional presidents under the Articles of Confederation (1781–1789). The Articles made no provision for a president of the fledging nation, as did the later Constitution.

4. In 1648, Oliver Cromwell and his supporters had enacted a statute, the Self-Denying Ordinance, that barred altogether members of the House of Commons and House of Lords from serving in any military capacity. Cromwell excoriated military service by "members of the Commons and the Lords" because Cromwell thought "they were prosecuting the war incompetently and perhaps deliberately refusing to bring it to a quick end 'lest their own power should [terminate] with it.'" Barton Swaim, "A Plain Man, Warts and All," *Wall Street Journal*, December 28, 2001, at A-15, quoting Ronald Hutton, *The Making of Oliver Cromwell* (New Haven, CT: Yale University Press, 2021). Of course, no such statute was in force at the times of Mifflin's switches back and forth between political and military roles.

5. Wright and MacGregor, *Thomas Mifflin*, at 109.

6. Kenneth R. Rossman, *Thomas Mifflin and the Politics of the American Revolution*, at 10 (Chapel Hill: University of North Carolina Press, 1952).

7. See https://archives.upenn.edu/exhibits/penn-people/biography/thomas-mifflin (accessed January 16, 2023). Mifflin also was a trustee of the University of Pennsylvania from 1773 to 1791, characterized by the website as "one of those men who seem to have been everywhere and done everything."

8. Rossman, *Thomas Mifflin and Politics*, 35.

9. Rossman, *Thomas Mifflin and Politics*, at 13.

10. Rossman, *Thomas Mifflin and Politics*, at 30.

11. Wright and MacGregor, *Thomas Mifflin*, at 110.

12. See generally Jared D. Johnston, "Thomas Mifflin," Smith National Library for the Study of George Washington, http://www.mountvernon.org/thomas/mifflin (accessed September 11, 2022).

13. Charles Francis Adams, *John Adams Works*, vol. 9, at 348 (Boston, 1856).

14. Speech of April 25, 1775, quoted in William Rawle, "Sketches of the Life of Thomas Mifflin," pt. 2, at 110–11 (Philadelphia: Historical Society of Pennsylvania, 1830).

15. Dean and Adams, quoted in Rossman, *Thomas Mifflin and Politics*, at 40.

16. "Thomas Mifflin," https://www.conservapedia.com/Thomas_Mifflin (accessed September 10, 2022).

17. Adams's diary entry, quoted in Adams, *John Adams Works*.

18. Stephen R. Taaffe, *Washington's Revolutionary War Generals*, at 141 (Norman: University of Oklahoma Press, 2019).

19. James Craik to George Washington, January 6, 1778, in W. W. Abbot et al., eds., *The Papers of George Washington: Revolutionary War Series*, vol. 13, at 161 (Charlottesville: University of Virginia Press, 1985–2003).

20. Taaffe, *Washington's Revolutionary War Generals*, at 30.

21. Rossman, *Thomas Mifflin and Politics*, at 45.

22. Rossman, *Thomas Mifflin and Politics*, at 53.

23. See, for example, Rick Atkinson, *The British Are Coming: The War for America, Lexington to Princeton, 1775–1777*, at 264–66 (New York: Henry Holt, 2019). The main British force sailed from Boston on March 20, 1776.

24. Washington appointed Mifflin quartermaster of the army by his general orders for September 28, 1776.

25. Richard Henry Lee to George Washington, September 26, 1775, in Abbot et al., *Papers of George Washington*, vol. 2, at 252.

26. "Thomas Mifflin," https://www.conservapedia.com/Thomas-Mifflin (accessed September 10, 2022). Mifflin was present earlier than Trenton and Princeton, although there is no evidence that he actively participated in the Battle of Long Island.

27. Taaffe, *Washington's Revolutionary War Generals*, at 52.

28. See generally Rossman, *Thomas Mifflin and Politics*, at 47.

29. Thomas Mifflin to Matthew Irwin, November 5, 1775, on file, Historical Society of Pennsylvania, Philadelphia.

30. "Side jobbing" and its cousin, double dipping, receive varied treatment depending on the fields of endeavor involved. For example, firefighters augment their municipal salaries by conducting brick laying, plumbing, or carpentry on days off from the firehouse. Universities commonly permit professors to use one day a week for outside consulting. By contrast, many private employers forbid the practice. Evidence seems to indicate that Mifflin and his Philadelphia relatives and acquaintances were engaged in outside businesses in addition to and utilizing Mifflin's quartermaster position.

31. George Washington to Joseph Reed, November 1775, in John C. Fitzpatrick, *Writings of George Washington: Revolutionary War Series*, vol. 2, at 428–30 (Washington, DC: United States Government Printing Office, 1931–1944).

32. Rossman, *Thomas Mifflin and Politics*, at 51.

33. Joseph Reed to George Washington, March 7, 1776, in Fitzpatrick, *Writings of George Washington*, at 428.

34. Professor Kenneth Rossman in *Thomas Mifflin and Politics*, at 52.

35. As noted, Mifflin was present at Trenton and the second Battle of Trenton; however, he "had little chance to distinguish himself in those actions." Rossman, *Thomas Mifflin and Politics*, at 78.

36. Taaffe, *Washington's Revolutionary War Generals*, at 137.

37. Rossman, *Thomas Mifflin and Politics*, at 55.

38. George Washington to Israel Putnam, March 19, 1776, in Fitzpatrick, *Writings of George Washington*, vol. IV, at 429–30.

39. Rossman, *Thomas Mifflin and Politics*, at 3.

Chapter 25—Dereliction of Duty and Abandonment of His Post

1. Mifflin had success with those missions. On one occasion, he brought fifteen hundred recruits into the army, and on another two thousand. See, for example, Kenneth R. Rossman, *Thomas Mifflin and the Politics of the American Revolution* (Chapel Hill: University of North Carolina Press, 1952), at 76, 88.

2. Quoted in Rossman, *Thomas Mifflin and Politics*, at 86.

3. Rossman, *Thomas Mifflin and Politics*, at 88.

4. Stephen R. Taaffe, *Washington's Revolutionary War Generals*, at 65 (Norman: University of Oklahoma Press, 2019).

5. Jared Johnson, "Thomas Mifflin," https://www.mountvernon.org/.../article/Thomas=mifflin (accessed January 11, 2023).

6. Letter from Thomas Mifflin to John Hancock, October 8, 1777, excerpted in Rossman, *Thomas Mifflin and Politics*, at 88.

7. See, for example, Rossman, *Thomas Mifflin and Politics*, at 110: On November 19, 1777, "Mifflin repaired to York and there got into the middle of things."

8. See, for example, Octavius Pickering and Charles Wentworth Upham, *The Life of Timothy Pickering*, at 187–88 (New York: Wentworth Press, 2016).

9. Chapters 2–4 and 5–7, respectively, chronicle the downfalls of Arthur St. Clair and Adam Stephen.

10. See Taaffe, *Washington's Revolutionary War Generals*, at 76–77.

11. See generally https://www.history.com/topics/american-revolution/valley-forge (accessed September 28, 2022).

12. Rossman, *Thomas Mifflin and Politics*, at 109.

13. Rossman, *Thomas Mifflin and Politics*, at 110.

14. Taaffe, *Washington's Revolutionary War Generals*, at 155 ("the quartermaster department quickly disintegrated" for want of "the presence of its head").

15. John Boyd, *Mad Anthony Wayne*, at 104 (New York: Charles Scribner & Sons, 1929).

16. Boyd, *Mad Anthony Wayne*, at 105.

17. Edmund C. Burnett, *Letters of Members of the Continental Congress*, vol. III, at 11–14 (Boston, 1921–1936; republished, Whitefish, MT: Kessinger, 2016).

18. Robert K. Wright Jr. and Morris MacGregor, *Thomas Mifflin: Soldier-Statesman of the Constitution*, at 110–11 (Fort McNair, DC: US Army Center of Military History, 1987).

19. Taaffe, *Washington's Revolutionary War Generals*, at 155.

20. Alexander Graydon, *Memoirs of His Time* (Philadelphia: J. S. Little; repr. Applewood Books, 2009). See also Rossman, *Thomas Mifflin and Politics*, at 98: "Mifflin openly criticized Washington's favorites like Greene and Knox who Mifflin thought had an undue influence in Washington."

21. See Taaffe, *Washington's Revolutionary War Generals*, at 16 (Greene) and 30 (Mifflin).

22. Rossman, *Thomas Mifflin and Politics*, at 56.

23. See, for example, Rossman, *Thomas Mifflin and Politics*, at 3.

24. Rossman, *Thomas Mifflin and Politics*, at 67.

25. Rossman, *Thomas Mifflin and Politics*, at 63.

26. Rossman, *Thomas Mifflin and Politics*, at 80. Washington responded to Mifflin's veiled criticism thus: "I agree but little I do [can] affect action of civil authorities."

27. Rossman, *Thomas Mifflin and Politics*, at 95.

28. Rossman, *Thomas Mifflin and Politics*, at 97.

CHAPTER 26—THOMAS MIFFLIN'S GREATEST SIN

1. Along parallel lines, the army chief of commissary, the "hapless" William Buchanan, was also a failure in supplying the army. See Mark Edward Lender, *Cabal: The Plot Against General Washington*, at 187 (Yardley, PA: Westholme, 2019). See also chapter 20.

2. Chapter 17 reviews Horatio Gates's role in the affair, characterized as aware but not an active participant, an assessment many question.

3. "Thomas Mifflin," https://archives.upenn.edu/exhibits/penn-people/biography/thomas -mifflin (accessed January 16, 2023). Thomas Mifflin was a University of Pennsylvania graduate and a university trustee (1773–1791), serving as treasurer of the Board of Trustees from 1773 to 1775.

4. Stephen R. Taaffe, *Washington's Revolutionary War Generals*, at 142 (Norman: University of Oklahoma Press, 2019).

5. Chalmers Gaston Davidson, *The Life and Times of Major General William Lee Davidson*, at 47 (Davidson, NC: Davidson College, 1951). See also Albert Louis Zambone, *Daniel Morgan: A Revolutionary Life* (Yardley, PA: Westholme, 2018).

6. Lender, *Cabal*, at xiii.

7. Professor Kenneth Rossman, in his biography of Thomas Mifflin, concluded that "it cannot be established that [Horatio Gates] actively joined in any such plot." Kenneth R. Rossman, *Thomas Mifflin and the Politics of the American Revolution*, at 134 (Chapel Hill: University of North Carolina Press, 1952). General Washington believed otherwise—namely, that Mifflin "bore the second part in the conspiracy" and that Gates "bore the first" (at 5).

8. Rossman, *Thomas Mifflin and Politics*, at 41.

9. Rossman, *Thomas Mifflin and Politics*, at 44. See also at 56: Mifflin had "a close association" with Gates from the war's earliest days.

10. Rossman, *Thomas Mifflin and Politics*, at 101.

11. See also Rossman, *Thomas Mifflin and Politics*, at 63.

12. Recounted in chapter 20.

13. Lovell (also) had in mind his fellow New Englander Israel Putnam, then in the Hudson Highlands. See James Lovell to General Horatio Gates, November 5, 1777, in Paul H. Smith and Ronald M. Gephart, *Letters of Delegates to Congress 1771–1784*, vol. 8, at 237 (Washington, DC: Library of Congress, 1976–2000).

14. Congressman Jonathan Dickinson Sergeant to James Lovell, November 20, 1777, in Smith and Gephart, *Letters of Delegates to Congress*, at 302–3.

15. See Lender, *Cabal*, at 245n47.

16. Lender, *Cabal*, at 28.

17. Lender, *Cabal*, at 29.

18. General Thomas Mifflin to General Horatio Gates, November 17, 1777, in Horatio Gates Papers, Archives Division, New York Public Library.

19. Lender, *Cabal*, at 35.

20. See Stephen Fried, *Rush: Revolution, Madness, and the Visionary Doctor Who Became a Founding Father* (New York: Crown, 2018). See also Harlow Giles Unger, *Benjamin Rush: The Founding Father Who Healed a Wounded Nation* (New York: Da Capo Press, 2018).

21. At Saratoga, Colonels Daniel Morgan and Henry Dearborn, along with Generals Benedict Arnold and Enoch Poor, carried the day. Other than protecting the turf he had marked out for himself next to the river, Gates did nothing—indeed, less than nothing. He cowered in a farmhouse far behind the battle lines, nearly snatching defeat from the jaws of victory by refusing to commit additional troops and then doing so in an untimely and inadequate manner.

22. "Ultimately, Gates did release . . . reinforcements to Washington [following Brandywine and Germantown] in numbers too small and too late to support" the Middle Department. See Lender, *Cabal*, at 76–77.

23. General George Washington to Henry Laurens, January 30, 1778, on file, South Carolina Historical Society, Charleston, SC.

24. See generally John A. Ragosta, *Patrick Henry's Last Stand: For the People, for the Country* (Charlottesville: University of Virginia Press, 2023). Most know Patrick Henry only for his stirring March 1775 oration to the Second Virginia Convention: "Give me liberty or give me death" (chapter 27). Both in the fledging union and in Virginia, Henry did much more of note, including being twice the governor of the commonwealth and, in 1775, the founder of Hampton-Sydney College.

25. Rossman, *Thomas Mifflin and Politics*, at 104.

26. Rossman, *Thomas Mifflin and Politics*, at 111.

27. Lender, *Cabal*, at 118.

28. Rossman, *Thomas Mifflin and Politics*, at 108.

29. George Washington was "incensed to learn about Conway's impending promotion to major general." The Continental Congress awarded a promotion whereby Conway "would be jumped over twenty more senior American brigadiers." Ron Chernow, *George Washington: A Life*, at 317 (New York: Penguin, 2011).

30. Lender, *Cabal*, at 123.

31. See, for example, General George Washington to Thomas Conway, December 30, 1777, in Theodore Crackel, ed., *The Papers of George Washington*, vol. 13, at 66–67 (Charlottesville: University of Virginia Press, 2007).

32. General George Washington to President of the Congress Henry Laurens, January 2, 1778, in Crackel, *Papers of George Washington*, vol. 13, at 199.

33. Major Alexander Hamilton to George Clinton, February 13, 1778, in Harold C. Syrett and Jacob Cooke, eds., *The Papers of Alexander Hamilton*, vol. 1, at 428 (New York: Columbia University Press, 1961).

34. Lender, *Cabal*, at 152.

35. Wayne Bodle, "The Vortex of Small Fortune: The Army at Valley Forge, 1777–1778," vol. 1, Valley Forge Research Report 222 (Department of the Interior, 1980).

36. Lender, *Cabal*, at 148.

37. Lender, *Cabal*, at 145.

38. Lender, *Cabal*, at 183–84.

39. Lender, *Cabal*, at 177–80.

40. Oliver Cromwell and the Rump Parliament enacted a statute, the Self-Denying Ordinance, that barred Lords and House members from serving in the military. See chapter 24, note 4.

41. Lender, *Cabal*, 232.

42. See, for example, "Thomas Mifflin," https://www.constitutionday.com/mifflin-thom as-pa-html/ (accessed January 22, 2023), also positing that "he excelled as Quartermaster General."

43. Rossman, *Thomas Mifflin and Politics*, at vii.

44. See Joshua Dressler, *Understanding Criminal Law*, 9th edition, at 121 (Durham, NC: Carolina Academic Press, 2022).

45. More accurately, the plot to corner the market would be the penultimate object, the means to an end. The end, or objective of the conspiracy, would be achievement of an ability to fix prices.

46. Dressler, *Understanding Criminal Law*, at 124. The agreement may be written, oral, or tacit—that is, deduced from the facts and circumstances. Principles do not specify that there must be a written document or documents with all or most of the rough edges sanded off. An exchange of telephone calls, texts, emails, or, as here, letters will suffice.

47. Dressler, *Understanding Criminal Law*, at 127.

CHAPTER 27—VIRGINIA PLANTER: A BRIGADIER AS A BENT TREE

1. Perhaps Benedict Arnold would top the list of "bent tree" brigadiers, but by virtue of his treason Arnold was beyond "bent"—hence beyond the scope of this book. See generally Stephen Brumwell, *Turncoat: Benedict Arnold and the Crisis of American Liberty* (New Haven, CT: Yale University Press, 2018); Nathaniel Philbrick, *Valiant Ambition: Benedict Arnold and the Fate of the American Revolution* (New York: Penguin, 2017).

2. See, for example, Douglas Branson, *Southern Brigadier Generals in the Revolutionary War: Eighteen Commandeers Instrumental in the American Victory* (Jefferson, NC: McFarland, 2024).

3. See *Southern Brigadier Generals*, chapter 20 ("Rivalries and Resignations"), at 156–61.

4. All told, thirteen of fifty-six brigadiers died of wounds in combat or of combat-related causes. Henry Augustus Muhlenberg, *The Life of Major-General Peter Muhlenberg, of the Revolutionary Army*, appendix, at 453–55 (Philadelphia: Carey & Hart, 1849), lists eighty-four generals who served, twenty-eight major generals and fifty-six brigadier generals. Excluding the twelve non-Americans who came to the United States only for the purpose of serving in the army yields seventy-two, several of whom did not serve. The major generals in the "foreign" category included Lafayette, De Kalb, du Coudray, Conway, Steuben, and Duportail. The brigadier generals in the category included de Woedtke, Fermoy, de Barre, Pulaski, Armand, and Kosciusko. The US generals who died included James Hogun, Hugh Mercer, Richard Montgomery, James Moore, Francis Nash, Enoch Poor, John Thomas, Joseph Warren, William Woodford, and Daniel Wooster. The generals from abroad who perished were De Kalb, de Woedtke, and Pulaski.

5. See generally Harry M. Ward, *Charles Scott and the Spirit of '76*, at 17 (Charlottesville: University of Virginia Press, 1988).

6. Congress elevated Hugh Mercer to his new rank in March 1777. See Stephen R. Taaffe, *Washington's Revolutionary War Generals*, at 30 (Norman: University of Oklahoma Press, 2019).

7. Michael Cecere, *General William Woodford of Virginia, Revolutionary War Patriot*, at 115 (Berwyn Heights, MD: Heritage Books, 2019).

8. Colonel William Woodford to General George Washington, July 6, 1776, in W. W. Abbot et al., eds., *The Papers of George Washington*, vol. 5, at 228–30 (Charlottesville: University of Virginia Press, 1993).

9. Cecere, *General William Woodford of Virginia*, at 121.

10. Ron Chernow, *George Washington: A Life*, at 260 (New York: Penguin, 2010).

11. George Washington to Samuel Washington, December 18, 1776, quoted in Chernow, *George Washington: A Life*, at 271.

12. See Taaffe, *Washington's Revolutionary War Generals*, at 78. Of the four generals ranked last, three were the southerners of the group: seventh, George Weedon (Virginia); eighth, Peter Muhlenberg (Virginia); tenth and last, William Woodford (Virginia).

13. Cecere, *General William Woodford of Virginia*, at 126 (footnote omitted).

14. General George Washington to William Woodford, March 3, 1777, in W. W. Abbot et al., eds., *The Papers of George Washington*, vol. 8, at 507 (Charlottesville: University of Virginia Press, 1998).

15. Douglas Southall Freeman, *George Washington*, vol. 4, at 613 (New York: Scribner & Sons, 1952). See also chapter 16.

16. Great military leaders often have "emphasized grinding rather than genius. . . . Winning the day of the battle is not enough, you have to win the campaign, then the year, then the decade." Cathal J. Nolan, *The Allure of Battle* (New York: Oxford University Press, 2017).

17. See William Woodford, "Revolutionary War Biography," http://www.battlefields.org /learn/biographies/william-woodford (accessed March 22, 2020).

18. Library of Virginia, "William Woodford (1734–1780)," http://edu.lva.virginia.gov /online_classroom/william_woodford (accessed March 23, 2020).

19. "William Woodford," http://www.encyclopedia.com/history/encyclopedias-alma nacs-transcripts-and-maps/william-woodford (accessed March 23, 2020).

20. Woodford, "Revolutionary Biography," at 2.

21. Woodford also became one of five residents selected to serve on Caroline County's Non-Importation Committee. William Rind, *Virginia Gazette*, January 17, 1771, at 2.

22. "William Woodford," at 1. See also Cecere, *General William Woodford of Virginia*, at 33–35.

23. Quoted in William Wirt, *Sketches of the Life and Character of Patrick Henry*, at 139 (Philadelphia, 1817).

24. Cecere, *General William Woodford of Virginia*, at 132.

25. Cecere, *General William Woodford of Virginia*, at 118.

26. Quoted in Cecere, *General William Woodford of Virginia*, at 119 (shortly before the Battle of Gwynn's Island).

27. Ward, *Charles Scott and the Spirit of '76*, at 74.

28. Colonel John Neville to General Daniel Morgan, November 9, 1779, at *Founders Online*, National Archives, available http://founders.archives.gov/documets/morgan (visited March 3, 2022).

29. See generally Cecere, *General William Woodford of Virginia*, at 140–43.

30. Harry M. Ward, *Duty, Honor or Country: General George Weedon and the American Revolution*, at 88 (Philadelphia: American Philosophical Society, 1979). See also at 123 (Woodford "appears to have been rather pompous and a dandy").

CHAPTER 28—MONMOUTH COURTHOUSE AND CHARLES TOWN

1. See, for example, Jim Piecuch, *The Battle of Camden*, at 10–11 (Charleston, SC: The History Press, 2006).

2. Michael Cecere, *General William Woodford of Virginia, Revolutionary War Patriot*, at 171–72 (Berwyn Heights, MD: Heritage Books, 2019).

3. Varying accounts of that June day exist, including one that a pullback by General Scott on the left precipitated what occurred. See, for example, Harry M. Ward, *Charles Scott and the Spirit of '76*, at 49–50 (Charlottesville: University of Virginia Press, 1988).

4. Cecere, *General William Woodford of Virginia*, at 173–74.

5. Cerece, *General William Woodford of Virginia*, at 176.

6. Major General Charles Lee faced a court-martial that included Woodford sitting in judgment. The court found Lee guilty. Washington affirmed judgment on the verdict: Lee was cashiered from the army, returning to his estate in Berkeley County, Virginia.

7. See, for example, "Monmouth Courthouse," https://www.battlefields.org/learn/revolu tionary-war/battles/monmouth (accessed February 19, 2023).

8. See, for example, John Jakes, *Charleston*, at 489 (New York: Dutton, 2002).

9. "You will put everything in train and march the whole with Tents & baggage as soon as possible to Philadelphia, where you will await further orders." George Washington to William Woodford, December 8, 1779, in *Papers of George Washington*, vol. 23, at 559 (Charlottesville: University of Virginia Press, 2015).

10. Cecere, *General William Woodford of Virginia*, at 212.

11. Jakes, *Charleston*, at 44.

12. Cecere, *General William Woodford of Virginia*, at 214.

13. Jakes, *Charleston*, at 45.

14. See Banastre Tarleton, *A History of the Campaigns of 1780–1781 in the Southern Provinces of North America*, at 16 (1787; Manchester, NH: Ayer, 1999).

15. Captain Hinrichs, describing the dire situation in May 1780 Charleston, quoted in Jakes, *Charleston*, at 7.

16. See Jakes, *Charleston*, at 46 (twelve thousand British force) and 64 (fifty-six hundred American troops).

17. See generally Carl P. Borick, *A Gallant Defense: The Siege of Charleston, 1780* (Columbia: University of South Carolina Press, 1980).

18. After the surrender of Charleston, Brigadier James Hogun (born Hogan, in Ireland) died on January 4, 1781, a British prisoner at Haddrell's Point.

19. French volunteer and engineering officer Louis Lebeque Duportail, quoted in Ward, *Charles Scott and the Spirit of '76*, at 78 (footnote omitted).

20. The Pennsylvania Packet, December 16, 1780, quoted in Catesby Willis Stewart, *The Life of Brigadier William Woodford of the American Revolution*, vol. 2, at 1187 (Richmond, VA: Witten & Shepperson, 1973).

21. On land, the DUMBO (Down Underneath the Manhattan and Brooklyn Bridge Overpasses) neighborhood lies south of the Brooklyn Navy Yard area. It has become a very trendy area.

22. A. Roger Ekirch, "Hell Afloat Wallabout Bay," *Wall Street Journal*, August 23, 2017, at A-13.

23. See generally Robert P. Watson, *The Ghost Ship of Brooklyn: An Untold Story of the American Revolution* (New York: Da Capo Press, 2017).

24. Colonial numbers were sixty-eight hundred killed, sixty-one hundred wounded, and twenty thousand imprisoned. See http://www.battlefields.org/combat/deaths/revolutionary/war (accessed April 30, 2020).

25. See also Edwin G. Burrows, *Forgotten Patriots: The Untold Story of American Prisoners during the Revolutionary War* (New York: Basic Books, 2008).

CHAPTER 29—SEDITION AFLOAT

1. The stereotypical Irishman is red haired and freckle faced; in contrast, a black Irishman has dark hair, dark eyes, and an alabaster complexion.

2. See, for example, chapter 21, "Pretenders, Parvenus, and Armchair Generals," in Douglas Branson, *Southern Brigadier Generals in the Revolutionary War: Eighteen Commandeers Instrumental in the American Victory* (Jefferson, NC: McFarland, 2024).

3. Michael Schellhammer, "Duels of Honor," *Journal of the American Revolution*, August 7, 2014, https://allthingsliberty.com/2014/08/duels-of-honor (accessed March 1, 2023).

4. Kenneth R. Rossman, *Thomas Mifflin and the Politics of the American Revolution*, at 116 (Chapel Hill: University of North Carolina Press, 1952).

5. A principal exception, of course, was the service of Marquis de Lafayette, a young general whom Washington came to regard as akin to a son.

6. In late 1777, Congress finally promoted the Irishman: "Thomas Conway to Major General over twenty-three brigadier generals. . . . Several major generals and nine brigadier generals—including Weedon—protested to Congress and threatened to resign." Cf. Ron Chernow, *George Washington: A Life*, at 317 (New York: Penguin, 2010) (twenty).

7. *Letters of Richard Henry Lee*, vol. 1, at 338–39 (1911; New York: Wentworth Press, 2016).

8. Rossman, *Thomas Mifflin and Politics*, 117.

9. Mark Edward Lender, *Cabal: The Plot Against General Washington*, at 84 (Yardley, PA: Westholme, 2019).

10. Rossman, *Thomas Mifflin and Politics*, 117.

11. See, for example, Stephen R. Taaffe, *Washington's Revolutionary War Generals*, at 140 (Norman: University of Oklahoma Press, 2019).

12. Lender, *Cabal*, at 88.

13. Lender, *Cabal*, at 91; Rossman, *Thomas Mifflin and Politics*, at 18.

14. See chapters 24–26.

15. Lender, *Cabal*, at 126.

16. Lender, *Cabal*, at 127.

17. Lender, *Cabal*, at 126.

18. Thomas Fleming, *Washington's Secret War: The Hidden History of Valley Forge*, at 108, 329 (New York: HarperCollins, 2005).

19. Fleming, *Washington's Secret War*, at 329.

20. See, for example, David Hackett Fischer, *Washington's Crossing* (New York: Oxford University Press, 2005).

CHAPTER 30—FINAL THOUGHTS AND CONCLUSIONS

1. Information about genealogy was readily available for fifty-one brigadiers. One, Seth Pomeroy of Massachusetts, refused to accept the brigadier's commission offered him. Seven (de Woedtke, Fermoy, de Borre, Pulaski, Neuville, Armand, and Kosciusko) immigrated to the colonies at the war's commencement or thereafter. Of the forty-three remaining, they immigrated earlier, as boys or young men, or their antecedents had done so. Five of those forty-three, however, were of continental European stock (two French, two Dutch, and one German) rather than having a heritage linked to Great Britain or Ireland. Calculations by the author.

2. Lynne Cheney, *The Virginia Dynasty: Four Presidents and the Creation of the American Nation* (New York: Viking, 2020).

3. Cheney, *Virginia Dynasty*, at iv.

4. Winston Groom, *The Patriots: Alexander Hamilton, Thomas Jefferson, John Adams, and the Making of America* (Washington, DC: National Geographic, 2020), reviewed in Jonathan Jordan, "Founding Brothers," *Wall Street Journal*, January 9, 2021, at C-12.

5. See generally H. W. Brands, *The First American: The Life and Times of Benjamin Franklin* (New York: Doubleday, 2000).

6. See, for example, Stacy Schiff, *The Revolutionary: Samuel Adams* (Boston: Little, Brown, 2022) (Sam Adams and Thomas Paine), reviewed by Adam Gopnik, "Finding the Founders: How Samuel Adams Helped Ferment a Revolution," *New Yorker*, October 31, 2022, at 62; Stephen Fried, *Rush: Revolution, Madness, and the Visionary Doctor Who Became a Founding Father* (New York: Crown Books, 2018); Harlow Giles Unger, *Benjamin Rush: The Founding Father Who Healed a Wounded Nation* (New York: Da Capo Press, 2018).

7. Brooke Barbier, *King Hancock: The Radical Influence of a Moderate Founding Father* (Cambridge, MA: Harvard University Press, 2023).

8. Quoted in William Anthony Hay, "*King Hancock* Review: The Biggest Name in Boston," *Wall Street Journal*, October 6, 2023, at C-5.

Bibliography

Abbot, W. W., et al., eds. *The Papers of George Washington: Revolutionary War Series* (Charlottesville: University of Virginia Press, 1985–2003).

Adams, Charles Francis. *John Adams Works*, vol. 9 (Boston, 1856).

Ahnlund, Nils. *Gustavus Adolphus, the Great Warrior King* (Des Moines, IA: History Book Club, 1999).

Alden, Richard John. *General Charles Lee: Traitor or Patriot?* (Baton Rouge: Louisiana State University Press, 1951).

Alder, Ken. *Engineering the Revolution: Arms and Enlightenment in France* (Chicago: University of Chicago Press, 2010).

Ambler, Charles H. *Washington and the West* (Whitefish MT: Kessinger, 2010).

Anderson, Fred. *Crucible of War: The Seven Years' War and the Fate of Empire in British North America, 1754–1763* (New York: Vintage, 2001).

Atkinson, Rick. *The British Are Coming: The War for America, Lexington to Princeton, 1775–1777* (New York: Henry Holt, 2019).

Ayrault, Theodore. *Gustavus Adolphus: A History of the Art of War after the Middle Ages to the End of the Spanish Succession War, with a Detailed Account of the Campaigns of the Great Swede* (Salisbury, NC: Pervasive Books, 2019).

Babbits, Lawrence E. *A Devil of a Whipping: The Battle of Cowpens* (Chapel Hill: University of North Carolina Press, 2011).

Baigent, M., Leigh, R., and Lincoln, H. *Holy Blood, Holy Grail* (New York: Dell, 2005).

Ballagh, James Curtis. *The Letters of Richard Henry Lee* (New York: Macmillan, 1911).

Barbier, Brooke. *King Hancock: The Radical Influence of a Moderate Founding Father* (Cambridge, MA: Harvard University Press, 2023).

Bennett, Charles E., and Lennon, Donald R. *A Quest for Glory: Major General Robert Howe and the American Revolution* (Chapel Hill: University of North Carolina Press, 1991).

Biddle, Charles B. *The Case of Major André* (Philadelphia: Historical Society of Pennsylvania, 1884).

Borick, Carl P. *A Gallant Defense: The Siege of Charleston, 1780* (Columbia: University of South Carolina Press, 1980).

Boyd, John. *Mad Anthony Wayne* (New York: Scribner & Sons, 1929).

Bragg, C. L. *Crescent Moon over Carolina: William Moultrie & American Liberty* (Columbia: University of South Carolina Press, 2013).

Brands, H. W. *The First American: The Life and Times of Benjamin Franklin* (New York: Doubleday, 2000).

Branson, Douglas. *Southern Brigadier Generals in the Revolutionary War: Eighteen Commandeers Instrumental in the American Victory* (Jefferson, NC: McFarland, 2024).

Browne, Stephen Howard. *The First Inauguration: George Washington and the Invention of the Republic* (College Park: Pennsylvania State University Press, 2020).

———. *The Ides of War: George Washington and the Newburgh Crisis* (Columbia: University of South Carolina Press, 2016).

Brumwell, Stephen. *Turncoat: Benedict Arnold and the Crisis of American Liberty* (New Haven, CT: Yale University Press, 2018).

Brydon, Robert. *The Guild, the Masons, and the Rosy Cross* (Jacksonville: Grand Lodge of Florida, 2012).

Buchanan, John. *The Road to Guilford Courthouse: The American Revolution in the Carolinas* (New York: Wiley & Sons, 1997).

Burnett, Edmund C. *Letters of Members of the Continental Congress*, vol. 3 (Boston, 1921–1936; republished, Whitefish, MT: Kessinger, 2016).

Burrows, Edwin G. *Forgotten Patriots: The Untold Story of American Prisoners during the Revolutionary War* (New York: Basic Books, 2008).

Butterfield, Lyman H. *Letters of Benjamin Rush*, vol. 2 (Princeton, NJ: Princeton University Press, 1951).

Carbone, Gerald M. *Nathaniel Greene: A Biography of the American Revolution* (New York: St. Martin's Press, 2010).

Catton, Bruce. *Stillness at Appomattox* (Garden City, NY: Doubleday, 1962).

Cecere, Michael. *General William Woodford of Virginia, Revolutionary War Patriot* (Berwyn Heights, MD: Heritage Books, 2019).

———. *Second to No Man but the Commander in Chief: Hugh Mercer, American Patriot* (Berwyn Heights, MD: Heritage Books, 2015).

Chase, Philander, ed. *Papers of George Washington* (Charlottesville: University of Virginia Press, 2001).

Chernow, Ron. *Alexander Hamilton* (London: Penguin, 2008).

———. *George Washington: A Life* (New York: Penguin, 2010).

———. *Grant* (New York: Penguin, 2017).

Cohen, Stan. *Historic Springs of Virginia* (Charleston, WV: Pictorial History Publishing, 1981).

Cole, Ryan. *Light-Horse Harry Lee: The Rise and Fall of a Revolutionary Hero* (Washington, DC: Regnery History, 2019).

Crackel, Theodore, ed. *The Papers of George Washington*, vol. 13 (Charlottesville: University of Virginia Press, 2007).

Custis, George Washington Parke. *Recollections and Memoirs of Washington* (Richmond, VA, 1860).

Dann, John C. *The Revolution Remembered: Eyewitness Accounts of the War of Independence* (Chicago: University of Chicago Press, 1980).

Davidson, Chalmers Gaston. *Piedmont Partisan: The Life and Times of Major General William Lee Davidson* (Davidson, NC: Davidson College, 1951).

Davis, Charles Luken. *North Carolina Society of the Cincinnati* (1907; New York: Legare Street Press, 2022).

DeMond, Robert O. *The Loyalists of North Carolina during the Revolution* (Durham, NC: Duke University Press, 1940; Greenville, SC: Southern Historical Press, 2019).

Draper, L. C. *King's Mountain and Its Heroes* (Cincinnati, OH, 1881).

Dressler, Joshua. *Understanding Criminal Law*, 9th edition (Durham, NC: Carolina Academic Press, 2022).

Drury, Bob, and Clavin, Tom. *Valley Forge* (New York: Simon & Schuster, 2018).

Dwyer, William M. *The Day Is Ours: An Inside View of the Battles of Trenton and Princeton, November 1776–January 1777* (New Brunswick, NJ: Rutgers University Press, 1998).

Evans, Emory G. *Thomas Nelson and the Revolution in Virginia* (Williamsburg: Virginia Bicentennial Commission, 1978).

Evans, Willis F. *History of Berkeley County* (Martinsburg, WV: n.p., 1928).

Fischer, David Hackett. *Washington's Crossing* (New York: Columbia University Press, 2004).

Fitzpatrick, John C. *The Writings of George Washington*. 28 vols. (Washington, DC: United States Government Printing Office, 1931–1944).

Fleming, Thomas. *Washington's Secret War: The Hidden History of Valley Forge* (New York: HarperCollins, 2005).

Flexner, James Thomas. *George Washington: The Forge of Experience* (Boston: Little, Brown, 1965).

Ford, Worthington Chauncey. *Journals of the Continental Congress*, vol. 10 (1937; London: Forgotten Books, 2014).

Forsythe, Gary. *A Critical History of Rome: From Prehistory to the First Punic War* (Berkeley: University of California Press, 2006).

Foster, Francis Apthorp. *The Institution of the Society of Cincinnati, 1783–1920* (Boston: General Society of the Cincinnati, 1923).

Freeman, Douglas S. *George Washington*, vol. 4 (Washington, DC: Library of Congress, 1949).

Fried, Stephen. *Rush: Revolution, Madness, and the Visionary Doctor Who Became a Founding Father* (New York: Crown Books, 2018).

Gallagher, Jon J. *The Battle of Brooklyn, 1776* (Edison, NJ: Castle Books, 2002).

Garden, Alexander. *Anecdotes of the American Revolution, Illustrative of the Talents and Virtues of Heroes and Patriots* (Charleston, SC: Miller, 1828).

Gavin, James M. *On the Road to Berlin: Battles of an Airborne Commander, 1943–1946* (New York: Viking, 1978).

Godbold, E. Stanly, Jr., and Woody, Robert H. *Christopher Gadsden and the American Revolution* (Knoxville: University of Tennessee Press, 1982).

Goolrick, John T. *Historic Fredericksburg* (Richmond, VA: Whittel & Shepperson, 1922).

———. *The Life of General Hugh Mercer* (1906; Hungerford, UK: Legare Street Press, 2022).

Graff, Alan D. *Field of Corpses and the Death of the American Army* (Brentwood, TN: Knox Press, 2023).

Graham, William A. *General Joseph Graham and His Papers on North Carolina Revolutionary History* (Raleigh: North Carolina Department of Archives and History, 1904).

Graydon, Alexander. *Memoirs of His Time* (Philadelphia: J. S. Little; reprinted Applewood Books, 2009).

Greenwood, Isaac. *The Revolutionary Service of John Greenwood* (1922; New York: Legare Street Press, 2022).

Grove, Max W. *Reconstructed Census of Berkeley County, Virginia* (Colesville, MD: Eastern West Virginia Press, 1970).

Hannah-Jones, Nikole, Roper, Caitlin, Silverman, Ilene, and Silverstein, Jack, eds. *The 1619 Project: A New Origin Story* (New York, Random House, 2021).

Henry, Robert. *Narrative of the Battle at Cowan's Ford* (Greensboro, NC, 1891).

Higginbotham, Don. *Daniel Morgan: Revolutionary Rifleman* (Williamsburg, VA: Omohundro Institute of Early American History and Culture, 1979).

———, ed. *The Papers of John Iredell* (Raleigh: North Carolina Division of Archives, 1976).

Hocker, Edward W. *The Fighting Parson of the American Revolution: A Biography of General Peter Muhlenberg* (Mechanicsburg, PA: Sunbury Press, 1936).

Hutton, Ronald. *The Making of Oliver Cromwell* (New Haven, CT: Yale University Press, 2021).

Isaacson, Walter. *Benjamin Franklin: An American Life* (New York: Simon & Schuster, 2004).

James, Alfred Procter. *Writings of General John Forbes* (Menasha, WI: Collegiate Press, 1938).

Jackson, Harvey H. *Lachlan McIntosh and the Politics of Revolutionary Georgia* (Athens: University of Georgia Press, 1979).

Jakes, John. *Charleston* (New York: Dutton, 2002).

Johnson, Daniel McDonald. *This Cursed War: Lachlan McIntosh in the American Revolution* (Allendale, SC: Self-published, 2018).

Kapp, Friedrich. *The Life of Frederick William von Steuben, Major General of the Revolutionary Army* (CreateSpace, 2015).

Karels, Carol. *A Disobedient Servant: The Revolutionary War and the Times That Tried Men's Souls* (Cheltenham, UK: The History Press, 2007).

Kars, Marjoleine. *Breaking Loose Together: The Regulator Rebellion in North Carolina* (Chapel Hill: University of North Carolina Press, 2002).

Lee, Henry. *Memoirs of the War in the Southern Department*, vol. 2 (Philadelphia, 1812).

———. *The Revolutionary War of General Henry Lee* (New York: Da Capo Press, 1998).

Lee, Noel Moore. *Patriot Above Profit* (Nashville, TN: Rutledge Hill Press, 1988).

Lender, Mark Edward. *Cabal: The Plot Against General Washington* (Yardley, PA: Westholme, 2019).

Lender, Mark Edward, with Garry Wheeler Stone. *Fatal Sunday: George Washington, the Monmouth Campaign, and the Politics of Battle* (Norman: University of Oklahoma Press, 2016).

Lengel, Edward. *General George Washington: A Military Life* (New York: Random House, 2005).

Lessler, Charles H. *The Sinews of Independence: Monthly Strength Reports of the Continental Army* (Chicago: University of Chicago Press, 1976).

Lingley, Charles R. *The Transition in Virginia from Colony to Commonwealth* (1910; New York: Legare Street Press, 2021).

Lint, Gregg, ed. *The Papers of John Adams* (Cambridge, MA: Belknap Press, 1996).

Lossing, Benson J. *Pictorial Field Book of the Revolution* (Philadelphia, 1860).

Lumpkin, Henry. *From Savannah to Yorktown* (New York: Paragon, 1981).

Lundin, Leonard. *Cockpit of the Revolution: The War for Independence in New Jersey* (1972; New York: Legare Street Press, 2023).

Luzader, John R. *Decision on the Hudson: A Military History of the Decisive Campaign of the American Revolution* (New York: Savas Beatie, 2010).

Mahan, Alfred Thayer. *The Influence of Sea Power upon History: 1660–1783* (Boston: Little, Brown, 1890).

Mantel, Hilary. *Wolf Hall* (New York: Picador, 2009).

Marambaud, Pierre. *Byrd of Westover* (Charlottesville: University of Virginia Press, 1971).

Marquis de Chastellux. *Travels in North America in 1780 & 1781*, vol. 1 (Chapel Hill: University of North Carolina Press, 1963).

———. *Travels in North America in the Years 1780–1782* (New York, 1828).

Marshall, John. *The Life of George Washington*, vol. 2 (Fredericksburg, VA: Citizens Guild, 1926).

Martin, James K. *Benedict Arnold, Revolutionary Hero: An American Warrior Reconsidered* (New York: New York University Press, 2000).

Mayo Clinic. *Family Health Guide*, 2nd ed. (New York: William Morrow, 1996).

Mazzagetti, Dominick. *Charles Lee: Self Before Country?* (New Brunswick, NJ: Rutgers University Press, 2013).

McBurney, Christian. *George Washington's Nemesis: The Outrageous Treason and Unfair Court-Martial of Charles Lee during the Revolutionary War* (El Dorado Hills, CA: Savas Beatie, 2020).

McCullough, David. *John Adams* (New York: Simon & Schuster, 2001).

———. *The Pioneers: The Heroic Story of the Settlers Who Bought the American Ideal West* (New York: Simon & Schuster, 2000).

———. *1776* (New York: Simon & Schuster, 2005).

McGuffey, William Holmes. *McGuffey's Fifth Eclectic Reader*, rev. ed. (Cincinnati, OH: Van Antwerp & Bragg, 1979).

McIlwaine, H. R. *Legislative Journals of the Convention of Virginia*, vol. 3 (Richmond, VA, 1918–1919; republished, New York: Wentworth Press, 2016).

Mekeel, Arthur J. *The Relation of the Quakers to the American Revolution* (Washington, DC: University Press of America, 1979).

Mintz, Max. *The Generals of Saratoga: John Burgoyne and Horatio Gates* (New Haven, CT: Yale University Press, 1990).

Mobley, Joe E. *North Carolina Governor Richard Caswell: Founding Father and Revolutionary Hero* (Charleston, SC: The History Press, 2016).

Montross, Lynn. *Ragtail and Bobtail: The Story of the Continental Army, 1775–1783* (New York: Harper, 1952).

Moore, George Henry. *Mr. Lee's Plan—March 29, 1777: The Treason of Charles Lee, Major General, Second in Command in the American Army of the Revolution* (Port Washington, NY: Kennikat Press, 1860).

Moultrie, William. *Memoirs of the American Revolution*, vol. 1 (1802; New York: Arno Press, 1968).

Muhlenberg, Henry Augustus. *The Life of Major-General Peter Muhlenberg, of the Revolutionary Army* (Philadelphia: Carey & Hart, 1849).

Nagy, John A. *Rebellion in the Ranks: Mutinies of the American Revolution* (Yardley, PA: Westholme, 2007).

Nash, Hugh Owen, Jr. *Patriot Sons, Patriot Brothers* (Nashville, TN: Westview, 2006).

Neilson, Charles. *An Original, Compiled, and Corrected Account of Burgoyne's Campaign* (Port Washington, NY: Kennikat Press, 1970).

Nickerson, Hoffman. *The Turning Point of the Revolution: Burgoyne in North America* (Boston: Houghton Mifflin, 1928).

Nolan, Cathal J. *The Allure of Battle* (New York: Oxford University Press, 2017).

Packman, Francis. *Montcalm and Wolfe* (1884; New York: Wentworth Press, 2019).

Palmer, David. *The River and the Rock* (New York: Greenwood Press, 1969).

Pancake, John S. *This Destructive War: The British Campaign in the Carolinas, 1780–1782* (Tuscaloosa: University of Alabama Press, 1985).

Pappas, Phillip. *Renegade Revolutionary: The Life of General Charles Lee* (New York: New York University Press, 2014).

Patterson, Samuel White. *Knight Errant of Liberty: The Triumph and Tragedy of General Charles Lee* (New York: Lantern Press, 1958).

Philbrick, Nathaniel. *Valiant Ambition: Benedict Arnold and the Fate of the American Revolution* (New York: Penguin, 2017).

Phillips, R. W. Dick. *Arthur St. Clair: The Invisible Patriot* (Bloomington, IN: iUniverse, 2014).

Pickering, Octavius, and Upham, Charles Wentworth. *The Life of Timothy Pickering* (New York: Wentworth Press, 2016).

Piecuch, Jim. *The Battle of Camden* (Charleston, SC: The History Press, 2006).

Plank, Geoffrey. *Rebellion and Savagery: The Jacobite Rising and the British Empire* (Philadelphia: University of Pennsylvania Press, 2005).

Polhemus, Richard V., and Polhemus, John F. *Stark: The Life and Wars of John Stark* (Delmar, NY: Black Dome Press, 2014).

Powell, William S. *North Carolina Through Four Centuries* (Chapel Hill: University of North Carolina Press, 1989).

Powell, William Stevens. *The War of Regulation and the Battle of Alamance, May 16, 1771* (Raleigh: North Carolina Department of Archives and History, 1957).

Preston, David L. *Braddock's Defeat: The Battle of Monongahela and the Road to Revolution* (New York: Oxford University Press, 2015).

Puls, Mark. *Henry Knox: Visionary General of the American Revolution* (New York: Palgrave Macmillan, 2008).

Ragosta, John A. *Patrick Henry's Last Stand: For the People, for the Country* (Charlottesville: University of Virginia Press, 2023).

Rand McNally, Inc. *2022 Road Atlas* (Chicago: Rand McNally, 2021).

Rankin, Hugh. *The North Carolina Continentals* (Chapel Hill: University of North Carolina Press, 1991).

———. *North Carolina in the American Revolution* (Raleigh: North Carolina Division of Archives and History, 1959).

Reid, Stuart. *Culloden Moor 1746: The Death of the Jacobite Cause* (Oxford: Osprey, 2002).

———. *Like Hungry Wolves: Culloden Moor 16 April 1746* (London: Windrow & Greene, 2000).

Reynolds, William R., Jr. *Andrew Pickens: South Carolina Patriot in the Revolutionary War* (Jefferson, NC: McFarland, 2012).

Rhodehamel, John. *George Washington: Writings* (New York: Library of America, 1997).

River, Charles, and Fluxman, Colin. *Little Turtle's War: The History and Legacy of the 18th Century Conflict between the United States and Native Americans in the Northwest* (Audible Books, 2020).

Robinson, William P. *The Revolutionary Sketches of William R. Davie* (Chapel Hill: University of North Carolina Press, 1976).

Robinson, Blackwell, ed. *Sketches of William Davie* (reprint, Raleigh: North Carolina Department of Archives and History, 1976).

Ronald, D. A. B. *The Life of John André: The Redcoat Who Turned Benedict Arnold* (Haverton, PA: Casemate Publishers, 2019).

Rose, Ben Z. *John Stark: Maverick General* (Waverly, MA: TreeLine Press, 2007).

Rossman, Kenneth R. *Thomas Mifflin and the Politics of the American Revolution* (Chapel Hill: University of North Carolina Press, 1952).

Rupp, Israel D. *Early History of Western Pennsylvania* (Los Angeles: HardPress, 2019).

Rush, Benjamin. *A Memorial Containing Travels through Life of Sundry Incidents in the Life of Dr. Benjamin Rush* (Philadelphia: Louis Biddle, 1905).

Russell, David Lee. *The American Revolution in the Southern Colonies* (Jefferson, NC: McFarland, 2000).

Ryan, Dennis P. *A Salute to Courage: The American Revolution as Seen through the Wartime Writings of Officers of the Continental Army and Navy* (New York: Columbia University Press, 1979).

Sargent, Winthrop. *The Life and Career of Major John André, Adjutant-General of the British Army in America* (New York: Legare Street Press, 2022).

Saunders, William L. *Colonial Records of North Carolina*, vol. 10 (Raleigh, NC, 1886–1890).

Schaw, Janet. *Journal of a Lady of Quality; Being the Narrative of a Journey to the West Indies and North Carolina in the Years 1774–1776* (New Haven, CT: Yale University Press, 1939).

Schiff, Stacy. *The Revolutionary: Samuel Adams* (New York: Little, Brown, 2022).

Schuricht, Hermann. *History of the German Element in Virginia* (Baltimore: Theo. Kroh & Sons, 1898).

Shelton, Hal T. *General Richard Montgomery and the American Revolution* (New York: New York University Press, 1994).

Smith, Paul H., and Gephart, Ronald M. *Letters of Delegates to Congress 1771–1784*, vol. 8 (Washington, DC: Library of Congress, 1976–2000).

Smith, Samuel S. *The Battle of Princeton* (Monmouth Beach, NJ: Philip Freneau Press, 1967).

Snow, Dean. *1777: Tipping Point at Saratoga* (New York: Oxford University Press, 2016).

Sparks, Jared. *The Writings of George Washington*, vol. 4 (Boston, 1840).

Specht, Johann Friedrich. *A Military Journal of the Burgoyne Campaign* (Westport, CT: Greenwood Press, 1995).

Stewart, Catesby Willis. *The Life of Brigadier William Woodford of the American Revolution*, vol. 2 (Richmond, VA: Witten & Shepperson, 1973).

Stryker, William S. *The Battles of Trenton and Princeton* (1898; Trenton, NJ: Old Barracks Association, 2001).

Swager, Christine R. *Heroes of Kettle Creek, 1779–1782* (West Conshohocken, PA: Infinity Publishing, 2008).

Swisher, James K. *The Revolutionary War in the Southern Backcountry* (Gretna, LA: Pelican, 2008).

Syrett, Harold G. *The Papers of Alexander Hamilton* (New York: Columbia University Press, 1961).

Taaffe, Stephen R. *Washington's Revolutionary War Generals* (Norman: University of Oklahoma Press, 2019).

Tarleton, Banastre. *A History of the Campaigns of 1780–1781 in the Southern Provinces of North America* (1787; Manchester, NH: Ayer, 1999).

Thacher, James. *A Military Journal during the American Revolutionary War* (Plymouth, MA, 1823).

Thayer, Theodore. *The Making of a Scapegoat: Washington and Lee at Monmouth* (Port Washington, NY: Kennikat Press, 1976).

Tuchman, Barbara. *A Distant Mirror: The Calamitous 14th Century* (New York: Ballantine Books, 1978).

Unger, Harlow Giles. *Benjamin Rush: The Founding Father Who Healed a Wounded Nation* (New York: Da Capo Press, 2018).

Ward, Harry M. *Charles Scott and the Spirit of '76* (Charlottesville: University of Virginia Press, 1988).

———. *Duty, Honor or Country: General George Weedon and the American Revolution* (Philadelphia: American Philosophical Society, 1979).

———. *Major General Adam Stephen and the Cause of American Liberty* (Charlottesville: University of Virginia Press, 1989).

Waterman, Joseph M. *With Sword and Lancet: The Life of General Hugh Mercer* (Richmond, VA: Garrett & Massie, 1941).

Watson, Robert P. *The Ghost Ship of Brooklyn: An Untold Story of the American Revolution* (New York: Da Capo Press, 2017).

Webb, James. *Born Fighting: How the Scots-Irish Shaped America* (New York: Random House, 2011).

Weeks, Steven Beauregard. *Church and State in North Carolina* (1893; New York: Wentworth Press, 2019).

Wilkinson, James. *Memories of My Own Times*, vol. 1 (Philadelphia: Abraham Small, 1816).

Wilkinson, Lauren. *American Spy* (New York: Random House, 2019).

Williams, Ortho Holland. *The Papers of General Nathanael Greene*, vol. 1 (Charleston, SC, 1822).

Wilson, David K. *The Southern Strategy: Britain's Conquest of South Carolina and Georgia* (Columbia: University of South Carolina Press, 2005).

Wirt, William. *Sketches of the Life and Character of Patrick Henry* (Philadelphia, 1817).

Wolke, Lars Erickson. *Gustavus Adolphus, Sweden, and the Thirty Years War* (Barnsley, South Yorkshire, UK: Pen & Sword Military, 2022).

Woodward, Sandy. *Memoirs of the Falkland Island British Group Commander* (Annapolis, MD: Naval Institute Press, 1992).

Wright, Robert K., Jr., and MacGregor, Morris. *Thomas Mifflin: Soldier-Statesman of the Constitution* (Fort McNair, DC: US Army Center of Military History, 1987).

Young, Calvin M. *Little Turtle (Me-she-kin-no-quah): The Great Chief of the Miami Indian Nation* (CreateSpace, 2014).

Zabin, Serena. *The Boston Massacre: A Family History* (New York: Houghton Mifflin Harcourt, 2019).

Zambone, Albert Louis. *Daniel Morgan: A Revolutionary Life* (Yardley, PA: Westholme, 2018).

Index